EDUCATION IN EDINBURGH
IN THE
EIGHTEENTH CENTURY

ALEXANDER LAW, OBE, MA, PhD

UNIVERSITY OF LONDON PRESS LTD
Warwick Square, London EC4

1965

Printed in Great Britain
by T and A CONSTABLE LTD, Hopetoun Street
Printers to the University of Edinburgh

CONTENTS

PREFACE

THIS study has occupied my leisure time for some ten years, and has introduced me to many people in universities and libraries whose help I should like to acknowledge. It is part of a thesis submitted to the University of Edinburgh, and I should like first of all to thank the University authorities for permission to reproduce it, and to record my special indebtedness to Professor Gordon Donaldson, of the chair of Scottish History, who supervised my work and helped me in many details. Many librarians have helped me, like my friend Dr William Beattie of the National Library and his staff, the late Dr C A Malcolm of the Signet Library, the late Miss Marie Balfour of Edinburgh Public Library, and the late Rev Dr Campbell of the Church of Scotland Library. Miss Helen Armet, of the Town Clerk's department, City Chambers, gave me much assistance with the records of Edinburgh, and I also had help from H M Record Office, the British Museum, the libraries of Edinburgh and Glasgow Universities, and the Baillie Library, Glasgow. The Clerk of the Heriot Trust and the Secretary of the Merchant Company of Edinburgh allowed me access to their records. To the Rector and staff—past and present —of The Royal High School, I bear a very special relation, for my interest in the history of education in Edinburgh began when I was a member of the staff and was privileged to be a colleague of the late W C A Ross, historian of the school and an authority on the history of Edinburgh. For a grant towards the publication of this book I am indebted to the Carnegie Trust for the Universities of Scotland.

I should like also to express my gratitude to the Scottish Council for Research in Education, who have agreed to publish this work as one of their volumes. The Director and his staff have been most helpful to me.

Chapter I

INTRODUCTORY

THIS study is an attempt to describe education in Edinburgh in the eighteenth century, a period which saw such a remarkable flowering of the intellectual life of the city that it is impossible for the student of literature or history not to feel curious about the circumstances that helped to produce it. One of the contributing factors was the educational system, and its special significance has not been studied in detail before. Fortunately, information about the schools is in existence in official records, books, and newspapers.

Many elements combined to create the circumstances in Edinburgh at the end of the century that were favourable to the development of genius. Historians and critics have pointed to the expansion of the city boundaries, the imaginative design of the New Town, the completion of public works like the North and South Bridges and the Royal Exchange, the quickening of interest in drama, art, and music, as all helping to produce an atmosphere congenial to the intellectual growth of men like Henry Mackenzie, Scott, Horner, Jeffrey, and Cockburn, and stimulating to the ordinary men of the day. In previous assessments, the importance of the educational system of Edinburgh has not been stressed, which is unfortunate, not only because it was different from that of other Scottish and English cities, but also because at the very time when most of these men of genius were young in Edinburgh, the University under the Principalship of William Robertson, one of the distinguished historians of the day, was attracting able men as teachers and students, and the High School, where the ablest boys were trained, was in the charge of a great teacher in its Rector, Alexander Adam.

Books have been written on the University, the High School, George Heriot's Hospital, and other schools in Edinburgh, but

9

no attempt has yet been made to give a complete picture of the various kinds of schools that existed in Edinburgh in the eighteenth century. It is the intention of this study to try to provide such a comprehensive view. It will include, for example, information about the Charity and English schools, where most of the children learned to read and write; the High Schools of Edinburgh, Canongate, and South Leith; the Hospitals of George Heriot and George Watson, and those for the Merchant Maidens and Trades Maidens associated with the name of Mary Erskine; and the great variety of private schools, private teachers, and boarding schools. There will also be some consideration of the books used in these schools, particularly those written by Edinburgh teachers.

Before a detailed study of the schools can be begun, it is necessary to sketch, in outline, something of the background. Accordingly, in this first chapter there will be some consideration of the size and growth of the city in the period under review, and of the Town Council which was responsible for it. Secondly, since the place of the Church of Scotland is of prime importance in any study of Scottish education, some estimate must be given of the powers of the Church in general, and of its position in Edinburgh in particular. Thirdly, something must be said, however briefly, about the special and indeed peculiar place of the University in the city.

THE TOWN AND ITS TOWN COUNCIL

Edinburgh grew rapidly in the course of the eighteenth century; at the beginning of the century, its population is estimated to have been 25,000, by 1750 it was 50,000, and by the end of the century, 100,000.[1] It was the largest city in Scotland. Glasgow had increased even more rapidly than Edinburgh, but was still at the end of the eighteenth century considerably smaller than the capital.[2] In that period, too, the prestige of a town often depended less on population, wealth, and trade than on the number of aristocratic families that lived in it, and from

---

[1] Ferguson, *Dawn of Scottish Welfare*, p 70.
[2] The population of Glasgow was 12,766 in 1708; 17,034 in 1740; 23,546 in 1755; 42,832 in 1780; and 66,578 in 1791. Ferguson, *op cit*, p 71.

this point of view, Edinburgh was pre-eminent in Scotland. Some noble families lived there, and many more visited it for long periods every year. Edinburgh also possessed a permanent aristocracy, that of the Court of Session, a group of men of the highest intellectual ability. The end of the Scottish Parliament after the Union of 1707 temporarily depressed the capital by depriving it of the members of the Estates: this was the cause of complaints made by the Rector of the High School in 1718.[1] But, after the turn of the century, there are indications that the number of noble families living in Edinburgh was growing again; private schools, for example, increased from this time, particularly those for girls. This probably reflected the general economic prosperity of Scotland. The prosperity of the city was also to be seen in its trade and industry, in buildings like the Royal Infirmary and the Orphan Hospital which were the products of local wealth as well as of Christian charity, and in that expansion of the burgh boundaries which ultimately led to the exciting development of the New Town.

Though the intellectual, social, and artistic life of Edinburgh owed much to the presence of 'the quality', the young advocates, and professors at the College, the city organisation was in the hands of a Town Council whose members came in the main from quite a different class. The Town Council continued throughout the eighteenth century on a pattern laid down in 1583.[2] It consisted of the Lord Provost and twenty-four members, of whom the majority were merchants and the remainder craftsmen. Only merchants and craftsmen could be members, and of these two groups, the merchants held permanent power, for the principal offices of Lord Provost, Bailies (of whom there were four), Dean of Guild, and Treasurer, could be held only by merchants.[3] Like most of the Town Councils in Scotland, it was self-electing, and the craftsmen councillors were chosen by the magistrates and council from lists prepared

[1] See *infra*, p 59.
[2] The Decree Arbitral of King James VI of 22 April 1583. See *Edinburgh 1329-1929*, p 280.
[3] *Edinburgh 1329-1929*, p 281. 'If, however, any craftsman engaged in trade should be chosen for office "for his guid qualiteis", he might not use his craft or allow his servants to use it while he was in office or thereafter until permission had been obtained by him from the Magistrates and Council.' Bailies in Scotland correspond to Aldermen in England.

by the Deacons of the fourteen incorporated crafts.[1] Membership, restricted to merchants and craftsmen, was in practice even more limited, for there was a tendency for these groups to choose members of their own particular cliques for membership of the Town Council. In such a close corporation, opportunities for nepotism and favouritism abounded.[2] Yet it did produce at least one distinguished man in George Drummond, six times Lord Provost and the founder of modern Edinburgh.

Educational matters, when they arose at all in the Town Council, were for the most part dealt with by one of the Committees. After 1698, the regular practice was to appoint four Committees after the election; these were (1) Treasurer's Accounts, (2) Public Works, (3) the College, Paul's Work, and Trinity Hospital,[3] and (4) the Supply Bills (for the poor). No powers were automatically delegated to the College Committee, which could only consider matters which were referred to it by the Town Council. Its recommendations were usually accepted. From 1722, it was called 'The Committee for affairs of the College and what else was remitted to them'. The College affairs which were normally referred to this Committee were consideration of the College accounts, vacant bursaries, the allocation of rooms in the College, and repairs or alterations to the buildings. Some of the business concerning the High School was also referred to this Committee. In 1733, for instance: 'Bailie Colhoun and the Committee anent College affairs to visit the High School on the first Monday of every quarter at 10 a.m., and to call what ministers and professors they shall think proper in order to take trial of the boys' proficiency and the masters' care and diligence, and to make a report of what regulations and methods may be found necessary for the same.'[4] The arrangements for the annual visitation were frequently put in the hands of the 'College Bailie', in other words the Third Bailie, who was the convener or preses of the College Committee. In 1771, this committee was assigned

---

[1] Complete details of the procedure and the officials are given in *Edinburgh 1329-1929*, p 282.
[2] Cockburn, *Memorials of His Time*, p 71. 'Within this Pandemonium sat the town council, omnipotent, corrupt, impenetrable.' But it is fair to say that Cockburn disliked the Town Council.
[3] Paul's Work and Trinity Hospital were old charitable foundations.
[4] Minutes of the Town Council of Edinburgh, 4 April 1733, 10 Oct 1733.

quite definitely, 'High School and what else shall be remitted to them'. The visitations of the elementary or 'English' schools seem also to have been arranged by the College Bailie; these took place at the same time of year as the High School visitations and were carried out by some of the same people, so it was sensible for the arrangements to be made by the College Bailie. The only definite reference to such an arrangement, however, is in the year 1782.[1]

Educational matters were sometimes handled by other committees of the Town Council. For example, a special committee was set up in 1726, including in its membership the First and Second Bailies, with the following remit: 'Considering that the by-laws and regulations made touching the administration and government of the University ought to be enquired into how far such or any part thereof ought to be continued or altered' . . . the committee is appointed . . . 'who shall meet immediately and shall have power to adjourn themselves from time to time and to call for and bring before them persons, papers and records necessary, and report'.[2] This committee was entirely different from the Committee on College Affairs, which had been appointed as usual in October 1726 with the Third Bailie as convener. In a somewhat similar fashion it was the Committee on Public Works, and not the Committee on College Affairs, that was asked in 1734 to visit the fabric of the High School and report.[3] The appointments of masters and of the rector of the High School were at least on some occasions made on the recommendations of the Committee on College Affairs.[4] On another occasion, a special committee was set up for the purpose.[5]

From 1698 to 1721, the Committee on College Affairs consisted of nine members: a Bailie, Dean of Guild, Treasurer, old (ie ex-) Bailie, old Dean of Guild, old Treasurer, the Deacon Convener, and two Council Deacons. In 1722, two members were added, a merchant, and a trades councillor. In 1730, the composition of the Committee took a form that

[1] Minutes of the Town Council of Edinburgh, 7 Aug 1782.
[2] ibid, 15 Dec 1726.
[3] ibid, 2 Jan 1734.
[4] ibid, 1 Feb and 8 Feb 1710.
[5] ibid, 5 Feb 1735.

remained for the rest of the century, and was as follows: Third Bailie, Dean of Guild, Treasurer, Third ex-Bailie, ex-Dean of Guild, ex-Treasurer, Third merchant councillor, First trades councillor, Deacon Convener, two Council Deacons, and two extraordinary Deacons, a total of thirteen members.

The Committee on College Affairs, while on occasions acting on matters to do with the High School or the English schools, was clearly nothing like a modern Education Committee. It acted only on subjects remitted to it, and not all school matters were so remitted. The tendency of the Town Council to take all major decisions itself is that of a body that wished financial control to remain in its own hands. Perhaps it is fortunate that there were other influences at work, looking at education not purely from the financial point of view. These influences were to be found in the Presbytery, and especially, as far as the Town Council was concerned, in the Edinburgh ministers. It was the Town Council's custom to consult the Edinburgh ministers on many educational matters. As we shall see, the moving spirits in the establishment of Charity schools and English schools were in the first place the ministers.

THE CHURCH

The First Book of Discipline of the reformed Church had stressed the importance of education, and the General Assembly of the Kirk in 1562 had wished the setting up of schools to proceed at the same time as that of churches.[1] The comprehensive system of government in Church and State that was in the minds of the early reformers did not come to pass, but the Scottish Parliament indicated in the series of Acts which it passed in the course of the seventeenth century that the Church had a definite responsibility in education. An Act of the Privy Council of 1616 said that, in every parish 'where convenient means may be had for entertaining a school', a school should be

[1] See Knox, *History of the Reformation*, ed Dickinson, Vol II, pp 295-6: 'Of necessity, therefore, we judge it, that every several church have a schoolmaster appointed, such a one as is able, at least, to teach Grammar, and the Latin tongue, if the town be of any reputation. If it be upland where the people convene to doctrine but once in the week, then must either the Reader or the Minister there appointed, take over the children and youth of the parish, to instruct them in their first rudiments, and especially in the Catechism.'

established and a teacher appointed at the expense of the parish-
ioners, 'at the sight and by the advice of the bishop of the
diocese in his visitation'.[1] An Act of the Parliament of Scotland
incorporated this Privy Council Act in 1633, and added powers
whereby the bishop could finance the setting up of schools by
laying a 'stent' on the heritors.[2] Unfortunately this Act of 1633
incorporated the phrase from the Privy Council Act which has
already been quoted, about 'convenient means', and this was
a loophole for those heritors who did not wish to spend money on
schools. The Scottish Parliament passed another Act in 1646,
this time to the effect that a school should be established and a
schoolmaster appointed 'by advice of the presbytery' in all
parishes where none existed. The heritors were to be responsible for the arrangements but, if they did not convene, or if
they disagreed when they did convene, the Presbytery could
hand over the responsibility to 'twelve honest men within the
bounds of the presbytery'.[3] This act was cancelled by the
General Act Rescissory of 1661. The Act of 1633, however,
remained in force. In 1696, the Act for Settling of Schools was
passed by the Scottish Parliament, embodying much of the
spirit of the 1633 Act and some of the ideas of the 1646 Act.
Instead of the 'twelve honest men' the 1696 Act mentioned the
Commissioners of Supply of the shire; the power of appeal to
these Commissioners, who had been set up under an Act of
1667, was an effective threat against recalcitrant heritors.[4]

The General Assembly and the various Presbyteries had not
been inactive. It was a petition from the General Assembly
in 1639 that led eventually to the 1646 Act, and Presbyteries
tried whenever possible to get schools founded in parishes
where there were none.

The foundation of the powers of the Presbyteries in the
eighteenth century, as regards the appointment of schoolmasters, is to be found in an Act of the Scottish Parliament of
1693, the 'Act for Settling the Quiet and Peace of the Church'.[5]

[1] Register of the Privy Council of Scotland, X, 671-2.
[2] Acts of the Parliament of Scotland, V, 21, c 5. A 'stent' was a tax, and
the heritors were the landholders in a parish.
[3] ibid, VI, pt 1, 554, c 171.
[4] ibid, X, 63, c 26. Nevertheless, several generations passed before every
parish in Scotland had its school.
[5] ibid, IX, 303.

This stated that all schoolmasters were liable to the 'trial, judgment, and censure' of the presbytery for 'sufficiency, qualifications, and deportment'. Some notion of what this meant can be gained from the terms of an Act of the same Parliament of 1690 which laid down that masters of schools had to subscribe the Westminster Confession and take the oath of allegiance.[1] This was repeated in the later 'Act for Securing the Protestant Religion and Presbyterian Church Government', which forms an integral part of the Act of Union of 1707.[2] This Act explicitly states that the profession of faith and subscription of the Confession must take place 'before the respective Presbyteries of their bounds'.

The supervision of schools by the Presbyteries went further than the mere approval of schoolmasters. It took two distinct forms, the visitation of parishes and the visitation of schools. In the visitation of a parish, the Presbytery, in the course of questioning the various bodies concerned with the parish church, made an investigation into the provision of schools in the area. This was a review of educational and religious facilities that took place at intervals of some years. The visitation of schools, on the other hand, was concerned with the work and standards of the teachers and pupils. The frequency of visitations varied at different times and in different places, but an Act of the General Assembly of 1700 said 'that presbyteries do visit all the public grammar schools within their bounds by some of their number appointed for that effect, at least twice every year'.[3]

The general position was that the Presbyteries, carrying out the policies approved from time to time by the General Assembly, had powers regarding the appointment of masters, and duties to inspect schools. The application of these powers in Edinburgh requires more detailed consideration.

The relationship between the Town Council and the Presbytery is at first glance confusing. The churches within the burgh boundaries were built, endowed, and maintained by the Town Council, who also appointed the ministers. Precentors—who

---

[1] Acts of the Parliament of Scotland, IX, 164a.
[2] ibid, XI, 402, c 6.
[3] Acts of the General Assembly. Act of 13 April 1706, 395.

conducted the praise—were usually also schoolmasters, and were also appointed by the Town Council. The appointments of session and elders were in the hands of the Town Council, and it was a matter of grievance to the Presbytery and dispute with the Town Council at the end of the seventeenth century that there was only one Kirk Session for the burgh. The Presbytery of Edinburgh covered a much larger area than the city, and its membership consisted of ministers and elders drawn from the parishes of Cramond, Corstorphine, Colinton, Currie, Liberton, Leith, Ratho, Kirknewton, and Duddingston as well as from the nine churches of the capital. The most important men in the Presbytery were, however, undoubtedly the ministers of the large city churches, whose appointments were in the gift of the Town Council. The danger which one might expect, that the ministers would become the creatures of the Town Council, does not, in fact, appear to have existed. The impression gained from the records of both bodies, indeed, is rather one of continual bickering between them.

There was a formal visitation of Edinburgh by the Presbytery in 1706, a record of which exists. The Presbytery convened in the High Church, where the magistrates, ministers of the Burgh churches, members of the Town Council and Kirk Session were present. Various questions about church affairs were put by the Preses to the ministers and magistrates, of which the last two were the following:

'*Undecimo*: If the Town be provided of schoolmasters? *Duodecimo*: If the schoolmasters have subscribed the Confession of Faith? If they be qualified for their offices, and other necessary qualifications? If they be diligent and faithful in their stations and have competent salaries?' The Town Council's reply mentioned the High School, three Hospital schools, and a Charity school, and also reported 'that there are French papists who keep schools in this city'. The masters of the High School, Heriot's Hospital, and the Free School were summoned to a later meeting. The Rector of the High School explained in answer to a question that he had already signed the Confession of Faith before the Commission of Parliament for the Visitation of Schools and Colleges. The Schoolmaster of Heriot's had not previously been required to sign the Confes-

B

sion of Faith, and this both he and the master of the Free School were ordered to do. Ministers and sessions represented at the visitation were asked to enquire what schools existed in their parishes, and to report them and the names of the school-masters to the Presbytery.[1]

General visitations of this kind were regularly held in the various parishes outside the burgh, including the burgh of Canongate, but there is no other record of a general visitation of Edinburgh.

The visitation of schools, however, was much more systematic. Committees of the Presbytery were appointed to visit certain schools, or groups of schools. For example, in 1712, a committee consisting of eight ministers 'or any three of them' was instructed to visit the High School, Heriot's Hospital, Canongate High School, the Free schools, the schools in the Merchants' and Trades' Hospitals and other schools in the city and Canongate.[2] In 1724, a different arrangement was made and four committees were set up to visit the schools in the following groups:

1 High School of Edinburgh, Liberton, Trades Maiden Hospital.
2 Heriot's Hospital, Merchant Maiden Hospital, West Kirk School.
3 Colinton, Currie, Kirknewton, Ratho, Corstorphine, Cramond.
4 North Leith, South Leith, Canongate, Duddingston.[3]

On the occasions of these visits the Presbytery's committee asked the following questions, among others: 'Had the school-master subscribed the Confession of Faith? Was there sufficient evidence that he had been diligent and faithful? What were his manner of teaching, school government, and discipline? Had young people profited from his teaching? Was the school maintained financially as laid down by law?'[4]

The minutes of the Edinburgh Presbytery contain much information about the provision of schools in the city, especially in the first quarter of the century. There are reviews of the general provision of schools in the city, and some reports of visits to individual schools. In response to an Act of the General

---

[1] Edinburgh Presbytery Minutes, 14 Feb 1706, 6 March 1706.
[2] ibid, 28 May 1712.
[3] ibid, 26 Aug 1724.
[4] ibid, 14 June 1710.

Assembly of 1700, the Presbytery prepared a list of all school-masters, tutors, and papists. A duty like this kept before the Presbytery not only the need to establish and supervise schools, but also the importance of keeping a careful check on the numbers of Roman Catholics.[1]

The Presbytery kept a watch on all who did not accept the Revolution settlement of the Church as well as on all Roman Catholics. Episcopal clergymen, other than those with whom a settlement was reached by the various Acts of Parliament,[2] and extremists like the Cameronians who had refused to accept the Revolution settlement, were investigated from time to time. Presumably some of these were also suspect on political grounds of being Jacobites. As an example of the Presbytery's method, there is the case of ten teachers of private schools who were summoned to appear before a committee of the Presbytery in November 1721. Only two actually appeared, and both had already signed the Confession of Faith and were both precentors in Episcopalian meeting-houses and kept small schools.[3] Among those who did not appear was John McMain, a Cameronian, who afterwards described the whole process in a pamphlet.[4]

There were fairly frequent disputes between the Presbytery and the Town Council in the first quarter of the century. In 1718 the Town Council had to admit that it had been mistaken in appointing some schoolmasters before they had been qualified by law in the presence of the Presbytery.[5] In the following

[1] The list of Roman Catholics in the bounds of the Presbytery in the years 1701-1705 is in the *Maitland Club Miscellany*, Vol III. There were apparently some 139 known Roman Catholics. Of these, 40 were in Canongate, 41 in College Kirk, 15 in Tron Kirk, 4 in New Kirk, 9 in Old Kirk, 2 in North New, 1 in Lady Yester's, 1 in Duddingston, 8 in Liberton, 4 in Colinton, 8 in West Kirk, 2 in North Leith, 4 in South Leith, and none in Tolbooth, Greyfriars, Currie, Kirknewton, Ratho, Corstorphine, and Cramond parishes. Four women are specially named as schoolmistresses; Mrs Badham and Mrs Wood in College Kirk parish, Margaret Thomson in Tron Kirk parish, and Mrs Lamb in West Kirk parish.

[2] Acts of the Parliament of Scotland, IX, 303 and 449. Act of Parliament of 1712 (7 April).

[3] Edinburgh Presbytery Minutes, 26 April 1721. The Minutes record that some of these teachers had been informed against as persons disaffected to the existing establishment in Church and State.

[4] *The Summons Dismiss'd; or the Process of Edinburgh against Mr McM—n, discussed with his answers and declinature. In a Letter to a Friend.* Copy in National Library of Scotland.

[5] Edinburgh Presbytery Minutes, 29 Jan 1718.

August, the Presbytery objected to the 'planting' of Edinburgh churches—that is to say, the filling of vacancies—but the Town Council drily replied that 'they did not know what concern the Presbytery had in the vacancies of the Town', and went on to say that 'they had ministers of their own to converse with on that subject'.[1] Thereupon the Presbytery appointed a committee to see the Town Council on the appointments of both schoolmasters and ministers. This led, after much argument, to the reconsideration of the case of Robert Spence, who had been appointed to the High School by the Town Council.[2] During a later quarrel, which had nothing to do with schools but was concerned with the constitution of the sessions in Edinburgh, the Town Council's excuse for not dealing expeditiously with the matters raised by the Presbytery was that the members of the Council were 'at present thrang with other affairs'.[3]

References to schools are to be found in the Presbytery minutes throughout the eighteenth century, and the ministers took part regularly in school visitations. As regards the High School, the Town Council had for long been in the habit of inspecting it annually, and there may have been a period early in the eighteenth century when visitations were carried out by Town Council and Presbytery separately. After 1714, however, a compromise was reached, and the Town Council always included at least two of the ministers from the Presbytery on the visiting committee which carried out the annual inspection.[4] A similar arrangement was made for the Canongate High School and the Free (or Charity) schools, and was continued for the English schools founded in 1759. Generally speaking, it was about the year 1733 that the establishment and management of schools ceased to be matters of controversy between Town Council and Presbytery, and the references to schools and schoolmasters in the Presbytery minutes become routine.[5] The

---

[1] Edinburgh Presbytery Minutes, 6 Aug 1718.
[2] See page 65.
[3] Edinburgh Presbytery Minutes, 16 April 1729.   [4] See also Chapter III.
[5] From about that time, the Church was involved in the disputes about patronage. One is tempted also to wonder whether the Moderate party in the Church, which began to make its influence felt from this period, did not exercise a beneficent power on the development of schools. Some of the most important Moderates were ministers in Edinburgh.

ministers were the Town Council's advisers on education, and
no important decision was made without their opinion being
sought. The ministers were also represented in the management and carried out the inspection of the Hospital schools.
In connection with the High School, on the other hand, the
Town Council often sought the advice of the Principal and
Professors of the College.

There are no kirk session records of the city churches, but
those of South Leith parish have been preserved, and indicate
in a vivid way the close control the session had over the schools
in the parish. The principal school was the Grammar School
and it naturally figures frequently in the minutes, but the session
also supported English schools for the teaching of reading,
writing, arithmetic, and church music. Several schoolmasters
were paid small salaries for which they were expected to teach
free of charge any 'poor scholars' sent to them by the session,
the annual salary paid to one such master in 1728 was 50 merks,
or £2 15s.[1] At least one of the schools was under a woman.
Both boys and girls attended them. In 1729, Robert Robertson,
who kept an English school, stated that he had taught several
of the session's poor scholars writing as well as reading, and
asked a special payment for what was considered extra work.
He was given an allowance and told in future to teach both
reading and writing.[2] The session was watchful over the setting
up of new schools. Colin McKenzie in 1724 was interviewed
by the session for unlawfully starting an English school: he was
the precentor in the Episcopal meeting-house, and the session
insisted that he produce a testimonial of good character from his
previous parish. He ultimately did so, but not before the
session had passed his case to the magistrates 'to execute the
law'. The case was, however, stopped.[3] Later, another man
started a small Grammar School: he had only five pupils, but
the session took counsel's opinion on whether this could be
reckoned a private school and how far the session had powers
to suppress private schools. Mr Dundas of Arniston gave it as
his opinion that 'this is not such a schooll as can legally be

---

[1] Kirk Session records, 23 May 1728.
[2] ibid, 8 May 1729.
[3] ibid, 26 Nov 1724.

suppressed'. The session described this school as follows: 'it cannot properly be accounted a Schooll but a Pedagogy'.[1] Vigilant supervision of schools in ways similar to those followed in these few examples from Leith must also have existed in Edinburgh, especially in the first half of the century.

THE COLLEGE

The College occupied a position in Edinburgh that was unlike that of the Universities in Glasgow, Aberdeen, and St Andrews, for it was 'Our Tounis College', and the Town Council was its patron. Appointments and finance were in the early days matters purely for the Town Council, and even educational policy came within its powers. In theory, the Town Council had the final say in directing education in Edinburgh from the earliest stages right to the end of a University course. Gradually, however, as the eighteenth century progressed, the College gained in independence. The use of the term 'University' is itself an indication of that growth; it was used more and more frequently by members of staff in the course of the eighteenth century, though the Town Council usually stuck to the old term, 'College'. 'The College', too, was the familiar, colloquial, name. It will be used in this study because it recalls the relationship that existed between the growing University and the Town Council.

For most of the seventeenth century, the teaching organisation of the College was the same as that in the other Scottish Universities; the staff consisted of a Principal and four Regents, and each Regent took his class through all the subjects of a four-year course. The system was indeed similar to that of the High School, where a Master took his class for the four-year course, only in the High School the pupils were then handed on to the Rector for the last year. Such an organisation in the College did not encourage specialisation or advanced study. The first departure from it was the appointment of James Gregory to be Professor of Mathematics in 1674. His tenure was short, but the principle had been established, and other

[1] Kirk Session records, 7 Aug 1729.

specialist professors were appointed in the next thirty years.[1] These appointments, like all previous ones, were made by the Town Council, but in 1702 an innovation occurred when the Queen appointed a Professor of Ecclesiastical History. This, the first Regius chair, was accepted by the Town Council under protest. In 1708, the Town Council took a momentous step when it ended the system of rotating Regents, and appointed specialist Professors of Humanity, Greek, Logic and Metaphysics, Natural Philosophy, and Moral Philosophy who constituted what we now call the Faculty of Arts.[2] What became later the Faculty of Law began when the Regius chair in Public Law was founded in 1707. The post of Professor of Civil Law was created in 1710, and that of Professor of Universal Civil History and Greek and Roman Antiquities in 1722, when the chair in Scots Law also was established. The Faculty of Medicine grew from the College of Physicians and the College of Surgeons, and developed with great strides under Alexander Monro, *Primus*, who became Professor of Anatomy in 1722. The first Professor of Anatomy was appointed by the Town Council in 1705, and the first Professor of Chemistry in 1713. Chairs in Midwifery (1739), Botany (1738), and Natural History (1770) followed, and with the opening of the Royal Infirmary clinical lectures began in 1746. The developments that in this way took place in Arts, Law, and Medicine, were not paralleled in Divinity, where the arrangements and methods remained much as they had been in the seventeenth century.[3]

Two other chairs of some interest were established. In 1785, a chair of Practical Astronomy was founded, but the Professor apparently never lectured in the whole of his forty years' tenure of office. Sir Alexander Grant suggests that, when it established this chair, the Town Council had in mind the needs of mates and skippers from Leith. This is probable; the advertisements of private teachers of navigation in the press of the time indicates that there was a demand. The other chair was in

[1] Three members of the College of Physicians were appointed Professors of Medicine in 1685. The Keeper of the Botanic Garden was made Professor of Botany in 1695.
[2] Minutes of the Town Council of Edinburgh, 16 June 1706.
[3] 'Jupiter' Carlyle said that divinity students at Edinburgh were all the livelier intellectually because their professors were dull. *Autobiography* (1860), p 56.

Agriculture, set up in 1790, as the result of the beneficence of Sir William Pulteney.

The establishment of specialist chairs raised the standard of instruction, and increased the prestige of the College. The number of students grew, and they came in large numbers from Ireland and England, especially to the medical classes. For the first fifty years or so of the century, most of the lecturing was still done in Latin. Somerville tells us that Monro *Primus*, the Professor of Anatomy, lectured in English, but Logic and Church History he specially mentions as having been in Latin. As an aid, the lectures in Church History began with a summary in English of the previous talk.[1]

At the end of the seventeenth and beginning of the eighteenth century, the Town Council treated the College much as it treated the High School, appointing the staff and expecting to dictate policy. An example of the Town Council's determination to retain power in its own hands was the incident in 1703 when a group of professors agreed to hold a graduation ceremony in private. It had been the custom in the past for the Lord Provost and magistrates to be present on such occasions, and the Town Council sensed that this proposal by the College staff was a reflection. The Lord Provost made a formal visitation to the College, and summoned the staff to meet him, the magistrates, members of the Town Council, two assessors, and eight of the city ministers. As a result of this meeting, the staff withdrew their proposal. The Lord Advocate, who was one of the assessors, produced a minute which affirmed that the magistrates and the Town Council 'have had and exercised the only and full government of the said College'. The Town Council was therefore confirmed in the use of its powers.

Another cause of disagreement between Town Council and College arose in 1703 over the election of a representative from the College to the General Assembly of the Church of Scotland, and at the time the College staff had to admit that the right to elect a member of Assembly lay with the Town Council. The matter was raised again in 1719, and on this occasion the General Assembly accepted the College's nomination, in spite

---

[1] Somerville, *My Life and Times, 1741-1814*. Edin, 1861, pp 12, 21. He went to Edinburgh University in 1756.

of the Town Council's protests. Another conflict on Church matters broke out in 1728, when the Town Council objected to the Principal and Professors acting 'as a Faculty' in the discussions on heresy at that time. It seems strange that the Town Council should have objected so strongly to the College staff acting as a body, but this was a matter of dispute for a long time. It was, of course, the idea of the College taking independent action that was deplored. The Town Council in fact did not recognise the collective opinion of the Faculty or its powers of managing College affairs until the case, referred to in Chapter III, of Dr Adam's Latin Grammar. This arose in 1785, when the Town Council referred to the 'Principal and Faculty of the College', the problem of settling whether Adam's or Ruddiman's Grammar should be used in the High School.[1]

Finance was in the hands of the Town Council. In the middle of the eighteenth century, the expenses usually exceeded the income from endowments and fees, and the deficit was made up by the Town Council out of the Common Good fund of the city. In 1776, this payment amounted to £340.[2]

It was the practice for professors to sell their professorships with the approval of the Town Council. For example, Robert Hunter, Professor of Greek, sold his chair in 1772 to Andrew Dalzel for £300 and a life-rent of his salary. George Stuart, Professor of Humanity, made a bargain of a similar type with John Hill in 1775, and both arrangements were sanctioned by the Town Council.

The range of subjects provided by the College was greatly extended in the course of the eighteenth century. With the end in 1708 of the old Regenting system, and the development of specialist professors, the practice developed of students merely taking a number of classes, and not graduating.[3] The resulting freedom of choice, coming at a time when the College had some very able professors, had a stimulating effect on the students. Walter Scott did not graduate, but attended classes

---

[1] Minutes of the Town Council of Edinburgh, 2 Feb 1785. See also page 77.
[2] Grant, *The Story of the University of Edinburgh*, Vol II, p 222.
[3] Grant, *The Story of the University of Edinburgh*, Vol II, p 265, says that in 1704, 65 graduated in Arts, and in 1705, 104, but by 1749, there were only 3 graduates, and thereafter only one or two each year to the end of the century.

in Latin, Greek (in which he did not distinguish himself), Ethics, Moral Philosophy (under Dugald Stewart) and History, before he proceeded to Law classes. To some extent the lectures of such men as Joseph Black provided a centre of scientific interest in Edinburgh that made the development of academies on the English model unnecessary. (Such academies were founded in Scotland in towns where there was no University, like Perth, Ayr, Dumfries, Stirling.)

Topham's account of the University in 1774 gives an illustration of the range of interests it encouraged, and the cosmopolitan nature of the student population. 'As the University of Edinburgh is celebrated through Europe for its instruction in particular branches of philosophy and literature, the number of young persons that crowd here from different countries is prodigious. They are under no restraint from the College, but have lodgings in the City. In general they are very extravagant, especially those from Ireland, who too often forsake the calm, retired paths of learning and science, to revel in the public scenes of dissipation and debauchery. But the students who are natives of this country, present a different picture. The miserable holes which some of them inhabit, their abstemiousness and parsimony, their constant attendance to study, their indefatigable industry, even border on romance. But, in general, they apply themselves to too many of the Professors, to pay a proper attention to each; and their excessive earnestness to obtain an universal knowledge, hinders them from gaining that proficiency in any one science, which ought to be the subject of great minds.'[1]

One other contribution which the College made to the life of the city must be mentioned. Of all the Scottish cities, Edinburgh was most open to influences from England and the Continent. By coach and ship from London many visitors came, companies of actors, musicians, charlatans advertising remedies for many ills, merchants, and literary men doing a tour of Scotland, who imparted a cosmopolitan flavour to Edinburgh. As far as education is concerned, however, the most potent influence came through the students from all parts of the United Kingdom, and the visiting lecturers who spoke both in the

[1] Topham, *Letters from Edinburgh*, Vol II, p 17.

College and to a more general public in the town. These visitors, attracted by the prestige of the College, brought many new ideas with them, and not least important were their ideas on education. It so happened that Edinburgh had also developed as a centre of the printing trade, and thus it came about that many textbooks for schools, embodying new ideas, were printed in Edinburgh for distribution all over Scotland. New ideas, from England in particular, were spread from Edinburgh.

It must not be thought that the Town Council, the Presbytery, and the College combined in any recognisable or logical way to organise or further the educational arrangements of Edinburgh in the eighteenth century. There was no organisation in the modern sense. The Town Council had inherited its High School from a past age, and did what was necessary to keep the institution going, but suggestions for rebuilding the school were considered for long periods before anything was done, and the notion of erecting an additional High School to meet the needs of the growing city was coldly received. Towards the College, too, the Town Council carried out its responsibilities, and paid what it had to pay, but looked long and closely at any scheme of development that was likely to cost money. Some of the remarkable advances in the College came not from the patrons' resources but from endowments by private persons and the establishment of Regius chairs.

The self-electing Town Council, like the group of merchant families from which it was largely drawn, had as objectives the increase of the wealth and influence of its members as well as the prosperity of the city. Councillors and magistrates were busy over the expansion of their own and the city's trade, the sale and purchase of lands, mortgage arrangements, local taxation, representations to the local Members of Parliament, negotiations with aristocrats and other gentlemen of influence, and many other projects. The affairs of the High School and the College take up a small part of the Town Council records, and with the exception of the setting up of the Town's English schools in 1759 and a few references to Charity schools, there is relatively little other mention of education at all.

There was nevertheless development in education in Edinburgh during the period, the initiative coming from the Church.

The Presbytery in the early part of the eighteenth century kept on approaching the Town Council about the provision and control of schools, and in mid-century the Presbytery started the movement towards English schools, helped by the Society in Scotland for the Propagation of Christian Knowledge. The prestige of the Presbytery was helped by the fact that one of its members was the Principal of the College, a minister of the Church, and usually high in the Church's councils. But it took all of the Presbytery's efforts to make any progress in the face of the Town Council's unwillingness to spend public money. The English schools would probably not have been established if the Lord Provost had not happened to be George Drummond, a man of strong religious views and sympathetic to the Presbytery's point of view.

Though it would be too much of a simplification to say that the Town Council was concerned with conserving traditions and spending as little money as possible on schemes which did not promise a pecuniary return, that the Presbytery represented on the whole generous ideas about education, and that the College brought the city into touch with contemporary European culture, yet there is something in it. The Presbytery, powerful in the first quarter of the century, had less influence later, when internal quarrels split the Church. The prestige of the College, on the other hand, grew steadily, and by the end of the century it was so widely renowned that independence from control by the Town Council appeared to be ultimately possible. The influence of all three—Town Council, Presbytery and College—in different ways and at different times can be traced in the Elementary and Charity schools, the High schools, Hospital schools, and Private schools, which will be described in the chapters that follow.

THE SCHOOLS

Before a detailed study can be made of the schools of Edinburgh in the eighteenth century, a brief word is perhaps necessary to explain the names they were given. The following notes indicate roughly the functions of the various kinds of schools, but no clear definition can be given of schools, particularly private schools, which changed their nature according to the interests of the master or the popular demand of the moment.

Free (or Charity) Schools. These were schools where the rudiments of reading, spelling, and a little counting were taught. No fees were charged, the expenses being met by charitable donations. They were attended by the children of the poor.

English Schools. At one time called *Lecture Schools*, these were private adventure schools where the rudiments of reading, spelling, and counting were taught. The teacher depended on fees for his livelihood. In many cases the teachers also conducted more advanced classes in subjects like book-keeping, navigation, modern languages, and even—though this was disliked by the High School—Latin and Greek. It was a departure from tradition when the Town Council established English Schools of its own in 1759.

Private Schools is the modern term which most nearly describes the great variety of independent schools which did not necessarily teach only reading and writing. There were schools for mathematics and languages, cookery and dancing. Some of them accepted boarders: small boarding establishments for girls were a feature of the late eighteenth century in Edinburgh.

Hospitals were residential schools for children whose parents had died or had suffered some calamity. The original Hospital was George Heriot's, whose fine building houses today the famous secondary school for boys. George Watson's Hospital was smaller in those days, but is the forerunner of the large and distinguished George Watson's Boys' College. For girls there were two Hospitals founded largely through the efforts of Mary Erskine: of these the Merchant Maiden Hospital is now the Mary Erskine School, and the Trades Maiden Hospital alone remains as a residence for schoolgirls.

Parish Schools. The Parish Schools were provided under Act of Parliament, and existed to teach reading, writing, and some arithmetic. The masters also taught Latin, and scholars could go from them direct to the University. There were no Parish Schools in Edinburgh, but they existed outside the city bounds in places like West Kirk (ie St Cuthbert's), North Leith, Liberton, Colinton, Cramond, and Duddingston.

High Schools were Grammar Schools; that is to say, they existed to teach Latin Grammar and so to prepare boys for entry to the University. Sometimes a little Greek was also taught. There were three High Schools, those of Edinburgh, Canongate, and South Leith. The Canongate High School is sometimes called the Canongate Grammar School, and the school in South Leith is usually called the Grammar School of South Leith. Boys stayed at these schools for four or five years beginning at about the age of 9. The Canongate High School has ceased to exist, but the other High Schools remain today as Leith Academy and The Royal High School.

Chapter II

ELEMENTARY EDUCATION

ELEMENTARY education was provided either in private schools or in schools which were to some extent under the control of public bodies like the Town Council, or the Society in Scotland for the Propagation of Christian Knowledge. The private schools will be discussed in Chapter V. Those for which public bodies were responsible are the concern of the present chapter.

The public provision of elementary education at no time in the eighteenth century resembled the modern system of primary schools under public ownership and direction, yet a certain measure of control of schools by the Town Council which had existed in earlier times was continued, and there were developments in the course of the century which led to a greater degree of public control. The Church, represented locally by the Edinburgh Presbytery, directed and inspired the charitably minded people who founded Charity schools and the Orphan Hospital. Though the Society in Scotland for the Propagation of Christian Knowledge was mostly concerned with the Highland areas of Scotland, there are some interesting examples of its work in Edinburgh. These three bodies, the Town Council, the Presbytery, and the SSPCK, are the only public authorities concerned with elementary education at this time.

The Town Council had for long been accustomed to appoint teachers to schools other than the High School. The earliest references in the post-Reformation period are of 1585, when the Town Council forbade the masters of 'Lecture' schools from teaching unless they had been licensed by the Kirk Session and

31

the Town Council.[1] The ten schoolmasters who at that time were subsequently licensed were also readers in the city churches. The control of schools in these days appears to have been in the hands of the Kirk Session, for the Town Council records state that the Kirk Session decided in 1590 to have separate schools for boys and girls.[2] In the course of the seventeenth century there are numerous references in the Town Council Minutes to the appointment of schoolmasters, but the term 'appointed' meant that the schoolmaster was approved as a fit and proper person to hold a school, and did not mean that he was paid a salary or provided with a schoolroom. Some schoolmasters, however, were granted allowances to help them to pay the rents of schoolrooms. The Town Council did not always insist that all schoolmasters should be licensed, and as a result there were times when the number of private school-masters in the city increased. Sometimes these men also taught Latin, and then there were complaints from the masters of the High School that their privilege was being infringed.[3] After the Revolution of 1688, the Town Council scrutinised with particular care the appointment of teachers, and in 1694 the keepers of private schools were warned to make application to the Town Council for licences to teach in such parts of the town as should be appointed for them. This implies a degree of planning and control that was not continued.[4] There were undoubtedly more schoolmasters in the city than were formally licensed by the Town Council, but it was a privilege to be licensed, as can be seen in the advertisements of one school-master, James Porterfield, whose work will be discussed later.

[1] Minutes of the Town Council of Edinburgh, 11 March 1585-86 and 7 Sept 1586.

[2] ibid, 6 Nov 1590. '. . . the session of the kirk . . . has thought expedient to make a separation in the lecture schools between the lads and lasses put to learn there, and has designed and appointed three masters to have the sole teaching of lasses.'

[3] ibid, 26 July 1656 and 28 Jan 1680. On the latter occasion, five school-masters were forbidden to teach Latin and signed a declaration accordingly.

[4] ibid, 6 June 1694. The Council recommended to the Magistrates that they should forbid the keeping of all Private schools that were contrary to the 'several acts and constitutions of the good town' until the masters of these schools 'make particular application to the Council and have their licences accordingly for keeping of Private schools in such places as shall be appointed for them alone'.

THE SCOPE OF ELEMENTARY EDUCATION

A word is necessary about the scope of elementary education as it was understood in Edinburgh in the eighteenth century. For boys who were later to proceed to the High School to learn Latin, elementary education provided a knowledge of reading and writing English. This could be given in the two years or so before the age of 9, when a boy might expect to begin his studies at the High School. In the early part of the century arithmetic did not occupy an important place in this training. As the interest of people grew in the development of commerce, however, arithmetic gradually gained a more regular place in school studies, and advanced pupils were also taught simple book-keeping. But reading was the basic subject and, in the eyes of the Church of Scotland, the teaching of reading meant the spreading of the knowledge of the Bible. The Bible was frequently used as a textbook, and most of the reading books contained passages from it, and from later works of a religious nature. The very name that was given to these schools shows that they were regarded first and foremost as the schools where children learned to read English, for they were called 'English' schools. The development of the use of this name is interesting. In the sixteenth century, similar schools were known as 'Lecture' schools, obviously because their main duty was the teaching of reading.[1] At the same period, these schools were also called 'Vulgar' schools, that is, schools where the native tongue was taught, as distinct from schools where Latin was taught.[2] In the seventeenth century, the vulgar tongue is twice mentioned in Town Council records as being Scots.[3] It was at the end of the seventeenth century that these schools were beginning to be known as 'English' schools. The term

---

[1] Minutes of the Town Council of Edinburgh, 11 March 1586, 23 Oct 1594, and other dates.

[2] ibid, 23 Oct 1594. This, the last reference to Lecture schools, contains also the first reference to 'Vulgar' schools. Henry Bryntoun was ordered to be reader in the East Kirk, and to read there on Sunday afternoons like other masters 'of the vulgar schools'. The last reference to Vulgar schools is in 1661, in the session records of South Leith, when David Forbes was allowed to keep a Vulgar school, and to teach reading, arithmetic, accounts, and Dutch.

[3] ibid, 12 Feb 1658, 7 Nov 1660. See Appendix I.

C

had been the normal one in England, and its use was probably borrowed from that country. The first official use of the term occurs in the Town Council minutes in 1694.[1]

On 9th June 1694, the Town Council appointed James Porterfield to be an English schoolmaster in the city. They agreed to pay him a hundred merks yearly (a sum approximately equal to £5 10s sterling) 'for his encouragement and for payment of his house rent'. Obviously, Porterfield drew his income from fees, an arrangement that had been usual in Edinburgh in the past and was to continue during the whole of the eighteenth century as the practice in all schools other than Charity schools. He seems to have been a distinguished teacher; in an advertisement attached to one of his books he claimed 'a rare and excellent method' of teaching children to read and write.[2] He retired in 1715, and the Town Council granted him a small sum of about £2 10s, whether as a pension or as a single payment is not clear.[3] In 1718, Archibald Keith petitioned the Town Council in respect of his 'singularity in teaching of English', and was granted an annual payment similar to that given to Porterfield, and on similar conditions.[4] Keith's appointment lasted until 1738. That there was need for properly authorised teachers of reading and writing may be gathered from a Presbytery recommendation of 1721 that there should be 'several schools in different parts of the city for teaching English by masters legally authorised'.[5] The Town Council did nothing on these lines until 1758 when, as will be described later, they established English schools in certain parts of Edinburgh. After Keith's appointment there is no reference to another being legally authorised in this way, and it is impossible to say why the Town Council did not continue the practice of appointing English teachers. One may guess, however, that the magistrates felt that the Charity schools could meet the needs of the poor,

---

[1] Minutes of the Town Council of Edinburgh, 9 June 1694.
[2] For details of his writings and methods, see Chapter VI.
[3] Minutes of the Town Council of Edinburgh, 3 June 1715.
[4] *ibid*, 3 Sept 1718.
[5] Edinburgh Presbytery Minutes, 18 Oct 1721.

and private schools those of the middle and upper classes. The numbers of both Charity and private schools increased in the first half of the eighteenth century.

The earliest reference to Charity or Free schools occurs in a minute of the Town Council of 1699.[1] It was then reported that there were many children in the city whose parents could not afford to pay fees for their children's education 'in these hard times'.[2] To satisfy their needs, the Town Council appointed George Clark, precentor in the Tolbooth Kirk, to be schoolmaster for as many of these children, boys and girls, as he could take. In the first instance he was to conduct his school in his own house and limit the numbers to forty. The subjects of instruction were reading, writing, a little arithmetic, and 'the common tunes of music', which were the twelve psalm tunes sung in church services. In addition, Mrs Clark was to instruct the girls in the working of stockings. The hours were nine to twelve and two to five, every weekday except Saturday afternoon. Clark's salary was fixed at £10 sterling annually, and he was forbidden to accept fees or other payments. There are two references to George Clark's school in the Minutes of the Presbytery. On the occasion of the Presbyterial visitation of Edinburgh in 1706, Clark told the visiting ministers that he taught his pupils to read and write English, and that his wife taught 'the poor girls' to 'work stockings and some things of that nature'. He then had over sixty pupils and had previously had more.[3] Of a visitation to certain schools in 1713, the Presbytery minute records: 'as to the Charity school, the scholars are taught to read the Holy Scriptures and other good books, writing and arithmetic, and the girls are taught to knit stockings'.[4] Clark died in 1714, and was succeeded by another precentor, John Finlater of the New North Kirk.

[1] Minutes of the Town Council of Edinburgh, 24 Feb 1699. See also Appendix II.
[2] Harder times were to come, for the news of the first failure at Darien was received in Edinburgh in Sept 1699.
[3] Edinburgh Presbytery Minutes, 14 Feb 1706.
[4] *ibid*, 1 April 1713.

By 1714, another Charity school had been established, for there is mention in a report from the Presbytery to the General Assembly of two Charity schools, 'one maintained by the Honourable Magistrates and Town Council, and the other by a voluntary collection at the church doors'. The latter is described in the Town Council Minutes as the Charity school in the east part of the city, taught by Arthur Cooper, formerly schoolmaster in Portsburgh, or West Kirk parish. Cooper's salary in 1723 was £12 sterling per annum.[1]

In 1718, money was left to the Town Council by Sir James McLurg of Vogrie to establish and maintain a Charity school. Sir James, a former Dean of Guild, left a sum of about £1225 sterling to various charities. As a benefactor to Edinburgh, his name should not be forgotten, but remembered along with those of George Heriot and Mary Erskine. For a Charity school, McLurg left the sum of £166 13s 4d sterling, of which the annual interest, amounting to £8 6s 8d sterling, went towards the salary of the schoolmaster.[2]

It appears from the Town Council minutes that the original intention of the Council may have been to divide the money from the McLurg bequest between the two schools, for the Treasurer was authorised to pay the interest 'to the respective Treasurers and Schoolmasters of the Charity schools'.[3] A later minute, however, records the decision that the money should be paid 'to the master of the Charity school to be named by the Magistrates and Council for the time being in the terms of the said mortification'.[4] This left it open to the Town Council to pay the money to the master of either of the Charity schools, but in fact the school 'in the West part of the city' was the one that received the money and was thereafter known as Sir James McLurg's Charity School. John Finlater was the first schoolmaster to be paid partly from the McLurg bequest; of his total annual salary of £11 5s stg (200 merks), the McLurg bequest gave £8 6s 8d, and the Town Council supplied the rest from the money received from a tax of two pennies on the pint of

---

[1] Minutes of the Town Council of Edinburgh, 9 July 1715 and 17 April 1723.
[2] ibid, 24 Dec 1718.
[3] ibid, 21 May 1718.
[4] ibid, 13 June 1718.

ale or beer.[1] Finlater's successor James Dewar, appointed in 1725, was paid £11 13s 4d stg (140 pounds Scots), 'by and with the interest of the sum mortified[2] by the deceased Sir James McLurg'.[3] In 1727, however, there was a change, and in response to Dewar's request, his salary of £20 sterling was made up of £8 6s 8d from the Kirk Treasurer and £11 13s 4d from the Town Treasurer. No mention is made of McLurg's bequest, which had presumably become part of the town's general income. The school continued to be known as 'the Charity School founded by Sir James McLurg',[4] though strictly speaking it had been founded earlier than the McLurg bequest.

The other Charity school, that 'in the East part of the city', depended for its existence on the voluntary church collections which were authorised yearly in December by the Town Council and Kirk Session.[5] But in 1740 this Charity school was closed because 'it has not served the design thereof', and, furthermore, the contributions were insufficient for its upkeep.[6] It is possible that the existence of other Charity schools had affected this one adversely.

In 1730, for instance, John Wightman of Maulsby, a former Lord Provost, left a sum of about £400 sterling, the interest of which was to be applied to maintaining a Charity school to be known as Wightman's School, to be under the patronage of the Tolbooth Kirk Session.[7] This school does not appear again in the Town Council minutes, but there is reference to it in the records of the SSPCK, when the Society agreed in 1758 to send the school 200 copies of the first page of Kerr's Spelling Book.[8]

Sir James McLurg's Charity school was in operation throughout the century, and there are several references to it in Town Council records. From 1740 to 1766, the master was Alexander Cleghorn, precentor in the College Kirk, to which, according to

[1] Minutes of the Town Council of Edinburgh, 24 Dec 1718.
[2] ie bequeathed to an institution.
[3] Minutes of the Town Council of Edinburgh, 8 Sept 1725.
[4] ibid, 28 April 1727.
[5] ibid, 24 Dec 1718, 20 Nov 1723, 6 Dec 1728, etc.
[6] ibid, 1 Feb 1740.
[7] ibid, 30 July 1730.
[8] Society in Scotland for the Propagation of Christian Knowledge, 30 Nov 1758.

a minute of 1751, this Charity school was attached.[1]   On Cleghorn's death in 1766, the Town Council arranged for three city ministers to examine and 'take trial' of the candidates for the vacant post, and James Tod, a teacher in the city, was successful. In less than a year he had petitioned the Council for help in furnishing the school. He said that he had spent 19s for a table and seats and other necessaries, and that the number of pupils was steadily increasing.[2]   The Council agreed that one of the bailies should arrange matters as he thought fit. Tod's next move to improve the status of his school reveals something of its nature. The Town's English schools, the founding and development of which will be des-cribed later in this chapter, were regularly inspected, and a report on their progress was published in the Edinburgh papers. In a manuscript note preserved in the City Chambers, Tod complains that the English schools were mentioned in the press, but 'Your Free school entirely neglected'. He adds a draft for submission to the press, as follows: 'Tuesday the 18th of August 1767 the Free School of Edinburgh taught by Mr Tod at his entreaty was visited by order of the Lord Provost and Town Council and the scholars being examined in presence of a Magistrate and a Doctor of Divinity had great approbation for their progress and good behaviour, and the judges highly approved of the diligence of the master.' (The last clause has been added to the original and is in a different hand.) In his note to the Town Council, Tod proceeds: 'It is true that this school may in some sense be said to be in its infancy, and taught by imitation and rules, only *viva voce*, for want of proper books, yet it is surprising they behave so well as they do. . . . It is a mistake to think that children of this school are only of the refuse of the people, for though a great many of their parents may be said to be in low life, yet they are in good repute and the children themselves are far from being street vagabonds....'[3] That the Charity school, like the others under the patronage of the Town Council, was regularly visited and examined is confirmed from the Presbytery minutes, where there is a refer-

[1] Minutes of the Town Council of Edinburgh, 17 April 1751.
[2] *ibid*, 25 March 1767.
[3] City Archives, MacLeod, Vol II, Bay D, Bundle 60, Shelf 17, Item 23.

ence to the appointment of a visiting committee for all the Charity schools.[1]

When Tod died in 1774, he was succeeded by George Fulton, one of the unsuccessful candidates for a vacancy in one of the Town's English schools. The committee was pleased with his 'manner of reading English both in prose and verse, as well as with his skill in arithmetic and writing'.[2] Five years later, Fulton was appointed to an English school, and there was again a vacancy in the Charity school. Some papers in the City Archives give us information about the candidates for the post, and the method of selection.[3] The candidates were James Ruthven, Alex Farquharson, Wm Davidson, James Graham, John Adams, William Brown, and James Muat, and the examiners were the Rev John Drysdale and Professor Andrew Dalzel. In his application, Gray gave as a sample of his handwriting the word 'Multiplication'; Ruthven merely stated that he was a printer in Edinburgh; Brown gave a sample of his handwriting and a testimonial from the minister of St Cuthbert's that he had taught a Private school in that parish since 1770, with entire satisfaction; Muat said that he had been trained in the English language. No doubt they had to read aloud to the examining committee, as Fulton in his time had had to do, and to show their skill in arithmetic, but no record remains of that part of the proceedings. There does exist, however, a sheet on which each of the candidates wrote a few words opposite his name. The words were, 'As Charles was the first prince', and there is no doubt that Muat (who wrote last and therefore knew what he had to beat) wrote best of all. At any rate, he was appointed.

The Charity school figures regularly in the Town Council Minutes, but for the most part only routine developments are noted. The most interesting entry falls in 1794, and consists of new regulations for the school.[4] The numbers were to be limited to forty, and no scholars admitted under 5 years of age. No scholar was to remain at the school for longer than five years. Absentees who had no satisfactory excuse were to be

[1] Edinburgh Presbytery Minutes, 31 Jan 1770, 27 Jan 1773, 31 Jan 1776.
[2] Minutes of the Town Council of Edinburgh, 9 Feb 1774.
[3] City Archives, MacLeod, Bay D, Bundle 119, Shelf 18.
[4] Minutes of the Town Council of Edinburgh, 5 March 1794.

reported to the College Bailie, who would make enquiries about their absence. Pupils who learned writing and arithmetic had to furnish their own pens, ink, and paper. The school was to open and dismiss with prayer, and the master was to be careful to instruct his pupils in the principles of religion. One interesting rule was that no scholar could be admitted without an order from the magistrates; in other words, only those who were known to be in poor circumstances could attend, an arrangement which protected the position of the many other schools where fees were charged. It is unlikely that the Charity school was very well supplied with equipment, though there is a record of the Town Council providing some books.[1]

Probably the last reference to Sir James McLurg's Charity school is to be found in the *Municipal Corporations Report* of 1835. There it is noted that the conditions of the bequest had been remodelled by the Town Council in 1824. The master at the time of the report had a salary of £52 9s 8d a year, and fees at the rate of 6d a month from each pupil. The number of pupils was not to exceed 100.

Humanitarian impulses have at all times found an outlet in the establishment of schools for the benefit of poor children but, as has been pointed out by Miss M G Jones, the movement was outstandingly strong among religiously minded people in the latter half of the eighteenth century.[2] Several Charity schools were founded either by Kirk Sessions or by groups of Church people in Edinburgh at this time. For example, a subscription Charity school was set up in Blackfriars Wynd in 1778 for poor and destitute children who, in the words of the advertisement for the school, 'are left to wander idly on the streets and exposed to almost every vice'. The notice continues: 'Though there are Charity schools which have been long established in this city, and have been attended with the most salutary effects, the children of the poor are now so numerous, and the funds already appropriated to their education are so much exhausted, that the establishment of new seminaries of this kind

---

[1] Minutes of the Town Council of Edinburgh, 24 Oct 1798. The Council agreed to supply three or four dozen copies of Gray's Spelling Book (a primer for the teaching of reading), and two dozen Testaments.
[2] Jones, *The Charity School Movement in the XVIII Century,* pp 1-14.

is become a matter not of mere expediency but of absolute necessity: especially at this time when the fathers of many destitute children are employed in the service of their country'.[1]

The aim of these schools was simple, to teach these poor children to read, and to instruct them in the principles of religion. Children were presented with Bibles when they left school. The master had a salary and a free house, and was not allowed to accept fees. A report by two visiting ministers in 1781 was as follows: 'Many of the children read and spell with great ease and propriety, and have been taught to sing the common church tunes.' The same notice ends with an appeal for funds, for the promoters of the school were 'affected by the consideration that, after all that has been done, the education of a great number of poor children is totally neglected'.[2] There were then 69 children attending this school. Two years later, the number of pupils was 60, and the visiting ministers' report read: 'Many of those in the higher classes read with great ease and propriety, and distinctly repeated important passages of a religious and moral tendency, judiciously selected from the Scriptures and their school books.'

THE CHARITY WORKHOUSES

The Charity Workhouse of Edinburgh was established by the Town Council in 1743 as a house of detention for the workless poor, and a teacher, William Halywell, was appointed to instruct the children who lived in it. The SSPCK approved of Halywell's appointment and paid him £25 sterling a year. From time to time the Society also sent books for the use of his pupils.[3] In 1744, the Presbytery Minutes record the information that it was necessary for the rules of the SSPCK, who paid Mr Halywell's salary, that the Charity Workhouse be visited by representatives of the Presbytery, and a committee

[1] *The Edinburgh Evening Courant*, 29 Jan 1781.
[2] *ibid*, 29 Jan 1781.
[3] Society in Scotland for the Propagation of Christian Knowledge, Minutes, 1744. The Society agreed to the request of Mr Halywell 'teacher of the poor house of this city . . . for 10 doz Syllabicating Catechisms and 5 doz of the Mothers' Catechism'. 'Syllabicating' means having the big words divided into syllables.

was appointed for this purpose.[1] That committee reported of the teacher: 'he teaches some of the people in the said house reading, and instructs them in the principles of religion. . . . that the Society had allowed them some books for the use of the boys and girls in the said house which books are carefully preserved except such as are distributed according to the Society's regulations.'[2]

Though children in the Workhouse had some training in reading and some instruction in religion, just as important in the eyes of the Town Council was the learning of trades. A report to the Town Council recommending a collection in aid of the Workhouse in 1752 is as follows: 'Young children left destitute are early trained up to virtue and religion by one employed for this purpose by the SSPCK, early accustomed to work, by which means they are prepared to be serviceable to tradesmen in the several branches of manufactures that have of late made great progress in this country, where more hands are still wanting.'[3] There is no full information as to what these trades were, but spinning, weaving and 'other branches of female industry' were taught by a woman teacher who was paid £5 a year by the SSPCK after 1766.[4]

In 1750 the Town Council decided that the revenue of the old pre-Reformation foundation called Paul's Work should be handed over to the Charity Workhouse for the following seven years, and that the Workhouse should be obliged to receive 20 children immediately, and then annually as many as it could accommodate. These children, to be called the 'Children of Paul's Work', were to live separately from the other children and to have a special uniform. The boys were to be in 'dark gray coloured cloth and mettall buttons' and the girls in 'coloured gowns faced with green'. The boys were to be taught writing and arithmetic, and might afterwards be bound apprentices in the manufacture in which they had been trained in the Workhouse. At the end of a satisfactory apprenticeship boys would be granted each £5 sterling. Girls would receive £2 sterling on

[1] Edinburgh Presbytery Minutes, 31 Oct 1744.
[2] *ibid*, 28 Nov 1744.
[3] Minutes of the Town Council of Edinburgh, 22 Jan 1752.
[4] *Account of Funds etc of SSPCK*, 1796.

leaving the Workhouse. In the course of that year 16 boys were admitted to the Workhouse from Paul's Work.[1] The training described above appears to be the same as had formerly been provided in Paul's Work where, as far back as 1718, boys were given training in weaving, reading, writing, and arithmetic, and a gift of 100 merks (or £5 sterling) and a suit of clothes on completing apprenticeship.[2]

Two other Charity Workhouses were set up in 1761, in the parishes of Canongate and West Kirk (St Cuthbert's), and each employed a teacher. An advertisement in the press in 1772 seems to indicate that little was done in the way of teaching reading and writing in the Canongate Charity Workhouse, for it mentions only instruction in the 'principles of religion' and 'some useful manufactures'.[3] An advertisement for a master for the West Kirk Charity Workhouse in 1780 specifies that the master should be able to teach reading and church music, and the principles of religion. He should also be acquainted with arithmetic and the keeping of accounts; since, however, the teaching of these subjects was not specifically demanded, it is possible that they were required only in connection with keeping the books of the manufactures carried on in the Workhouse.[4]

Little information is to be found about living conditions in these Charity Workhouses. Life was almost certainly hard for the children; the constant references to early training in virtue, and the value of being in youth accustomed to work, remind us that to the eighteenth-century mind, education was a discipline of mind and body, and that the poor were to be trained not only in virtue but in industry. A letter which appeared in the *Courant* in 1782, criticising the Workhouses, brought forth a reply which adds a little to the small store of our knowledge of these institutions.[5] At that time, says the anonymous but well-informed writer, one-third of the children in the three Workhouses were under 6 years of age. Of the 200 children in the Edinburgh Charity Workhouse, an average of 7 died every year; of 60-70 in West Kirk Workhouse, 13 had died in the

---

[1] Minutes of the Town Council of Edinburgh, 2 May 1750.
[2] *The Edinburgh Evening Courant*, 17 Nov 1718.
[3] *ibid*, 1 Jan 1772.
[4] *ibid*, 18 Dec 1780.
[5] *ibid*, 30 Dec 1782 and 6 Jan 1783.

previous five years, and of 56-66 in Canongate Workhouse, 8 had died in the previous five years. The boys and girls were in separate houses in the Edinburgh Workhouse, and were kept apart from the adult poor. The writer claimed that their education was well looked after, and that its quality compared favourably with that of the Orphan Hospital, to which compliments had been paid.

THE ORPHAN HOSPITAL

The Orphan Hospital was established in 1733. An interesting account of its foundation and early development is to be found in an article by John Richardson in the productions of the Old Edinburgh Club.[1] The management was in the hands of a committee of the original subscribers, but they quickly secured the goodwill and sponsorship of the SSPCK. They also approached the Edinburgh Presbytery, and invited its moderator, together with another minister and an elder, to join the board of governors. The Presbytery agreed, and arranged for church collections to be made in aid of the project. The Minute of Presbytery which records these matters also mentions that the aim of the Hospital was to teach the orphans reading, writing, and useful trades, a programme similar to that of the Charity Workhouse.[2] Many contributors in Edinburgh gave generous donations to the new hospital, and Mr Richardson gives a list of these, including sheets and blankets, a striking clock, shoes for the boys, and 25 dozen baps. There were at first 24 boys and 6 girls, selected from 73 applicants from many parts of Scotland, and aged between 8 and 11 years.[3]

In asking the Presbytery in 1736 to organise another church collection in aid of the Orphan Hospital, the governors gave a short report on its progress in the three years of its existence. The greater part of the new building had been built. There were 54 orphans, a Master, a Mistress, Doctor or Usher (ie a teacher), a woman who taught the children carding and spinning, wool combers, a master weaver and other weavers, and women

[1] In *Book of the Old Edinburgh Club*, XXVI (1949), pp 155-68.
[2] Edinburgh Presbytery Minutes, 30 Jan 1734.
[3] *The Caledonian Mercury*, 29 Oct 1733.

servants, in all 66 persons resident in the Hospital. The children were instructed in the principles of religion, and taught 'from the lowest part of the woollen manufacture, and brought that length so as to earn their own bread, and some others have been put out to apprenticeships under indentures, and girls to common service'.[1] In 1738 there were 70 orphans; the practical work consisted of 'pulling wool, carding, spinning, winding pirns, and divers on the linen weaving'. This was presumably the work of the boys, for a sentence specifically adds: "The girls were busy about linen manufacture.'[2] At a general meeting of the subscribers in the following year, the 66 orphans appeared 'all clothed with their own manufacture, and such an air of cheerfulness in their countenances that bespoke how thankful they are for their mercy'.[3] In the same newspaper report, the words about the need 'to sow the seeds of industry in their very infant years' strike strangely on modern ears, but remind the reader that the kindest of charitable people in those days felt that the poor should be trained early in habits of hard work. Patriotic Scotsmen no doubt also had in mind that if they could train poor children to be efficient in the manufacture of textiles, they could develop the wool and linen industries to the benefit of their country and themselves. The number of members of staff engaged on this practical training is significant.

Mr Richardson describes a typical day in the Orphan Hospital in 1736, basing his information on a report of that period. The children alternated 'work' with lessons. 'They commenced work at 6 o'clock in the morning and continued till 8 at night. The smaller children rose about 7 and got their questions until 8, when they got breakfast.' ('Getting their questions' means learning and reciting the catechism.) After family worship, school and work went on by turns throughout the day, two classes being at work while one was in school. The school subjects were reading, writing, arithmetic, and church music. The master catechised the children twice a week. At the date of this report, all the children except five were able to read the

---

[1] Edinburgh Presbytery Minutes, 29 Dec 1736.
[2] ibid, 25 Jan 1738.
[3] The Caledonian Mercury, 23 Oct 1739.

Bible, and '42 are learning to write and several of the boys and also some of the girls had got a considerable part of the Assembly's Larger Catechism by heart, some had the whole of it'.

Since the Orphan Hospital received children from all parts of Scotland, the SSPCK, which was founded to serve primarily the rural areas, was within its powers in helping by financial grants.[1] The Society gave a grant towards the salary of the teacher, of £10 10s in 1754 for example, and supplies of textbooks similar to those dispatched to schools all over the Highlands. In 1756, to take only one entry, the Society supplied 3 dozen Psalm books, 3 dozen Kerr's Spelling Books, 3 dozen 'syllabicating' Catechisms, 3 dozen simple Catechisms, and 60 copies of the first sheet of Kerr's Spelling Book.[2]

The number of orphan children accommodated in the Hospital increased and in 1784 there were 130, 70 boys and 60 girls. The curriculum remained basically as in the early days. The yearly accounts in the press of the amount of work carried out in spinning, weaving, and knitting are impressive. In 1786, for instance, there were between 130 and 140 children; the girls had spun the yarn for 483 yards of linen cloth which they had made into shirts 'for the whole family'. The girls made all their own clothes, did all the domestic work of the house, and some of the younger ones made lace which was sold at the Hospital. The boys spun yarn for 453 yards of woollen stuff to 'clothe the whole family', made and mended their own clothes, made and mended all the Hospital shoes, and bound all their own books. Boys and girls had together knitted 280 pairs of stockings. The report ends: 'When they are not at play out of doors to keep their young minds cheerful, they are encouraged to sing and dance in the house to their own music.'[3] This is a happier picture than most of the reports on the Orphan Hospital suggest.

---

[1] The position of the Society in Scotland for the Propagation of Christian Knowledge is discussed in detail on page 47.

[2] Society in Scotland for the Propagation of Christian Knowledge, Minutes, 14 Jan and 2 Dec 1756. It is typical of the careful and practical management of the SSPCK that when it was reported that the first page of Kerr's Spelling Book, being usually used by the youngest children, was often torn or destroyed and the whole book thereby spoiled, the Society decided to print a large number of separate first sheets for the use of beginners.

[3] *The Caledonian Mercury*, 26 July 1786.

Forty years earlier, the Presbytery had defined the object of the Hospital as to prepare the orphans 'for the business of life and the purposes of eternity',[1] and it is this sober attitude that characterises most of the reports on its work. These abound with descriptions of the home-made clothes, monotonous diet, diseases, hard work, and formidable lists of garments made and yards of material woven. There is something pathetic in the thought of these hard-worked children ever playing or singing or dancing, but no doubt, being children, they did find some interest or fun.

THE TOWN'S ENGLISH SCHOOLS

The establishment in 1759 of the Town's English schools is a most important development. It is significant because it is an early recognition of the town's responsibility for elementary education, though in that respect the arrangements did not go far. It is interesting because the movement towards the erection of these schools and of the Charity Working schools was the result of co-operation between the Town Council on the one hand, and the Edinburgh Presbytery and the SSPCK on the other. The minutes of the bodies concerned indicate incidentally something of the relationship that existed among them.

A preliminary word is necessary about the history and aims of the Society in Scotland for the Propagation of Christian Knowledge. Though founded earlier, this Society was given letters patent in 1709, and had as its object 'to erect and maintain schools in such parts of the Highlands and Islands of Scotland, as should be thought to need them most; in which schools the children of Popish as well as Protestant parents should be taught the English Language, reading and writing, and especially the principles of true religion'.[2] The headquarters of the Society was in Edinburgh, and from the beginning the Edinburgh Presbytery and the University were strongly represented on the committee of management; some of the Edinburgh ministers indeed undertook the day by day running

---

[1] Edinburgh Presbytery Minutes, 29 Dec 1742.
[2] *Account of the Funds etc of the SSPCK*, Edinburgh 1796.

of the Society's affairs. As has been noted in the cases of the Charity Workhouse and the Orphan Hospital, the Society, though most of its work was in the Highlands and Islands, also took an interest in work in Edinburgh.

The first move towards the founding of the Town's English schools came from the Presbytery. The minutes record the receipt of a letter from the SSPCK to all presbyteries, enquiring whether parish schools had been set up in all parishes, and urging presbyteries where no such schools had been established to take steps to force the heritors to comply with the law. In reply to this letter, the Edinburgh Presbytery, after stating that there was provision in the area for schools according to the law, proceeded to add the following interesting statement: 'And it being observed that the educating of children in this city to read English is at present on a very bad footing, and in particular in respect of the high fees exacted by many of the teachers thereof, therefore the Presbytery appoint a committee, Messrs Stevenson, Lindsay, Kay, Jardine, Walker, and Hyndman to enquire into that affair and to converse with the magistrates anent the same.'[1] The committee worked fast. On 15 November 1758 they had shown a memorial on the prevalence of ignorance in the city to the committee of the SSPCK, and on 28 November they presented it to the Presbytery. It was approved, and the committee was instructed to speak about the subject to the SSPCK and to the magistrates. On 13 December the Town Council appointed the Lord Provost and a committee to meet the Presbytery committee and representatives of the SSPCK, and on 20 December the Lord Provost, the distinguished George Drummond, presented a report to the Town Council which is substantially the memorial of the Presbytery, and the proposals were approved. The solution proposed was twofold. The Town Council should proceed to set up four English schools, the masters and curricula of which would require to be acceptable to the Presbytery, and the SSPCK should at the same time establish three Charity Working schools.

---

[1] *Fasti.* The Rev James Stevenson was minister of New Greyfriars, Rev George Lindsay of North Leith, Rev George Kay of New Greyfriars (Moderator of the General Assembly in 1759), Rev Dr John Jardine of Lady Yester's, Rev Robert Walker of St Giles, and the Rev John Hyndman of St Cuthbert's. Edinburgh Presbytery Minutes, 29 Sept 1758.

For a joint effort by three different committees this was very quick work, and one cannot help feeling that the city ministers —who were influential in all three of the interested parties— had done a great deal of persuasive argument before the formal actions of the committees took place at all. Be that as it may, the four English schools of the Town Council were opened on 18 June 1759, and the three Charity Working schools of the SSPCK by the end of July.[1]

The memorandum put forward by Drummond is valuable because it gives a picture of the school provision existing in 1758. The picture is incomplete, but it is exceptional to have such a survey at all. The memorandum says that there were 24 English schools taught by men in the city. Two of these schools were, as we have seen, the Charity schools. Of the remaining 22, four or five charged fees of at least 10s 6d per quarter, which, with other payments like 'Coal money', made a total of £2 10s or £2 15s per annum. About twelve of the schools charged 5s per quarter, four charged 4s and one charged only 3s per quarter. There were in addition five or six schools taught by women, at varying charges, none of which is given. The average attendance at the schools taught by men was 30, and at the women's schools, 15. The conclusion was that some 800 children, including those in the Charity schools, were being taught to read. It was calculated that there were in the city 3000 children 'fit to go to school', and the obvious conclusion was that more provision was urgently needed. We do not know what criteria were used in determining the numbers of those 'fit to go to school', but it would be in agreement with contemporary practice if these numbers included all the children between the ages of 6 and 9.[2]

In the eyes of the Presbytery there was another serious problem. Of the 22 schoolmasters, only 9 were members of the Church of Scotland, the others being 'Nonjurors, Seceders, Cameronians, etc.' Furthermore, several of the Church of Scotland teachers, especially those who were charging high fees, were not teaching the Catechism, and were not insisting on their

---

[1] Minutes of the Town Council of Edinburgh for the dates mentioned.
[2] See Appendix III for the complete minute of Council setting up these schools.

D

scholars reading from the Bible. The Presbytery therefore felt that religious training was being neglected, and that a considerable number of pupils was being brought up to regard the establishment in both Church and State with criticism and possibly aversion.

The regulations agreed for the English schools may be summarised here. First, the appointment of masters was to be in the hands of the Town Council. The Town Council agreed, however, to follow the regulations approved by the Presbytery in their memorial, and there may be said therefore to have been a compromise over the control of the schools. In practice, ministers were always on the committees which selected schoolmasters for the English schools. The schools were to open and close with prayer and a psalm. Each pupil was to read 'a large portion' of the Bible every day, and was to repeat first thing in the morning session a question from the Catechism. Saturday forenoons were to be devoted to Bible reading and Catechism. A visiting committee, consisting of at least a magistrate, a minister, and an elder, should visit quarterly and report to the Council, the master's salary being conditional on good reports. The schools were not free: fees were fixed at the modest rate of 2s per quarter, with an additional 1s from each pupil at Candlemas for coal and candle. The Town Council granted £10 sterling to each master annually, to defray the expense of renting a schoolroom and for his 'encouragement'. Finally, it was laid down that the schools should be established in convenient parts of the city; this met a complaint of long standing on the part of the Presbytery, that there were populous areas not served hitherto by schools.[1]

Before the English schools were opened, there was a change in the fees to be charged; the Town Council decided that these should be increased to 3s for English, and 2s 6d each for writing and arithmetic, and that the Candlemas charge for coal and candle should be 2s.[2]

---

[1] For example, in 1721 (Edinburgh Presbytery Minutes, 9 Nov 1721) the Presbytery complained to the Town Council that there ought to be several schools for teaching English in different parts of the city. The magistrates agreed that the Presbytery's case was good, and promised help, but nothing was done.

[2] Minutes of the Town Council of Edinburgh, 11 April 1759.

A committee of six of the city ministers was set up to 'publickly try' the applicants for the post of master, and the following were chosen. The situation of each school is given also:

Alexander Gairdner, bottom of Burnet's Close.
Thomas Young, bottom of Peebles Wynd.
James Stalker, second storey of second stair of the land above the Weigh house, North side of the Street.
John Watson, Drummond's Land in Blackfriars Wynd.

By request of the Town Council, the city ministers announced the opening of the schools from their pulpits, and exhorted their hearers not to miss such a favourable opportunity to get good and reasonably cheap education for their children.[1]

The schools were inspected the following February, and an excellent report was submitted on their progress. Stalker had 22 scholars, Gairdner 30, Young 23, and Watson 15. The visiting committee 'took trial' of the several classes at each school in writing, reading, and arithmetic, and the result was very satisfactory. The committee suggested that the city ministers might help to supply each school with a catechism suited to the age of the youngest pupils, 'who are very young in the lowest classes'. As a result of this favourable report, the masters got the salaries of £10 per annum they had been promised.[2] A paper in the City Archives of this date gives us some more information; it is a letter from the four masters to the Town Council saying that they have found it impossible to get suitable rooms below £12 or £14 rent, and asking the magistrates to provide schoolrooms.[3] Nothing came of this, but three years later the Town Council increased the annual grant by £5, provided that they were satisfied that the masters had taken houses 'with large well-lighted rooms for teaching in to the value of the sum hereby granted and allowed'. The Town Council took seriously this matter of accommodation, and when Dunsmuir, who had succeeded Watson, moved to Chalmers Close, his house was inspected and approved before any pay-

---

[1] Minutes of the Town Council of Edinburgh, 6 June 1759.
[2] ibid, 19 March 1760.
[3] City Archives, MacLeod, Vol IV, Bay D, Bundle 48, Shelf I.

ment was made.[1] Gairdner did not get the extra £5 grant until
he moved from his original house to other premises in 1766:
the grant was given 'in regard the place where he now teaches
is now good and commodious'.[2]

Visitation was carried out every year, usually by a Bailie and
two of the city ministers, and the reports are all good. The
Town Council agreed that they should be published in the
local press, and they are to be found in the *Edinburgh Evening
Courant* and *Caledonian Mercury* in September of each year
after 1764, generally about the same time as the annual report
on the High School. The report of 1761 gives some indication
of the kind of pupils who attended the English schools. 'The
greater part of the scholars are children of reputable burgesses
and others of considerable rank both in town and country, and
not of the lowest class of inhabitants only, as hath been indus-
triously propagated to the prejudice of the said schools.'[3]

When Dunsmuir resigned in 1772, his place was taken by
Alexander Masson, a brother of Arthur Masson, a well-known
schoolmaster in the city and author of many textbooks.[4]
Alexander Masson, like his brother, had been a private teacher
before his appointment to one of the English schools, and he
did not give up his private practice. His advertisement is
explicit.[5] He explains that he has been chosen by the Town
Council to fill a vacancy among the city's English schoolmasters, that his school is in Carrubber's Close, that he has an
assistant for writing and arithmetic, 'in a room so contiguous
to the school, that all the scholars are under the Master's eye',
and that he still continues private tuition, takes boarders, teaches
in boarding schools, all at any hour except those of his public
school, which are four hours a day. In the same year, the
masters in petitioning the Town Council for an increase in fees,
state that the fees are so low that the schools are attracting the
wrong type of pupil, and that private teachers who charged
higher fees were drawing larger classes. They say that the

[1] Minutes of the Town Council of Edinburgh, 24 Aug 1763.
[2] *ibid*, 3 Sept 1766.
[3] *ibid*, 3 Nov 1761.
[4] For details of Arthur Masson, see Chapters V and VI.
[5] *The Edinburgh Evening Courant*, 13 June 1772.

reason for Dunsmuir's resignation 'was the objection of all ranks above the very lowest class of the inhabitants against the above terms, as introductory of mean ill-dressed company into their schools'. And that 'Charity schools being set on foot at the same time when their schools were instituted it was evident from thence that theirs were not intended for the meanest of the people, but for the benefit of the middle rank; besides there are sundry schools in town where such of the poorer sort as do not incline to send their children to the Charity schools may have them taught to read the Scriptures with sufficient propriety at and below three shillings a quarter. . .'.[1] The Town Council ultimately agreed to increase the fees to 5s a quarter for reading, but administered a rebuke also, saying that some of the masters had been demanding, or at least receiving, higher fees than had been agreed by the Town Council.

Ten years later, the established English teachers made another appeal for an increase in emoluments. They claimed that the fees were only half of what private teachers were charging, and that rents for schoolrooms had risen. They proceed: 'the number of pupils at each school taken at a medium did not exceed forty; and the extreme difficulty of fixing their attention, and causing them to sit still and be quiet as they are mostly infants, together with the variety of exercises in which they were engaged in their several classes according to the different degrees of progress they made, rendered it a most laborious task to superintend even that number, that the petitioners finding the emoluments arising from the said schools not competent for the support of their families were under the necessity of giving a close application to private teaching, when they could obtain employment, which often impaired their health, and after all turned out to small account.' This appeal was refused, 'the state of the city's funds not admitting of any additional salary to the petitioners at this time'.[2]

Some of the town's English schoolmasters were distinguished men in their profession. George Fulton, for example, who, after being master of the Charity school, was appointed to

---

[1] Minutes of the Town Council of Edinburgh, 9 Dec 1772.
[2] *ibid*, 4 Sept 1782.

an English school in 1778, was an original and able teacher, well known for his methods in teaching reading. After quarrelling with the Town Council in 1789, he resigned his English school and set up a private school in the New Town, where he was most successful. The man who succeeded him as English schoolmaster was even better known, Alexander Barrie, author of many textbooks which were popular all over the country.[1]

It was the practice for the examiners at the annual visitations of the Town's English schools to give 'confections' as prizes to those who had distinguished themselves, but in 1786 the Town Council decided to give small books instead of sweets, the total expense not to exceed £5 annually.

All the references and reports indicate that these English schools became an institution in Edinburgh, and retained for many years a deservedly high reputation. In the early nineteenth century, the establishment of elementary day schools under the auspices of George Heriot's Trust affected them adversely, however, and by 1835 only two English teachers remained under the Town, and their appointments were not to be renewed.[2]

THE CHARITY WORKING SCHOOLS OF THE SSPCK

As has already been mentioned, the primary purpose of the SSPCK was work in the Highlands and Islands, but under a second patent, granted in 1738, the scope of the Society's activities was considerably widened. This patent gave the Society powers to erect schools 'for the instruction of children, and particularly female children, in some of the most necessary and useful arts of life'. The belief of the times in the need 'to sow the seeds of industry in their very infant years', found expression in the establishment of schools for spinning, sewing, and other manufactures. In this the Society was following the example of the Commissioners and Trustees for Improving Fisheries and Manufactures in Scotland, which had helped to

[1] See page 202.
[2] *Municipal Corporations Report*, 1835.

set up several spinning schools, among them one in Edinburgh, in 1727.[1] Nevertheless, the Society's principal interest lay in the remote areas, and it seems from the early announcements of the opening of the Society's schools in Edinburgh, that these were justified because considerable numbers of Highland folk had come to the city. There are certainly references in the contemporary press to numbers of 'poor Highlanders' in Edinburgh in 1756.[2] In announcing the opening of its schools, the Society stated: 'The SSPCK, considering the great expense of education of children within the city of Edinburgh, whereby the children of the poorer sort of people, of whom the far greater part have come from the Highlands and Islands, are not only altogether ignorant of the principles of religion, but entirely idle, being destitute of the means of instruction in any useful employment . . . have erected three Charity Working schools in the city for the education of orphans and of children whose parents are not able to pay for them. . . .'[3] These schools were established in the World's End Close near the Netherbow, in Castlehill, and at the foot of Forrester's Wynd, under masters called James Maitland, John Johnston, and James Anderson. The advertisement proceeds: 'In each of these schools there is a mistress for teaching the children the art of spinning and knitting of stockings, and such other branches of manufactures as the Society shall appoint.' The curriculum also included reading, writing, arithmetic, and church music.

These schools had a short but interesting history. They lasted for not quite ten years. The Society's records contain details about their organisation, and about some of the equipment provided. Each schoolmaster was to have £4 sterling annually for coals, and had to keep fires in the teaching rooms from 1 November to 1 April. One room was for reading and writing, and the other for spinning and the other crafts. The hours were 7-9, 10-12, and 2-5 in summer, and 10-12 and 2-4 in winter. The Society bought 30 spinning wheels for the schools at a cost of £9 4s 9d. Each school was supplied with the following textbooks:

---

[1] See Appendix IV.
[2] *The Edinburgh Evening Courant*, 21 Sept 1756.
[3] *The Caledonian Mercury*, 3 Sept 1759.

40 copies of the first sheet of Kerr's Spelling Book
6 Bibles
18 Proverbs
12 New Testaments
6 Music Books
36 Plain Catechisms
6 Copy Books
1 Copy of the abridgement of the Society's rules
1 Quair paper
30 Copies of the ABC.[1]

That the new schools were at first popular seems certain. According to the Society's minutes, in September 1759, pupils in outlying parishes like Canongate, Calton, West Port, and Potterrow were applying for admission, and the Society did not immediately agree to admit them.   In February 1760, a means test was employed to discourage parents who, in the opinion of the Society, could well afford to pay for their children's education, and they were asked to state what they earned per day or per week.   In the first session each school had an enrolment of 60.   Before the one month's summer vacation, prizes were awarded to the best scholars.   The best spinner got a wheel, the second a Bible, the third a New Testament with Psalms, the fourth *A Token for Children*.   The best scholar in reading received a Bible,   In addition, each spinner received 2d for each spindle of good yard spun.   When the schools met again after the holiday, the best scholar in reading and 'answering the questions' was to get a Bible, the second a New Testament, and the third Pringle's *Compassionate Address*.

Begun with enthusiasm, the Charity Working schools continued for a time with success, but by 1763 there were proposals to reduce the practical work which gave them their distinctive character.   It is impossible now to say why these schools lost their popularity.   There may have been duplication of effort, for spinning and similar crafts were taught in the Charity Workhouses.   It may be that the emphasis on practical work tended to lower the schools in popular esteem, as compared with the Town's English schools.   Whatever the causes of their decline, the Charity Working schools gradually ceased to func-

---

[1] Society in Scotland for the Propagation of Christian Knowledge, Minutes, 30 July 1759 and Dec 1759.

tion after 1766. In that year, the SSPCK noted that the many demands on their funds forced them to close the schools run by Anderson and Johnston as from Whitsun 1768, and that Maitland's school (now run by his sister) should close in 1766. Mary Maitland eventually closed her school in May 1767, and was allowed to keep her wheel and reel. Johnston's and Anderson's schools closed in 1768, and so ended a short-lived but interesting experiment.

Chapter III

THE HIGH SCHOOLS

THE schools to be described in this chapter are the High Schools of Edinburgh and Canongate, and the High School (or Grammar School) of South Leith. More fully than the Hospital schools and private schools, which will be described later, they represent the traditional Scottish education. They are the schools of Grant's *Burgh Schools of Scotland*, the schools praised in many histories as bringing democratic education to large numbers of people and so producing a higher standard of literacy in Scotland than obtained in other countries at the time. They are also the schools criticised by Johnson in the *Journey to the Western Islands*: 'The grammar schools are not generally well supplied; for the character of a schoolmaster being there less honourable than in England, is seldom accepted by men who are capable to adorn it, and where the school has been deficient, the college can effect little.' We have already noticed the schools, usually called English schools, where children were taught the elements of reading. The High Schools represent the next stage, where those who could read English were taught Latin. In the sense of teaching boys Latin, the High Schools prepared them for the Universities. The High Schools of Edinburgh and Canongate were definitely schools for boys only, and the Grammar School of South Leith was probably also only for boys. They entered at about the age of 9 and spent the next four or five years mostly in the study of Latin.

These three schools had been in existence for a long time before the eighteenth century. The Pre-Reformation records of schools in the Edinburgh area are scanty, but the absence of references should not be taken to mean that schools did not exist. It is inconceivable that there should be no High School in the largest town in Scotland, when smaller places like Perth, Aberdeen, Ayr, and Dumfries had High Schools, and we can take it for certain that the High School of Edinburgh had been founded before 1503, when it is first mentioned[1] and that the High School of the Canongate existed before 1529,[2] and the Grammar School of South Leith before 1521.[3]

The High School of Edinburgh was much the most important school in the city, and for long periods in the eighteenth century it was pre-eminent in Scotland. The influence of its best teachers was widespread, for many of them eventually became rectors of other schools. For example, John Love, a master from 1735 to 1739, became rector of the Grammar School of Dalkeith: John Rae, a master from 1739 to 1759, became rector of the Grammar School of Haddington, and James Anderson, a master from 1739 to 1752, became rector of the Grammar School of Kelso. James Barclay, a master from 1742 to 1750, succeeded Love at Dalkeith. (In passing, it may be noted that the Grammar Schools of Dalkeith and Haddington had very high reputations. Dalkeith produced, among others, Principal Robertson, the distinguished historian. At Haddington, the boys gave the first public performance of Allan Ramsay's *The Gentle Shepherd*.) But the greatest period of the High School of Edinburgh was that of Dr Adam's rectorship, from 1766 to 1809. Adam's scholarship was renowned, and his textbooks were used all over the country and widely abroad. The tributes of old pupils like Scott and Cockburn have added to his fame and that of his school.

From an early time the High School served not only Edinburgh but Scotland. Boys of noble families, or of the landed gentry, many of whom lived part of the year in Edinburgh, were accustomed to attend the High School along with the sons of burgesses. The rector, Arbuthnott, referred to this when he reported to the Town Council in 1718: 'it being well known . . . that there is a great decay of the inhabitants of this city, there being now scarce any of the nobility and very few of the gentlemen of the country residing here, whereby the petitioner comes very far

---

[1] Ross, *The Royal High School*, p 19.
[2] *Book of the Old Edinburgh Club*, XX (1935), p 3.
[3] Mackay, *A Sketch of the History of Leith Academy*, p 9.

short of the encouragement his predecessors had'.[1] Arbuthnott
went on to claim that he had 'youth under his charge who are
almost altogether the children of burgesses'. It was probably
this state of affairs that prompted James Paterson, one of the
masters, to advertise, jointly with Professor Scott of the Chair
of Greek, a proposal for boarding young gentlemen either of
the University or the High School. Their notice stresses, in
addition to the usual details, the learning of French, which was
to be spoken ordinarily in the house, tutoring in Latin and
Greek, Philosophy or Mathematics, and particular care of
English 'by exercises prescribed them every week', a 'fair hand
of writing', and some arithmetic.[2] What became of this project
is not known, but there are references to other masters keeping
boarders, which was indeed a common practice in most High
Schools. With the increasing prosperity of Edinburgh in the
course of the eighteenth century, the number of the aristocracy
who had houses in the city increased, and the High School
Library lists, which date from 1738, contain the names of quite
a number of the sons of well-known Scottish families.

The High School of the Canongate was a rival institution,
but smaller. Little definite information exists about the numbers
in attendance, but it appears from figures provided by Steven,
that the High School of Edinburgh enrolled about 156 boys in
1753, 318 in 1770, and 489 in 1799. The notes left by David
Laing suggest that the roll of the Canongate High School at
the end of the century was about 100.[3] The relative standing
of the High Schools of Edinburgh and Canongate may be
gathered too from the movement of masters. Arbuthnott, who
has already been quoted, was a High School master who became
rector of the Canongate High School but subsequently returned
to the High School of Edinburgh as rector. Two Canongate
High School rectors, William Cruickshank and William
Ritchie, resigned that post in order to become masters in the
High School of Edinburgh. The Grammar School of South

---

[1] Minutes of the Town Council of Edinburgh, 27 Aug 1718. 'Encouragement' is a euphemism for 'total emoluments, or salary plus fees and other
incidentals'.
[2] The Edinburgh Evening Courant, 8-10 Sept 1718. Paterson died in 1722,
having translated Paterculus, and compiled the first High School Vocabulary.
[3] Anderson in Book of the Old Edinburgh Club, XX (1935), p 21.

Leith figures less frequently in these moves, but in 1795 its rector left to become a master in the High School of Edinburgh. All of this stresses the pre-eminence of the High School of Edinburgh, but also makes clear that the Canongate High School and the South Leith Grammar School had a standing relative to the High School of Edinburgh that schools like the smaller parish schools did not have. There is no instance of the parish schoolmasters near Edinburgh becoming High School masters. Yet the Canongate High School and the Grammar School of South Leith were both under the control of Kirk Sessions, in this way resembling the parish schools.[1] But both were larger than the schools of Duddingston or Liberton, and their situation as well as their size lent them prestige.

A word should perhaps be said here about the parish schools of the Edinburgh neighbourhood. Under the general surveillance of the Edinburgh Presbytery, there were schools at Duddingston, Liberton, Corstorphine and Cramond as well as in the more remote parishes of Colinton, Currie, Kirknewton, and Ratho, and conditions were probably better than in most rural areas in Scotland. At least there is only one mention of the Presbytery's having recourse to the extreme powers mentioned in the Act of 1696. This occurred at Corstorphine, where the heritors for various reasons refused to put the school in order and pay the master his legal salary. With the help of the Commissioners of Supply for the county, the Presbytery was able to compel the heritors to carry out the necessary works. It is perhaps only to be expected that the prosperous and long-settled agricultural area near Edinburgh should early have its parish schools. The Presbytery Minutes and reports in the Edinburgh newspapers record the annual visitations by ministers from the Presbytery, sometimes accompanied by distinguished scholars like Thomas Ruddiman, Keeper of the Advocates' Library, or Dr Adam of the High School. Some of the schoolmasters in the villages kept boarders: the master at Liberton, for example, mentioned in his advertisement, 'Liberton has a pure and wholesome air'.

---

[1] For the special position of the Canongate High School, see below. The Bailies of the Canongate, with the Kirk Session of the Canongate, controlled the school.

It is possible that boys were sent as boarders from Edinburgh to the parish schools on the outskirts. We find from the records of Heriot's that the schoolmaster at Corstorphine had as occasional pupils boys from Heriot's who were sent there to recover from illness.

It is not the intention here to describe the growth and progress of these three schools. In the case of the High School of Edinburgh, that has been done several times, perhaps most notably by Dr Steven. The history of the Canongate High School has been covered as far as the scanty records will allow in an admirable article by H M Anderson in the publications of the Old Edinburgh Club. The South Leith Grammar School's history is told in works by Alexander Mackay and Charles McAra. The aim of the present study is, however, not so much to regard the progress of individual institutions as to present a general picture of education in Edinburgh as it was in the eighteenth century. The chapter that follows therefore considers how these schools were managed, how the staff were appointed, the salaries paid to masters, and the fees paid by pupils. It looks at the curriculum, which seems to us so narrow, but which, in the hands of an inspired teacher, was capable of width and subtlety. All three schools were rebuilt in the course of the century, and factual information is available about the buildings. The hours of attendance are of interest, too. In these schools, as in most Scottish schools then and now, a most significant figure was the janitor, and luckily some information is available about his position and duties. The annual inspections or 'visitations' were red letter days that led to the publication of a report in the press, from which we can deduce something of the work of the schools. And of course there are also the impressions of pupils. Unfortunately there are no notes written by pupils when they were actually at school—that is the kind of discovery every historian of education hopes for— but there are quite a number of recollections written by former pupils. These may perhaps be not without hindsight, but most of them seem to have the stamp of truth, and some of those by eminent men are vivid and memorable.

To avoid confusion, when the phrase 'the High School' is used, the reference is to the High School of Edinburgh, now The

Royal High School. The Canongate High School is always mentioned as such, though it was frequently called the Grammar School of the Canongate. The Leith school which is the fore-runner of the present Leith Academy is usually called the Grammar School of South Leith in the records.

GENERAL MANAGEMENT

The control of the High School of Edinburgh was in the hands of the Town Council, some of the details of administration being dealt with by the College Committee, which was also responsible for part of the administration of the Town's College. As is indicated in Grant's *Burgh Schools*, there were towns in Scotland where the Presbyteries claimed some control over the High Schools, but there was never any doubt about the position in Edinburgh. The Presbytery had statutory rights[1] to satisfy themselves about the conduct and qualifications of all school-masters and to see that they signed the Confession of Faith. In Edinburgh this right was conceded, but the Town Council did not yield up the powers it had always had of appointing and dismissing staff. The Presbytery inspected all schools, but the Town Council comparatively early in the eighteenth century came to an agreement with the Presbytery and in-corporated the Presbytery's inspections into their own existing method of annual 'visitations'. The new building of the High School was erected through the work of an independent com-mittee, which raised funds for the purpose but, when the school was built, the Town Council received it, and continued to administer it. In all circumstances the Town Council was defi-nitely in control of the High School.

The position was different in the other two High Schools. The Canongate High School appears to be at one moment under the Control of the Bailies of the Canongate, and at another under the Kirk Session of the Canongate. Two references to the appointment of masters illustrate the confusion. The *Acts of the Bailies of the Canongate*, preserved in the City Chambers, in recording an appointment in 1703 use the phrase: 'The which

---

[1] Under the Act for securing the Protestant Religion and Presbyterian Government, 1707 (Acts of the Parliament of Scotland, XI, 402, c 6).

day, William Neilson and David Denoon, Bailies, and John Cochran, Treasurer, sitting in Council, with advice and consent of the ministers and kirk session of the Canongate.'[1] Later in the century, in an advertisement in the *Caledonian Mercury*, the kirk session says it proposes to appoint a master 'with the advice' of the magistrates.[2] Unfortunately, the Acts of the Bailies of the Canongate are available only up to 1731, and it is impossible now to say which was the true controlling power and which only gave assent, or whether, indeed, a compromise was reached between them. Perhaps the simple solution of the conflicting phrases is that each body placed itself first in its own records. There was no such doubt about the Grammar School of South Leith. It was under the control of the Kirk Session, in which respect it was like the small parish schools, but its size and the prestige of its teachers gave it a high standing.

STAFFING, APPOINTMENTS, AND CONDITIONS OF SERVICE

In the appointment of staff to the High Schools, the Presbytery had important rights. The Act for Securing the Protestant Religion and Presbyterian Government, which formed part of the Act of Union of 1707, laid down that all masters of schools and all professors had to acknowledge the civil government and sign the Confession of Faith before the Presbytery.[3]

How the system worked may be seen in the records of the appointment of George Arbuthnott as a Master in the High

---

[1] Quoted in Anderson, *op cit*, XX, p 16.
[2] *The Caledonian Mercury*, 12 Aug 1786.
[3] Acts of the Parliament of Scotland, XI, 402, c 6: 'And that in all time comeing no Professors, Principalls, Regents, Masters or others bearing office in any University Colledge or School within this Kingdom be capable or be admitted or allowed to continue in the Exercise of their said functions but such as shall own and acknowledge the Civill Government in manner prescribed or to be prescribed by the Acts of Parliament. As also that before or at their admissions they do and shall acknowledge and profess and shall subscribe to the foresaid Confession of Faith as the Confession of their faith, and that they will practise and conform themselves to the Worship presently in use in this Church and submit themselves to the Government and Discipline thereof and never endeavour directly or indirectly the prejudice or subversion of the same, and that before the respective Presbyteries of their bounds by whatsoever gift presentation or provision they may be thereto provided.'

School in 1710. (Arbuthnott later became Rector of the Canongate High School, and after little more than a year returned to be Rector of the High School of Edinburgh.) The first step towards Arbuthnott's appointment was a Town Council recommendation that the 'Committee anent the Colledge' should submit a report on his qualifications for the post. A week later, the convener of the College Committee reported to the Town Council that the Principal of the College, the professors, and some of the city ministers 'had taken tryall of Mr George Arbuthnott his parts and found him qualified to be one of the masters of the High Schooll', and that he was well affected towards the civil government. The Town Council agreed to the appointment, and Arbuthnott thereupon appeared before them and signed the Confession of Faith as the confession of his faith.[1] This procedure seems to pay only lip-service to the Act, as there was no appearance before the Presbytery. No doubt the Town Council felt that the general principle was observed by the presence of ministers on the selection committee. A similar procedure was followed in 1716, when a committee was appointed consisting of three of the city ministers, the Professor of Divinity, the Rector of the High School, and six members of the Town Council, with instructions to be particular that the successful candidate was well affected to the establishment and constitution. Only one candidate appeared, but he proved satisfactory, and took the oath of allegiance to King George.[2] There is no mention in the Town Council minutes of the new master signing the Confession of Faith.

The matter of the Town Council's duty to follow the law of the land in appointing staff to the High School was raised by the Presbytery in 1718 in the case of Robert Spence. Steven, in his history of the High School,[3] gives the following account of Spence's appointment: 'Sir Hew Dalrymple, Lord President of the Court of Session, with other influential parties, brought Mr Robert Spence of Montrose under the favourable notice of the patrons. On the 11th September 1717, Mr Spence, without being asked to submit to an examination, was chosen to fill a

---

[1] Minutes of the Town Council of Edinburgh, 1 and 8 Feb 1710.
[2] ibid, 20 July 1716. The master appointed was James Paterson.
[3] Steven, The High School of Edinburgh, p 88.

E

situation left open by the death of one of the teachers.' When
this matter was raised in the Edinburgh Presbytery, the Town
Council's representatives there had to admit that the Council
'had admitted some schoolmasters of late before they had been
qualified in presence of the presbytery, and that the Council
had resolved that in all time coming they should observe
exactly what is enjoined by law as to the admission of masters
in their schools'.[1] But this was not the end of the affair. The
Presbytery, dissatisfied with the Town Council's explanation,
raised the question of Spence's appointment with the Synod of
Lothian and Tweeddale, and the Synod demanded of the Town
Council that it should dismiss Spence. From the Town Council's reply to this overture, it appears that Spence had been
admitted as a master at Montrose without being 'qualified
before the presbytery in terms of law'; he had been deposed from
his Montrose post by the presbytery on the grounds of not
being properly qualified and of disloyalty and disaffection to the
government. It was said that he had been 'Concerned in the
late Rebellion'. The Town Council of Edinburgh had appointed
him and he had appeared before the presbytery and signed the
Confession of Faith before any protests had been made by the
Presbytery of Brechin or the Synod of Angus. The Town
Council in its reply pertinently wonders why 'some of the reverend ministers of this city did not prevent this misunderstanding
by duly informing the reverend Synod of the true state of this
affair'. In the end, the Town Council agreed to follow what
the law laid down, Mr Spence offered to 'obtemperate what the
law requires', and there the matter rested.[2]

In 1719, the Town Council decided that all appointments of
professors and schoolmasters should mention that they were
held during the Council's pleasure.[3] This had formerly been
the normal practice in Edinburgh, but recent appointments had
not included the phrase, and the Council foresaw difficulties
if it were omitted.[4] 'During pleasure' was the common practice

[1] Edinburgh Presbytery Minutes, 29 Jan 1718.
[2] ibid, 6 Aug, 20 Aug, and 2 Oct 1718; Minutes of the Town Council
of Edinburgh, 1 and 8 Aug 1718.
[3] Minutes of the Town Council of Edinburgh, 28 Aug 1719.
[4] Grant, History of the Burgh Schools, p 239. The references are to 1593,
1594, and 1654.

for the appointment of masters in burgh schools. There are very few instances of the Town Council terminating a master's engagement. One Patrick Middleton, having been convicted of fornication before the Kirk Sessions of Edinburgh, was dismissed by the Town Council in 1702.[1] Complaints were received by the Town Council about the unpunctuality and poor teaching of James Gibb in 1737.[2] This is the master described nearly twenty years later by Henry Mackenzie as 'an old man, short and squabby . . . verging upon dotage'.[3] The Town Council sent a special committee consisting of Professor Ker and some of the city ministers to investigate. They found that Gibb was unpunctual, that his class was not as far advanced as it should have been, and that he had not followed the rules laid down by the Council. They then publicly rebuked Gibb and exhorted him to improve. The Council agreed that the Bailie who was convener of the College Committee should, along with the Dean of Guild, summon Mr Gibb and let him know that unless he attended to this admonition 'he will be dismist'.[4] Gibb promised to acquiesce, but we know from Henry Mackenzie that he was still, twenty years later, an unsuccessful teacher.

The practice of 'comparative trials' obtained at this time, and in the Town Council Minutes there is an interesting account of the procedure. When Creech died in 1739, the Town Council appointed a committee consisting of Principal Wishart of the University, Professor Ker, Rev Patrick Cumming, Thomas Ruddiman, Keeper of the Advocates' Library, and Mr Lees, the Rector of the High School, to try the candidates. There were nine candidates, on whom the judges finally reported as follows: 'As to the extemporary trials upon some passages out of Livy, Horace, and Buchanan's Psalms, eight . . . performed very well, and by their explication of the several passages discovered such a fine acquaintance with the Latin language that in our opinion any of them may with all respect be reckoned qualified for the vacant charge. . . . Mr Wilson declined to explain the passage in Horace yet on the rest of the passages he acquit himself tolerably well and deserves encourage-

[1] Minutes of the Town Council of Edinburgh, 1 May 1702.
[2] ibid, 26 Jan 1737.
[3] Mackenzie, *Anecdotes and Egotisms*, p 34.
[4] Minutes of the Town Council of Edinburgh, 26 Jan 1737, 9 Feb 1737.

ment. As to the last part of the trial prescribed them, viz the translating an English argument into Latin, though some were of a more elegant and polite turn of writing Latin than the rest . . . yet all were sufficient. . . .' One candidate, William Lauder, was said to be particularly good, but the Council, having considered the report, elected John Rae.[1]

Three years later, when another vacancy had occurred, the Council elected James Barclay to it without any comparative trial; the phrase used is 'being well informed of the literature, piety and good qualifications of Mr James Barclay Teacher of a private school in this city'.[2] One is forced to draw the conclusion that influence was used often to secure these desirable appointments.

From 1739 it seems to have been generally accepted practice for the Town Council to refer the examination of candidates for appointments to the High School to committees of learned men specially chosen for the purpose. An advertisement in 1750 asks applicants to appear at the Council chambers 'to give trial of their skill and proficiency in the Latin language before proper judges who are to be appointed thereto by the Magistrates and Town Council, each candidate bringing with him proper certificates of his moral character etc from the place of his former residence'.[3] In 1750, the interviewing committee consisted of Principal Wishart and the Rev Fred Carmichael, ministers, Professor Hunter of the chair of Greek, Professor Stuart of the chair of Humanity, and Thomas Ruddiman, or any three of them.[4]

An even more exacting procedure was followed in the appointment of a rector. Steven has recorded the experiences of Alexander Adam when he was examined for the post in 1768. He

[1] Minutes of the Town Council of Edinburgh, 14 Feb 1739. The candidates were: William Lauder, John Merns, James Innes, James Wilson, James Anderson, Walter Greig, Robert Anderson, William Brown, and John Rae. Rae is described by Henry Mackenzie as 'a severe harsh-tempered man, but an excellent scholar, a rigid disciplinarian, and the only frequent flogger in the school'.

[2] *ibid*, 2 June 1742. The Council's appointment was nevertheless a wise one, for Barclay became well known as an able teacher. He became Rector of Dalkeith High School, and one of his daughters was the mother of the Ballantyne brothers.

[3] *The Edinburgh Evening Courant*, 16 Oct 1750. The advertisement in 1759 is in the same words; *The Caledonian Mercury*, 25 Jan 1759.

[4] Minutes of the Town Council of Edinburgh, 31 Oct 1750.

was first of all seen privately by the Rev Dr MacQueen, and then by Professor George Stuart, 'who was known to be partial to another candidate'. Professor Stuart's examination 'was not so long as Dr MacQueen's'; but the passages which he selected for trial were very difficult—the 18th chapter of the Second Book of Livy, and the 6th Ode of the Fourth Book of Horace. 'I should probably have failed,' says Dr Adam, 'had I not providentially—so I have always considered it—some time before, talked over the chapter in Livy with Mr Matheson, and read the ode of Horace by myself. I have ever esteemed my being prepared on the passages Mr Stuart turned up as one of the most fortunate circumstances of my life, as it gained me the approbation of one who was rather unfriendly.'[1] This was not all, for Adam was then interviewed and examined by a committee of 'the most learned men about Edinburgh', who recommended him for appointment only after they had 'taken trial' of him.[2]

This practice of referring the testing of candidates to a special committee, on which, it will be noted, the Town Council itself was not represented, led to an extension of the committee's duties. When, in 1766, the Rector, Matheson, broke down in health, temporary help was engaged to take over his class. (Adam was employed for this work.) A month earlier a committee of 'examinators' had been appointed to examine the candidates for another post in the High School, and this committee was asked to visit Matheson's class, see how it was taught, and recommend how the vacancy could be filled.[3]

There was no scheme for the payment of pensions or widows' allowances, but on several occasions an arrangement was made whereby a new master made over his salary to his predecessor, but kept the fees. This was done in the case of James French, who succeeded Gibb in 1759 and agreed to pay to Gibb £20 a year during the latter's lifetime. French was a teacher of

[1] Steven, op cit, p 114 et seq, quoting from Dr Adam's MS memoranda.
[2] This committee included the Rev Dr MacQueen, Professor Stuart, and four others representing the ministers and the university.
[3] Minutes of the Town Council of Edinburgh, 29 Oct and 5 Nov 1766. The committee consisted of Principal Robertson, Professors Stuart, Hunter, James Robertson, and the Revs Dr Cumming, Dr Blair, Messrs Webster, MacQueen, and Dick—or any three of them.

fine reputation, and the Town Council probably realised they were fortunate to have him, for in 1763 they agreed to pay him an additional £20 to make up for the money he was paying Gibb. When Gibb died in 1764, the Council made a final payment to his widow of £20, of which £10 had been due before his death.[1] The following year Mr Lees, the former Rector, appealed to the Council for financial help because he had lost all his money through the bankruptcy of others. He was granted his former salary of 600 merks (£33 6s 8d stg) a year, and when he died in the following year the Council paid his widow an annuity of half that sum.[2] An arrangement was made between Matheson, Rector from 1759 to 1768, and Adam, who became joint-Rector with him in 1768. Matheson was in bad health and Adam agreed to pay him £40 a year for three years in addition to the salary of £33 6s 8d and at the end of the three years to pay him a total sum of £50 a year.[3] In 1782, Adam was still paying this money to his predecessor, and he petitioned the Council, adducing the precedent of their payment to French, and pointing out that when Cruickshank succeeded Farquhar in 1772, he was paid his full salary and the Council paid £30 a year to Farquhar. Adam would appear to have had logic and justice on his side, but his appeal was rejected. In fact the whole procedure seems illogical, for we find that when Christison succeeded French in 1786, French was granted his old salary of £20 plus an additional £10 a year, and this sum was deducted from Christison's salary.[4]

A Society of Teachers was formed in 1737 which established a provident association. This gave allowances to members who were in distress, grants to widows and children, and payments for funeral expenses.[5]

The responsibility for appointments to the Canongate High School rested either with the Bailies of the Canongate or with the Kirk Session, or, perhaps in some way we do not understand,

---

[1] Minutes of the Town Council of Edinburgh, 4 May 1763 and 21 March 1764.
[2] *ibid*, 24 July 1765, 6 Aug 1766.
[3] Steven, *op cit*, p 114, and Minutes of the Town Council of Edinburgh, 20 Nov 1782.
[4] Minutes of the Town Council of Edinburgh, 28 June 1786.
[5] Steven, *op cit*, p 95. See also Chalmers' *Life of Thomas Ruddiman*. That celebrated grammarian was one of the founders of the Society.

with both. The same terms and phrases are used in 1703, 1715, and 1720 in the appointment of rectors. The rector had to keep decent order in his school, and had to live in the house that was part of it. He had to charge as fees 'at least half a crown per quarter for himself and twenty shillings scots as the minimum per quarter for his doctors'.[1] Children 'whose capacities fit and incline them for learning and whose parents are fallen back and not able to pay their quarter payment' shall be educated free if recommended by the Magistrates and Kirk Session. The last item is that 'the doctors of the said school when vacant be chosen by the Bailies and Treasurer with advice of the ministers and Master'.[2] There is no mention here of the Confession of Faith or signing the formula of allegiance, but the Presbytery Minutes record the new rector's appearance to make confession of his faith in 1720.[3]

The staffing of the Grammar School of South Leith was in the hands of the ministers and Kirk Session. In 1703, the Kirk Session sharply told the Incorporation of Trades of Leith that they had no powers in the appointing of a schoolmaster, that matter being in the hands of the Kirk Session 'since the session paid the master's salary'.[4] Like the Town Council of Edinburgh, the South Leith Kirk Session sometimes appointed special committees to recommend candidates or conduct comparative trials. In 1735, a committee consisting of the Principal of the University, Professor Ker of the chair of Humanity, and Thomas Ruddiman took trial of Hugh Miller, an applicant for the mastership of South Leith, and recommended him.[5] A similar arrangement was made in 1787.[6]

SALARIES AND FEES

In 1709 the Town Council laid down a scale of fees for the High School. Each pupil paid five shillings a quarter, of which

---

[1] 'Doctors' were assistant teachers.
[2] Acts of the Bailies of the Canongate: 2 Dec 1715.
[3] Edinburgh Presbytery Minutes, 28 Sept 1720. 'The Presbytery did allow him to enter his post and teach.' The Canongate teachers all signed also on 23 March 1715.
[4] Mackay, *op cit*, p 13.
[5] *The Caledonian Mercury*, 17 April 1735.
[6] Mackay, *op cit*, p 14.

the Rector received one shilling from each scholar in the classes of the four masters. The master of the third class (ie that nearest the top of the school, the others being the Rudiments class, first class, and second class) received one shilling out of the five shillings paid by the pupils in the Rector's class. Since the masters each took their classes up the school to the third class, they received this extra payment in turn.[1] Presumably it was felt that the master of the third class had more responsible work, but a good case could have been put forward for the extra payment to be given rather to the master of the youngest class, for he had the task of teaching the 'Rudiments' to a very mixed collection of young gentlemen, some of whom had come from widely separated parts of Scotland.[2] In 1736, this change was in fact made, and at the same time it was stated that the Rector and masters were entitled to whatever extra payments their scholars felt inclined to give them at Candlemas.[3] These last payments are described in the Town Council minutes as 'intended and designed to be given severally to them by the parents', a system that looks like bribery. The writing master made his own separate charge.

To estimate what each master drew in salary and fees is difficult. The popular masters drew larger numbers and made more money than the others. The records of the school give the following numbers of boys in the earliest session of which there are details, 1738-39:

Lees (Rector)	34
Love	58
Rae	26

The rector would receive in fees 4s from each boy in his class for each of the four quarters of the year—Lammas, Hallowmas, No figures are given for Spence and Gibb, the other masters.[4]

---

[1] Steven, *op cit*, p 83.

[2] Steven, *op cit*, p 94.

[3] Steven, *op cit*, p 94, and Minutes of the Town Council of Edinburgh, 28 Jan 1736.

[4] Steven, *op cit*, Appendix No VII. The figures are based on the lists of boys who paid their library subscriptions. Love was a great teacher, who afterwards became Rector of Dalkeith High School. Rae was a hard man: see the quotation from Henry Mackenzie on page 68. Spence never submitted any library returns, and Gibb was a weak teacher who was several times threatened with dismissal.

Candlemas, and Beltane.[1] This would yield a sum of nearly £30 stg, to which should be added 84s for each quarter from the classes under Love and Rae, a total of, say, £16 16s. The Rector's income from fees was therefore at least £46 16s, and probably more when the money from Spence and Gibb's classes was added. If, however, a conservative estimate of £50 from fees is made, and to it is added the basic salary from the Town Council of 300 merks or £15, we can say that the rector received not less than £65 a year. This may be compared with the salaries given to the masters of Charity schools as detailed in Chapter II, where Arthur Cooper was given a total of £12 stg in 1723, and James Dewar £20 stg in 1725. A similar calculation shows that Love made about £58 10s in 1738-39, and Rae £32 10s. These sums include the basic salary paid to masters of 250 merks (approximately £12 10s).[2]

At a later period, in 1790, when the High School was enjoying a period of great distinction under Dr Adam, a writer estimated that the Rector's place was worth £400 a year, and a master's, £200.[3] In the late eighteenth century the masters of the town's English schools were being paid £15 a year plus 5s a quarter in fees, which would yield from a school of forty, about £55 a year.[4] It is clear that the masters of the High School were paid much more than other teachers in Edinburgh.

The fees charged at the High School of the Canongate were regulated by the Bailies, and are given in their records when new Rectors were appointed in 1703 and 1715.[5] The fees from the children of burgesses were to be half a crown at least per quarter to the Rector, and a minimum of 20 shillings Scots a quarter to his assistants (or doctors). The rector's fees were thus not much more than half of those paid to the rector of the High School.

The rector of the Grammar School of South Leith had a

---

[1] Grant, *op cit*, pp 469, 543.
[2] Grant, *op cit*, p 543.
[3] Brown, *History of the Shires of Scotland*, 1791, p 42.
[4] See Chapter II. The masters themselves said the average roll was 40.
[5] The 1703 minute is quoted in H M Anderson, 'The Grammar School of the Canongate' in *Book of the Old Edinburgh Club*, XX, p 16. The 1715 minute is in the Acts of the Bailies of the Canongate (City Chambers, Edinburgh).

salary of 200 merks a year in 1735, ie a little over £10 stg, and in addition he had half a crown from the scholars quarterly.[1]

CURRICULUM

On occasions the Town Council did not hesitate to prescribe the texts to be read in the High School, for example in 1696, when they pronounced as their opinion that the ordinary '*Latin Rudiments*' in use at the school—known as the Dunbar Rudiments—was too difficult, and that the volume by Wedderburn was 'more plain and easy learned'.[2] In 1709 a thorough review of the High School course was carried out. The College Committee of the Town Council got a small sub-committee consisting of the Principal and six professors of the College to outline the course that should be followed.[3] Naturally the professors had in mind those boys who were going to proceed to the College. The course they recommended was as follows:

Lowest Class—Vocables, Variae Loquendi Formulae Dicta Sapientum, Rudimenta Pietatis.

Fourth Class— Sulpitius de Moribus, Cato's Moral Distichs, Phaedri Fabulae.

Prose authors—Corderii, Erasmi, et Castalionis Colloquia.

Third Class— Poets—Phaedrus, Ovid's Epistles or Metamorphosis.

Prose Authors—Cicero's Select Epistles, Cornelius Nepos.

Second Class—Poets—Virgil's Pastorals, Claudian, Ovid's Metamorphosis, Buchanan's Psalms.

Prose Authors—Caesar's Commentaries, Velleius Paterculus, Justin, Curtius.

Highest Class—Poets—Terence, Virgil, Lucan, Horace, Juvenal, Buchanan's Psalms.

Prose Authors—Cicero's Select Orations, Livy, Florus, Sallust, Suetonius, Vossius' little compend of Rhetoric.

---

[1] Mackay, *op cit*, p 16.
[2] Steven, *op cit*, p 76, quoting Minutes of the Town Council of Edinburgh, 11 Sept 1696.
[3] Minutes of the Town Council of Edinburgh, 28 Oct 1709, 8 Feb 1710. Quoted in full by Steven, *op cit*, p 84.

This interesting report was produced after the professors had studied the curriculum of the High School as described to them by the Rector, and it includes some observations on the teaching of grammar and the type of classical texts to be studied. The professors recommended, for example, that the fourth part of grammar, ie that studied in the last year of the course, should be dropped in favour of a 'short compend of rhetoric'. As for the classic authors, they are in favour of the genuine classics themselves and not dialogues 'writ by learned men and great masters of the language'. On method, they advocate slow but sure progress and no skipping. The old practice of 'disputing' on Saturday afternoons should be reduced to once a month only, and in its stead there should be regular revision of work done during the week. This is clearly the curriculum of a school that concentrated on Latin. There was no Greek. Writing was available as a subject for boys whose parents thought they would benefit from it, but it was an extra. Writing usually included 'accounts'. A writing master was appointed in 1704, 'to teach such of the scholars in the High School of Edinburgh as have a mind to write', and the Town Council recommended James Alexander 'to the master and doctors to employ him for that effect'. Alexander was unable to carry out his duties, and his place was taken by Robert Godskirk.[1]

It would be wrong to think of the Latin classics as being dull, or as not providing the material for lively teaching. In the hands of poor teachers, Latin grammar can be intolerable for lively boys, but in the hands of good teachers Latin can be a most satisfactory medium for a literary education. The newspaper report of the annual visitation of the High School in 1738 throws up one of the interesting teachers. It describes the work of the fourth class under Mr Creech, and says that the master had prepared 'a very beautiful and nice model of Caesar's Bridge over the Rhine (done from the famous Palladio's Copperplate Design) of Wainscot; which being presented before the Honourable Magistrates, one of his scholars, a gentleman of an admirable lively genius, read to them Caesar's description of

---

[1] Minutes of the Town Council of Edinburgh, 17 May 1704 and 29 Oct 1707. Godskirk was a private teacher of writing, and also taught in Heriot's, where he was not very successful. See p 203.

the bridge, which he explained distinctly, and thereafter demonstrated to them the structure and several parts thereof to the great satisfaction, and with the approbation of all present'.[1]

There is mention of geography in 1715, when the city treasurer was authorised to spend 24 pounds Scots on geographical maps.[2] These were probably for use in connection with the Latin texts. The practice of adding to Latin grammar some knowledge of the history and geography of Rome and the Roman Empire grew with the century. In 1745, after an account of the annual visitation, James Barclay, the master who was to begin the Rudiments class the following session, gave this account of his methods: 'Mr Barclay begins the Rudiments class October next. Such as enter then continue with him four years: in which time besides grammar and the Latin authors commonly read, he proposes, if the parents incline, to give them some knowledge of mythology, Roman antiquities, geography and Ancient History. Nor are these instructions to interfere with the learned languages, as they are given at a separate hour betwixt four and five, when the Latin exercises are over.'[3]

In 1751, Mr Gibb advertised in most flowery language, but we know from Henry Mackenzie and the Town Council records that Gibb was not a successful teacher. Yet the advertisement, strictly accurate or not, gives us a fair idea of the content of education in the second highest class of the High School. 'Mr Gibb's class, after having explained Virgil's beautiful account of the zones, gone through the parts of speech and construction, the quantities and scanning of the verses, with the rules in all the different parts of grammar, were next examined upon the globe, without which they could not have understood that part of the author, where they distinctly marked out the constellations, the five zones, the uses of the several circles, longitude and latitude, as they relate to the globe of earth. After this, they explained Caesar's description of the Wooden Bridge which he laid over the Rhine; when, after parsing and construing the lesson, they applied the same to the timber model which belongs

---

[1] *The Caledonian Mercury*, 10 Aug 1738.
[2] Minutes of the Town Council of Edinburgh, 23 Sept 1715.
[3] *The Edinburgh Evening Courant*, 8 Aug 1745. (Incidentally this was the day that Sir John Cope heard of the landing in Scotland of Prince Charles Edward.)

to the school, and shewed the particular use of every part of it, except where it runs away from the true meaning of Caesar's words, which they pointed out, and shewed how they ought to be adjusted.'[1] In the following year, the visitation concluded with the boys of the highest class translating 'free English' into classical Latin, and 'pronouncing Latin Orations ... in order to initiate them in the art of oratory'.[2]

The grammar book used in the High School was Ruddiman's, and when, in 1772, Dr Adam, the Rector, proposed to introduce a grammar book of his own, there was a great deal of trouble. It is said that some in the Town Council were in favour of Ruddiman's grammar because of their acquaintance with the famous Thomas Ruddiman, Keeper of the Advocates' Library, and with his sons Walter and Thomas, printers and publishers. Some people objected to Dr Adam on political grounds, for he was said to hold republican views. It is unnecessary now to enter into the dead controversy, but Adam was not allowed to use his own book in the High School. He appears to have used it unofficially. Its particular merit is that in it Latin grammar is linked with English. His other publications, on Geography and History, and on Antiquities, show the trend of Adam's mind, and give some idea of the breadth of culture which this able teacher was spreading in the High School. Adam described his course of study in a letter to the Rector of Aberdeen Grammar School,[3] where he explained that boys stayed in his class for two years. In addition to Latin, which was taught to all, he taught the principles of Greek and Geography to the abler pupils. He wished to see English grammar, Mythology, Antiquities and History, some Science—he called it Natural Philosophy—and French, in the curriculum of most boys, but the course in the High School in his day was still narrow. One of his successors as Rector, Pillans, described the curriculum when he was a pupil under Adam, the thorough grounding in Latin translation and grammar, a very little Greek, so little that he scarcely knew the Greek characters when he left for the Uni-

---

[1] *The Caledonian Mercury*, 19 Sept 1751. Mr Creech's model was still doing good service.
[2] *ibid*, 19 Sept 1752 NS.
[3] Steven, *op cit*, p 146.

versity, and some interesting Ancient Geography, interesting enough to make Pillans wish there had been more details of foreign countries. But generally the atmosphere was one of rather tedious repetition.[1] Of Adam's distinguished pupils, Walter Scott writes of his High School reading with most affection. 'It was the fashion', he says, 'to remain two years in his class, where we read Caesar, and Livy, and Sallust in prose, Virgil, Horace, and Terence in verse. I had by this time mastered, in some degree, the difficulties of the language, and began to be sensible of its beauties. This was really gathering grapes from thistles; nor shall I soon forget the swelling of my little pride when the Rector pronounced, that though many of my schoolfellows understood the Latin better, Gualterus Scott was behind few in following and enjoying the author's meaning. Thus encouraged, I distinguished myself by some attempts at poetical versions from Horace and Virgil. Dr Adam used to invite his scholars to such essays, but never made them tasks.'[2]

The curriculum of the Canongate High School followed the same lines as that of the High School: Latin was the principal subject, and whether it provided a generous education depended on the tastes and ability of the teacher. An account of a visitation of the school by the Magistrates and Ministers of the Canongate appears in the *Courant* which talks of the children in the various classes being taught English, Latin, and Greek. In an advertisement appended to this account, the Rector, Mr Panton, announced that he would begin a 'Rudiments class' in October, an arrangement exactly similar to the High School one. He also proposed a course in Arithmetic 'at six o'clock at night'.[3] Two years later the same idea occurred again, of a course in Arithmetic between six and seven at night, and a course in Church Music between seven and eight.[4] The advertisement of the school in 1771 referred to the teaching of English, ie of read-

---

[1] *Municipal Corporations Report*, 1835, Vol 1.

[2] Lockhart, *Life of Scott*. One of Scott's earliest poems was an exercise handed in to Dr Adam. It is among the Rector's papers preserved in the High School.

[3] *The Edinburgh Evening Courant*, 15 Sept 1764. Panton published a textbook on arithmetic: see Chapter VI. The evening classes in Arithmetic and Church Music were probably private classes for which separate fees were charged.

[4] *ibid*, 1 Oct 1766.

ing, and it is plain that a special class had been formed for those who needed to learn English before they could proceed to Latin.[1] This is explicitly stated in the 1774 advertisement, where it is said that the curriculum consisted only of Latin; 'no other branch of science is carried on', but care was taken to instruct beginners in English grammar, and exercises were set daily in writing English as well as Latin.[2]

In 1784, the advertisement in the *Courant* indicates that the Rector of the Canongate High School was following the same lines as Dr Adam in the High School. 'To enlarge the mind and improve the taste of the fifth form, the beauties of the classical authors are pointed out, and the fine passages of the poets are exhibited in Poetical English. Classical Geography is taught and antiquities are illustrated as they occur.'[3] The report of the visitation of 1780 speaks of the extensive reading of the pupils and derides teaching shorter passages until all boys have them by heart (perhaps a reference to the methods of some High School masters).[4] The 1784 advertisement in the *Caledonian Mercury* also by implication refers to the High School; in the Canongate school, boys were put into classes according to their ability and promoted as soon as they are fit; 'This revives the sinking spirits of the slow, and gives additional vigour to the quick.'[5] One of the later pupils of the Canongate High School was David Laing, who wrote as follows about the course: 'When little more than seven years old (in or about 1800) I was put to the Grammar School, Canongate, to learn Latin— but the rector said I had much better go back to the English school to learn both to read and spell! . . . The Canongate School was then in a tolerably flourishing condition. The course extended over five years—but the first and second classes sitting together in one room under the charge of an assistant teacher—and the other three classes in the rector's room, it so happened that we sat half the day idle, unless when engaged with slate and pencil on lessons in Arithmetic. After that came the study of Geography—with Greek in the fourth and fifth years.

[1] *The Edinburgh Evening Courant*, 4 Sept 1771.
[2] *ibid*, 4 April 1774.
[3] *ibid*, 22 Sept 1784.
[4] *ibid*, 16 Aug 1780.
[5] *The Caledonian Mercury*, 18 Sept 1784.

In the fifth year the class to which I belonged had dwindled down from upwards of thirty scholars to five!'[1]

The curriculum of the Grammar School of South Leith followed very closely that of the High School which has already been quoted. When the school was inspected in 1729, the first (or highest) class was reading Virgil's Aeneid IV and Terence; the second class, Virgil's 1st Eclogue and Cornelius Nepos; the third class Ovid's Metamorphosis Book I and Erasmus Minor: the fourth class Ovid's First Epistle and Corderius; the fifth class had completed the declension of nouns and pronouns in Ruddiman's Grammar; and the sixth, or lowest, class had begun vocabulary. This visitation took place in May, and it is possible that the sixth class was a preliminary one to prepare pupils for beginning Latin at the start of the following session.[2] A later visitation quoted by Mr Mackay mentions only five classes. The texts then read were: first class, Horace Odes II, Buchanan's History; second class, Ovid's Metamorphosis XIII and Eutropius; third class, Kirkwood's Grammar, 'Lilus Monita Pedagogica' and Corderius; fourth class, Ruddiman's Rudiments; fifth class, declensions and vocabulary.[3] The account of the visitation of 1739 is a testimonial to the master's diligence, refers to the ability of the highest classes in dealing with Caesar and Virgil, and gives special praise to Latin versions.[4]

By 1779 there was a change in emphasis, and the visiting ministers speak of good work not only in the principles of grammar and knowledge of Latin, but also in Roman Antiquities.[5] The advertisement of the school in 1781 shows that in addition to the usual subjects of a grammar school, the master taught writing, geography, arithmetic, and book-keeping privately.[6] In 1785, the visitation report says: 'The different classes gave specimens of their acquaintance with the principles of grammar, of their knowledge of the Latin and Greek languages, Roman antiquities, and Geography, to the entire satisfaction

[1] Goudie, *David Laing: a Memoir*, pp 19-20.
[2] Records of Session of South Leith, 8 May 1729.
[3] Mackay, *op cit*, p 18.
[4] *The Caledonian Mercury*, 4 Sept 1739.
[5] *ibid*, 21 Aug 1779.
[6] *The Edinburgh Evening Courant*, 6 Oct 1781.

of all present.'[1] This is the first mention of Greek in the Leith curriculum.

We are fortunate in being able to catch a glimpse of the methods of teaching in the Grammar School in 1729. Thomas Kirkwood, the master, had been accused of neglecting his duties, and the school was said to be in a state of 'manifest decay'. Even boys in the advanced classes were said to be 'very lame and defective' in grammar, in such simple matters as the declension of nouns and conjugation of verbs. Kirkwood was interviewed and stated his defence, in the course of which he outlined the typical day in his school. 'Every Monday morning I take an account of the Sacred Lessons which were prescribed the Saturday before, together with the Repetition of their Catechism, and the notes of the Sermon. And in the afternoon I prescribe a Lesson on their Rudiments, Grammar, and Authors and appoints (sic) the Boyes to give an account of them next day, and likewise I prescribe Mondays nights a Generall preufe (ie a proof or explanatory passage from the Shorter Catechism) which I take an account of next morning immediately after prayers are said, the Superior classes having with the same preufe either a Theme or Version to write, and so on from Day to Day.'[2]

BUILDINGS

The Town Council was responsible for seeing that the High School building was kept in good condition, and those who conducted the annual visitation were accustomed to bring defects in the building to the notice of the Council. The building had been in use since 1578 and it is not surprising that defects were reported. In 1714, for instance, the Bailie in charge of the College Committee reported to the Council about a recent visitation by himself, the Professor of Divinity, and several ministers of the Presbytery, and after a brief account of the satisfactory state of learning in the school, the record proceeds: 'that the windows of the school needed to be mended and

---

[1] *The Edinburgh Evening Courant*, 27 Aug 1785.
[2] Session records, 13 March 1729.

they wanted a lamp to be fixed in the middle of the wynd . . .'[1]
The appropriate committee was the Committee of Public
Works, which inspected the building again in 1722 and, according to their report then, found it defective.[2] At this visit they
reported on the garret, which they state to be 'of great use to
the masters for working their classes separately, and does not
at all accommodate them as it is presently modelled'. This is
interesting as an indication that the masters were accustomed
to split up their classes, which were sometimes large, into
groups. This garret was 'altogether coomciled', and it was
agreed that the walls should be raised to overcome this awkward
construction. A major repair was carried out, which must have
caused the staff some inconvenience, for the Town Council
recorded their thanks to the masters for their care of the children's health 'during the time the school was repairing'.[3]

There are from time to time other references to repairs to the
building. Windows were broken, usually in the vacations. One
remedy suggested was keeping the windows open in the daytime
with iron cleeks'.[4] But the real problem was the replacement of
the old building of 1578. The method used for financing
the building of the new school is interesting. According to
Steven,[5] and also Ross,[6] the Town Council had no money for
a project like this, and therefore after a public meeting a committee of interested citizens was set up to collect money. There
is a reference to this meeting in the *Courant* of 31 August 1774,
where it is stated that the school was 'too confined for the great
numbers that have of late been taught Latin there', and that it
had been resolved to open a subscription list under the patronage of the Town Council. The matter was discussed in the
Town Council,[7] after representations had been made by the
masters about the inadequate size of their rooms. The Lord
Provost's Committee agreed that conditions were bad, 'especially

---

[1] Minutes of the Town Council of Edinburgh, 3 Dec 1714.
[2] *ibid*, 30 May 1722. 'Fand the roof therof veray defective and insufficient.
. . . Joysts are bended and thereby the roof holowed.'
[3] *ibid*, 10 April 1724.
[4] *ibid*, 20 Aug 1755.
[5] Steven, *op cit*, p 122.
[6] Ross, *op cit*, p 25 ff.
[7] Minutes of the Town Council of Edinburgh, 15 Feb 1775. This is the
earliest reference; Steven, *op cit*, gives 8 March.

in the summer season for the reception of the great number of boys resorting thither', but pointed to the poor financial position of the city. The Lord Provost reported that he had had conversations with 'some of the most respectable citizens', who had suggested a plan of raising the necessary sum by voluntary subscription. On 8 March, the Town Council agreed to contribute 300 guineas. The Committee contained some important people; Sir William Forbes, Bart, was the leading spirit, and with him were Provost Stodart, Professor John Hope, John Wauchope, WS, Alexander Wood, Surgeon (well known as 'Lang Sandy Wood'), Thomas Elder, James Hunter Blair, Andrew Crosbie, Lord Westhall, Principal Robertson, Alexander Cunnynghame, WS, and Provost Dalrymple.[1] The foundation stone was laid in 1777, on 25 June, with elaborate masonic ceremony.[2] The committee went about the business of collecting money with great thoroughness; they drew up a letter, which, with a subscription book, they proposed to offer at the houses of the principal citizens. The letter said that they were not pressing for subscriptions but wished citizens to know that the building might have to be discontinued because of shortage of funds. For those who did not wish to give their names 'a sealed box will be presented by the bearer'. The Town Council agreed to this collection.[3] In all these ways a sum of £2300 was raised, and the Council agreed to make up the deficiency over a number of years. It seems an extraordinary way for a Town Council to build its school, but the school was eventually built, and the city's Common Good fund was not raided as severely as it might have been.

The new building was erected at right angles to, and partly on the actual site of, the old building in High School Yards. Land was taken over from the nearby Royal Infirmary, and in place of the old building, which ran east and west, a new one was built running north and south. Organising the school while these complicated building operations were going on must have been trying.

To aid in writing off the debt on the new building, the Town

[1] Minutes of the Town Council of Edinburgh, 23 Dec 1778 and 21 April 1779.
[2] *The Caledonian Mercury*, 25 June 1777.
[3] Minutes of the Town Council of Edinburgh, 23 Dec 1778.

Council granted the Committee the proceeds of a dramatic production in the Theatre Royal every year. The play in 1781 was 'Henry IV', in 1782 'The Revenge', and in 1783 'The Merry Wives of Windsor'. Plays were given annually until 1790, when the Committee asked the Town Council to pay off the remaining debt of approximately £230, which the Council did.[1].

The completed building consisted of a hall and two smaller rooms on the ground floor, used as writing-room and library, and five classrooms on the upper floor.[2] The provision was the same as in the old school, though the rooms were better planned and more spacious. (The same pattern, indeed, forms the basis of the present school on the Calton Hill.) The 1779 building was completed sometime in the early 1780s, and exists today at the foot of Infirmary Street. An account of the school says that in total length from north to south it was 120 feet, and 36 feet broad in the middle, 38 feet at each end. 'The great hall where the boys met for prayers is 68 feet by 30.'[3] The library and writing-rooms were each 32 feet by 20.

The old Canongate High School was destroyed by fire in 1696 and the Town Council of Edinburgh allowed the master to find any suitable property for his school in Edinburgh until a new one could be built.[4] A petition from the Bailies of the Canongate to the Dean of Guild to erect the school on land purchased by the Kirk Session was granted in 1704.[5] The ground was 'at the north side of the Canongate on the west side of the Common Close'. There the session proposed to erect 'a common school, several conveniences as a house to the master'. This school was 75 feet long, and 23½ feet wide, and had three storeys and garrets. It was in existence until 1822, when it was sold, and Sir Daniel Wilson described it in his *Memorials* as being ornamented, with dormer windows and a pediment in the centre with a sundial with the date 1704. The playground in front of the school was 107 feet by 54, and at the back 73

[1] Minutes of the Town Council of Edinburgh, 3 Nov 1790.
[2] Steven, *op cit*, p 124.
[3] Brown, *op cit*, p 42.
[4] Minutes of the Town Council of Edinburgh, 11 Nov 1696.
[5] Inventory in City Chambers, see H M Anderson, *op cit*, XX, p 14.

feet by 64. The playground at the back, however, stretched to the Calton slopes, and that area alone would seem to justify the Rectors of the school in advertising its healthy site and facilities for exercise.[1] Mr Anderson reproduces a map in his article in the Old Edinburgh Club series that marks the site of the Canongate High School as midway between New Street and Leith Wynd and some distance north of the Canongate. The building has now disappeared.

It is unusual to find any references at all to games or the need for physical exercise in schools at this time. This makes the advertisement of the Canongate High School for 1776 all the more interesting.[2] There is a description of the 'pleasant and commodious situation', surrounded by large open spaces where the boys could play. No doubt this was meant to impress readers who were at the same time hearing how cramped and old-fashioned the buildings of the High School were. The advertisement continues: 'Elegant bounds have been formed for the hand-ball by raising part of the garden wall to an extraordinary height, and preparing the ground properly at the bottom of it. This, tho' extremely necessary for procuring health and strengthening the constitution of boys at the doubtful season of life, universally set apart for acquiring languages, and much attended to in England, yet it has been hitherto but too much neglected in Scotland.'

Part of the building was occupied by the Rector as his private dwelling. According to David Laing,[3] the master's quarters were originally the upper storey and attics, which were rented to him at £1 yearly, but later the master used the garden flat opening out on the slope to the north.

Laing states that the building of the school in 1704 cost £5944 4s 2d Scots, or about £500 sterling.

The Grammar School of South Leith had existed for a long time in the vaults of Trinity House,[4] but in 1710, owing to a dispute between the Kirk Session and the Masters of Trinity

[1] *The Edinburgh Evening Courant*, 15 Feb 1772, where the school is described as having 'a free air'. *ibid*, 1 April 1775.

[2] *The Caledonian Mercury*, 9 Sept 1776.

[3] Laing papers, Edinburgh University Library, Bundle 21, quoted by Anderson, *op cit*, XX, p 15.

[4] Mackay, *op cit*, p 11, quoting session minutes of 1636.

House over rent, the Session moved the school to the King James's Hospital in South Leith Churchyard. This building belonged to the Kirk Session. By 1792, this old building—it dated from 1614—was unsuitable as a school, and it was reported to the session that 'complaints having been long made of the present grammar schoolhouse being damp, confined, and otherwise unhealthy for the boys', a group of 'respectable inhabitants of Leith' proposed to petition the Town Council of Edinburgh for ground on which to build a new school. The session agreed to support this movement, and as a result a feu was obtained of a piece of ground on Leith Links. The ground was vested in the Police Commissioners of Leith, who decided to raise the money for the new school by public subscription. It is interesting that the same method was followed as for the building of the High School of Edinburgh in the 1770s. The advertisement in the press said: 'The want of public schools for accommodating the youth of Leith has long been a subject of complaint and regret. The rooms now occupied by the different teachers are too small, placed at a great distance from each other, and some of them in improper and even unhealthy situations.' The foundation stone was laid in 1804, and the new building was occupied in 1806. To it went not only the Master of the Grammar School and his pupils, but also the master of the English school which had, along with the Grammar School, been in the old King James's Hospital.[1] Though the development of the school on its new site is outwith the period of this study, it is important to mention one detail. The new school was to be under Trustees, including two ministers of South Leith, and the Trustees claimed the right to approve the appointments of teachers; this right appears to have been disputed by the Kirk Session certainly until 1831, and the session ceased to have an official connection with the school only in 1846.

HOURS

There is not much information about the hours of attendance in the High Schools. Steven, writing of the High School of Edinburgh, has a short but rather misleading paragraph, which

[1] Mackay, *op cit*, p 24.

commences: 'The patrons have uniformly attended to any representation, respectably signed, which might in any way contribute to the comfort of those attending, or otherwise connected with this seminary.' The Town Council record does not suggest that this was always true, for there was a protest by parents in 1696 against the early morning start at 7 am and the Town Council record says that the Council agreed that the hours from November to March should be 9-12.[1] The Council must have gone back on this agreement, for parents protested again in 1723 against the 7 am start. The Town Council on this occasion discussed the matter with the Rector and masters and again agreed that 9-12 should be the rule.[2] In 1754 occurred the protest to which Steven referred, when parents objected to the afternoon session beginning at 2 pm. It was then agreed that 9-12 and 3-5 should be the normal hours, but that in the winter months from November to February the hours would be 9-11 and 12-2 on Saturdays as well as week days.[3]

In 1781 the question of hours was raised again, this time by Sir William Forbes in the name of the High School committee and the Rector and masters. (This was the committee in charge of the new building.) They did not object to the winter hours, but thought the arrangements for the summer were not 'as well arranged as they may be for the instruction of the boys'. The summer times were 7-9, 10-12, and 3-5. The committee thought it prejudicial to the pupils' health to study immediately after dinner; they mentioned the alteration that time had produced in the hours of dining in the city, and suggested that all school should be over by 3 o'clock in the summer. The Town Council agreed and the hours were fixed as 7-9, 10-12, and 1-3.[4] This is an interesting confirmation of Miss Plant's statement in *Domestic Life in the Eighteenth Century*, page 111; 'So in Edinburgh, whereas in the 'sixties the "correct" dinner-hour was two o'clock, twenty years later it was four or five.'[5]

[1] Minutes of the Town Council of Edinburgh, 11 Sept 1696.
[2] *ibid*, 9 Oct 1723.
[3] Steven, *op cit*, pp 101-2. Minutes of the Town Council of Edinburgh, 9 Oct 1754.
[4] Minutes of the Town Council of Edinburgh, 28 March 1781 and 4 April 1781.
[5] See also Cockburn, *op cit*, p 27.

No information has been found about the hours of attendance at the Canongate High School.

It seems likely that the Grammar School of South Leith followed the same hours as the High School of Edinburgh. In the seventeenth century, the hours were from 6 am to 6 pm, with one hour breaks for breakfast and dinner, but the eighteenth century saw some mitigation of this harsh regime. In the middle of that century the hours were 7-9, 10-1, and 3-5 in the summer months, and shorter hours in winter.[1]

THE JANITOR

The post of Janitor at the High School was described by no less an authority than Dr Samuel Johnson as 'a mean office', of which William Mallet (or Malloch) preferred not to be reminded.[2] Dr Steven traced the record of Mallet's short tenure of the post in the City Chamberlain's records, and quoted Mallet's receipt for sixteen and eightpence, his half-year's salary.[3] Steven also gives a list of the janitors, from which it appears that many of those appointed in the early part of the century held the post for short periods only, and it is possible that these early holders were students. (Steven points out that at that time students on occasion held the post of janitor at the University.) After 1720, however, the janitors in succession held office for long stretches.[4] William Crawford, janitor from 1730 till 1759, was, according to the newspapers of the time, 'somewhat advanced in years, and has been for some time a widower'.[5] The story of his being jilted at the altar by a young woman was reported in some detail in the press.

In 1793, the Town Council adopted a set of regulations for the janitor of the High School, which give some indication of his position at that time. After the usual adjurations to be sober

[1] Mackay, *op cit*, pp 18-19.
[2] Johnson, *Lives of the Poets*.
[3] Steven, *op cit*, p 90. The date of the receipt was 2 Feb 1718.
[4] Steven's list includes: 1705, William Lyle; 1706, John Ewart; 1710, John Morrison; 1712, William Charles; 1717, William Malloch; 1718, James Finlay; 1720, Robert Scott; 1730, William Crawford; 1759, Thomas Elliot; 1775, William Carfrae; 1793, John Wright.
[5] *The Caledonian Mercury*, 29 Nov 1731.

and honest, there are instructions that the janitor was responsible for seeing that the rooms were kept clean and the fires lit, and the yard and 'the necessaries' in proper order. Regulation 6 says: 'That he allow no idle boys to enter the playground, climb on the walls, or mingle with the young gentlemen at their play.' The janitor was to ring the bell and keep a register of the names and addresses of the boys, and 'be always ready to serve any boy who may be taken suddenly ill, by seeing him to the place of his residence, or calling a chair for him should he not be able to walk'. Further, 'he may, if he chooses, sell to the boys play things such as hand balls, rackets, or marble bowls, rolls of good bread and ripe fruit, that he must not sell pease, unripe fruit, nor any thing by which a boy's health may be hurt, and on no account sell anything to a boy on credit'. Finally 'he shall have a basin, water, and a towel ready at all times for the boys, and assist them in cleaning themselves or their clothes if they shall be dirtied from a fall or otherwise; and provide them with a clean linen rag for tying up any wounds or bruises they may occasionally meet with'. The janitor must live in the house at the gate.[1]

ANNUAL VISITATIONS

The Presbytery made arrangements to visit all schools annually. The Town Council, for its part, had for many years conducted similar inspections of the High School. There is reference to this practice in the Council's minutes in 1646,[2] and in 1699 details are given, including the provision of 40 pounds Scots for prizes.[3] Similar arrangements were made in 1703 and 1704, but in none of them is the Presbytery mentioned as taking part. One must assume, however, that some of the city ministers did in fact conduct the visitation, for they, with the professors from the College, were the best fitted of the Town's servants to criticise public instruction in Latin grammar.

By an Act of the General Assembly of 1706, all Presbyteries were enjoined to visit 'public grammar schools within their

---

[1] Minutes of the Town Council of Edinburgh, 20 Nov 1793.
[2] Steven, *op cit*, p 59.
[3] Steven, *op cit*, p 78.

bounds . . . at least twice every year', and for several years the Edinburgh Presbytery seems to have done this, and indeed to have visited all the schools in the city in an agreed rota.[1] But this was too elaborate a system, and the High School was in danger of being over-inspected. A compromise was the sensible solution, and it took place by 1714, in which year the reports of visitation to Presbytery and Town Council clearly refer to the same occasion.[2] The Presbytery continued to record notices of visitation until 1727. The Town Council minutes, on the other hand, mention them annually, and from 1733 notices also appeared in the Edinburgh newspapers, from which it is clear that the Town Council included two of the city ministers on the visiting committee along with distinguished scholars like Ruddiman, Keeper of the Advocates' Library, and professors from the College.

The working of the joint system of inspection that prevailed in the early years of the eighteenth century can best be illustrated by an account of the inspection of the High School in 1707. A committee of the Presbytery visited the school in October[3] and again in December of that year, and reported that the Rector was 'much discouraged' by the number of Private schools in the city. The Presbytery agreed that the Town Council and the city ministers should investigate this complaint. There was a long delay, and the subject does not appear in the Town Council Minutes until 1709,[4] when the Lord Provost, magistrates, city ministers and professors, 'taking to their consideration the great decay of the school, called the master and doctors before them, to take trial of the cause thereof'. The Rector and his doctors—or assistants—were interviewed separately. The Rector denied that his discipline was at fault, praised the work of his staff, and asserted that the High School was suffering because of private schools. The assistants, in their turn, confirmed what the Rector had said about private schools. 'Thereafter the master was called in, and all of them,

---

[1] *Acts of the General Assembly*, p 395. Act of 13 April 1706.
[2] Edinburgh Presbytery Minutes, 8 Dec 1714; Minutes of the Town Council of Edinburgh, 3 Dec 1714.
[3] Edinburgh Presbytery Minutes, 15 Oct 1707.
[4] Steven, *op cit*, quoting Minutes of the Town Council of Edinburgh.

by the Lord Provost, in name of the council, were exhorted to a faithful and conscientious discharge of their respective duties. The council recommended to Bailie Brodie, and the committee anent the College, to consider what overtures might be given for recovering the said school to its former lustre, frequence, and reputation, and likewise to consider the method of teaching, and report the same with all convenient diligence to the council.' The College Committee reported in December 1709 that the masters were to be examined by some of the ministers and professors, but that in the meantime a new system of salaries and fees be set up.[1] Two months later the Committee submitted a further series of recommendations,[2] drawn up by the Principal and some of the professors of the College for a new organisation of the curriculum and methods of teaching. The whole process of visitations and reports and consideration thus took over two years, and many people were consulted; perhaps this was not a bad thing, for change in human institutions like schools is better brought about slowly.

In 1714, Presbytery and Town Council inspected the High School jointly, and each body recorded its own report. The ministers of the Presbytery[3] 'ordered the several masters to examine their respective classes and found that there was good order kept in that school and that many of the boys made good proficiency. And they are informed that the masters are diligent in their charge and found the school in a very flourishing condition.' The Town Council report[4] says: 'Bailie John Osburn reported that he with the Professor of Divinity and several ministers of the Presbytery visited the High School which they found to be under a good regulation and discipline, and they having taken trial of several of the scholars found they had made good progress in their studies.'

The Town Council Minutes usually specify that the visitors shall 'take trial of the boys' proficiency and the masters' care and diligence', and recommend 'what regulations and methods may be found necessary'.[5] Matters concerning the fabric of the

[1] For details see page 71.
[2] For details see page 74.
[3] Edinburgh Presbytery Minutes, 8 Dec 1714.
[4] Minutes of the Town Council of Edinburgh, 3 Dec 1714.
[5] *ibid*, 4 April 1733.

building were referred to the Council's Committee of Public Works.[1] There was no doubt that the annual visitations were meant to keep the teachers working satisfactorily; the visitation in 1735 was undertaken 'that it may be enquired into whether the Rector and Masters do their duties . . . and that good order and government be observed . . .'.[2]

A similar briefing of the visiting committee took place in 1737 'considering that there are several complaints made touching the government and management of the High School', but the report was favourable except for the conduct of Mr Gibb, who was publicly rebuked.[3] Prizes were awarded at these examinations. In 1736, the Town Council allowed an expenditure of £5 16s 1d stg for books to be given as prizes.[4] From 1745 to 1754 the allowance was £10 10s; from 1755 to 1775 it was £12, and from then to the end of the century, £20 was granted. The reports made after these visitations were usually formal and are nearly all to the effect that the masters are diligent and the boys are making good progress, but occasionally something fresh is said. In 1748, for example, the report says that 'the boys behaved extremely well. . . . Great numbers of them really outdo the expectation of the gentlemen examinators which gave universal content to all present, and did greatly add to the honour of their teachers.'[5] It became the practice to insert a notice in the press about the visitation, and the occasion was taken for advertisement; no doubt some of the laudatory remarks must be read with some caution. We know, for example, that Mr Gibb was not a satisfactory teacher, yet we find an account of the annual visitation in the *Caledonian Mercury* that praises him. Setting aside praise of Mr Gibb's achievements, however, we can form a fair idea of the method of the visitation. A whole day was taken, the lowest classes in the forenoon and the highest in the afternoon. 'Mr Gibb . . . had his scholars examined on the Fourth Eclogue of Virgil; when, besides the exposition of it they explained its design and the antiquities that served to illustrate it, and showed their knowledge

---

[1] Minutes of the Town Council of Edinburgh, 2 Jan 1734.
[2] *ibid*, 29 Jan 1735.
[3] *ibid*, 26 Jan 1737.
[4] *ibid*, 28 July 1736.
[5] *ibid*, 3 Aug 1748.

in all the different parts of grammar, in the analysis, quantities and scanning of the verses. They were next examined on the different sorts of verses in Buchanan's Psalms: in all which acquitted themselves to the general satisfaction. They likewise explained Caesar's description of his bridge over the Rhine, showed the use of every part, with the reason of its structure and particular position: and that all the schemes and models of it hitherto given have been faulty, through a misunderstanding of Caesar's words.'[1] The newspaper account for the next year is similar but an additional paragraph stated that the writing-master produced 'pieces of writ done by boys under his care, which were admired'.[2] Fathers of boys at the school attended on the visitation day. Many of the parents, we are informed in 1749, expressed satisfaction[3]; and in 1750 Professor Stewart and the other examiners were accompanied by several gentlemen who had sons at the school.[4] The 1752 report in the press defends the school organisation: 'the excellent method in which the boys are taught in that seminary, where they must certainly make a greater progress in their education than in most other schools, whose teachers have perhaps four, five, or more different classes, and consequently as many lessons to prescribe and examine; whereas in the High School of Edinburgh, every master has his particular class, who have one lesson in common which must be of great advantage to boys of a slow capacity or the more careless'.[5] On this occasion, the boys in the highest class translated several paragraphs of English into classical Latin, and pronounced Latin orations 'in order to initiate them in the art of oratory'. In 1762, the Lord Provost and magistrates were so pleased with the work of the High School masters that they honoured them and the Rector with the freedom of the city and made them burgesses.[6]

After this date, though the visitations continue, the reports, both to the Town Council and in the press, are generally stereotyped, mentioning the diligence of the masters, the good appear-

[1] *The Caledonian Mercury*, 20 Aug 1739 (*cf* p 77).
[2] *ibid*, 4 Sept 1740.
[3] *ibid* and *The Edinburgh Evening Courant*, 7 Sept 1749.
[4] *The Edinburgh Evening Courant*, 6 Sept 1750.
[5] *The Caledonian Mercury*, 19 Sept 1752.
[6] *ibid*, 1 Sept 1762.

ance of the boys, and the prizes consisting of copies of the classic authors stamped with the arms of the city.

The Canongate High School also was examined every year, 'in the presence of the Magistrates of the Canongate, some of the ministers of the Presbytery of Edinburgh, and several other gentlemen'.[1] In 1764, the press report gives a few more details, for the children were examined 'in the several classes in which they were taught English, Latin, and Greek'.[2] In 1772, when the school was under Cruickshank, 'the scholars of the several classes went through their exercises at great length to our entire satisfaction'.[3] Since these reports appeared in the press, there was a tendency to use them to advertise the teachers; the note of 1777 contains the phrase that the examiners were 'well satisfied that young gentlemen cannot be under the care of a more sufficient master'.[4] An appeal of another kind occurs the following year in the phrase 'a great part of the scholars consisted of sons of gentlemen of the first rank'.[5]

In 1780, the Canongate High School was examined in the presence of a 'numerous and genteel' company, and the boys translated and analysed 'the passages of the classic authors which were turned up to them'. The report continues: 'The extensive practice of the scholars in reading met with particular approbation. To teach a small portion of any author, and to repeat it until every boy has it by rote, is an easy matter, and very convenient for making a show; but it is very hurtful to young minds.' The dux of the school spoke 'the elegant speech of Galgacus the Caledonian chief, to his soldiers'. Finally, the report contains the statement that 'the number of genteel scholars in the Canongate School has, of late, increased considerably'.[6] The tenor of the announcement in 1782 is the same; the response of the boys gave 'universal satisfaction'; the older pupils 'translating the different classics with elegance and ease, applying the rules of grammar readily and distinctly'.[7]

Of all the reports of visitations published in the Edinburgh

[1] *The Caledonian Mercury*, 15 Sept 1762.
[2] *The Edinburgh Evening Courant*, 15 Sept 1764.
[3] *ibid*, 19 Aug 1772.
[4] *The Caledonian Mercury*, 27 Sept 1777.
[5] *ibid*, 28 Sept 1778.
[6] *The Edinburgh Evening Courant*, 16 Aug 1780.
[7] *The Caledonian Mercury*, 17 Aug 1782.

press none can equal that on the Grammar School of South Leith in 1739. It certainly gives the impression it was presumably meant to create, that the parents of Leith were lucky in Mr Millar. 'A committee appointed by the reverend Presbytery of Edinburgh to visit the Grammar School of South Leith, reported to the Presbytery Wednesday last, That in presence of the session and several other gentlemen, they examined the whole classes, and with pleasure observed the excellency of Mr Millar's teaching, and his scholars' great proficiency. The young ones are taught the rudiments, the properties of the several parts of speech, the nature of declension and construction in a most easy familiar way, instead of burdening their memories with tedious repetitions of things they don't understand, first principles are agreeably instilled into their minds, and they are gradually led in by such natural steps, as engages the attention of the most thoughtless, and makes grammar itself tolerable and pleasant. Those of the higher classes turned any given piece of English with the utmost ease and facility into a Latin style, not unworthy the best humanist; and with the same readiness translated Caesar's Commentaries, Virgil's Aeneids, etc, preserving almost the very spirit of their authors, tho' they had no occasion to read them for above twelve months past. While they learn the Latin, great care is taken to improve them in English, being accustomed to prove every word, decline every noun, conjugate every verb, and construct the whole in both languages, giving the proper rules. The examination continued six hours, and scarce any one boy was at a loss to give the rational account of what he had learnt, not being taught by rote, but instructed from the very beginning, so far as their capacities admit, in the true nature and reason of things. The committee observed it as none of the least of Mr Millar's qualifications, that he is not ashamed even in this age to act the part of a Christian teacher on proper occasions, warmly recommending to all under his care the practice of those divine virtues that will render them valuable members of the commonwealth, and prove the glory and comfort of their riper years. The Presbytery have ordered this report to be recorded in their register, in testimony of their regard to Mr Millar; and we think ourselves bound to publish the same, in justice to his character, whose abilities for his station, his diligence and success, entitle him to the esteem of all, and demand the highest encouragement.'[1]   Behind the exaggerations of this report, it is possible to discern the kind of teaching that went on in this school. Latin was the basis of instruction, but English was taught as well, and grammatically treated in the same way as Latin.   No mention is made of arithmetic, but this does not mean it was not taught; the chances are that writing and accounts were part of the curriculum, if not for everyone, at least for some, but it is unlikely that the visiting ministers were much interested in these subjects.   The next reference is forty years later, when Mr John Wilson was schoolmaster.   Then the school was examined in the presence of the magistrates, ministers, and a number of the principal inhabitants, and the pupils showed themselves to be well versed in the principles of grammar, a knowledge of Latin, and of Roman antiquities.[2]   The report for 1780 is similar, but that for 1785 mentions that the pupils in addition to the subjects already mentioned, professed Greek and geography.[3]

FROM THE BOYS' POINT OF VIEW

One of the difficulties about writing the history of education is that seldom can one get authentically the point of view of the boy on the benches.   The experiences of the boy and man combine to give a quality of hindsight to even the most vivid accounts of schooldays.   The High School at the end of the eighteenth century produced a group of pupils whose abilities bear comparison with those of any other school at any other time.   Henry Mackenzie, Walter Scott, Henry Cockburn, Francis Jeffrey, Henry Brougham are the most distinguished names, but there were many others, and it is not surprising that a number of these men have left fascinating accounts of the High School.   Cockburn seems to have been unhappy as a little boy at school, and this has coloured his attitude. Mackenzie, who wrote many years after he had left school in

[1] *The Caledonian Mercury,* 4 Sept 1739.
[2] *ibid,* 21 Aug 1779.
[3] *The Edinburgh Evening Courant,* 27 Aug 1785.

1757, also seems to emphasise the harshness of the regime. Scott, a pupil from 1779 to 1783, tells more of his exploits in the Yards with his fellows than of his class work, and perhaps this is natural. It is possible, however, by taking information from various sources, to build up a kind of picture of the High School as it appeared in the eyes of the pupils.

First of all there was that early morning start, so vividly described by Cockburn; 'They had the barbarity to make us be in school during summer at seven o'clock in the morning. I once started out of bed, thinking I was too late, and got out of the house unquestioned. On reaching the High School gate, I found it locked, and saw the yards, through the bars, silent and motionless. I withdrew alarmed, and went near the Tron Church to see the clock. It was only about two or three. Not a creature was on the street; not even watchmen, who were of much later introduction. I came home awed, as if I had seen a dead city, and the impression of that hour has never been effaced.'[1] This must have taken place after October 1787, when Cockburn entered Mr Christison's class. Thirty years earlier, from 1751 to 1757, Henry Mackenzie had the same hours: 'The hour of attendance was from seven to nine and after an interval of an hour for breakfast from ten to twelve; thereafter another interval of two hours for dinner, latterly I think in my time of three; returned for two hours in the afternoon.'[2]

Of the organisation of the High School Scott makes two criticisms in the autobiographical chapters in Lockhart's *Life*.[3] First he was entered in the second class, and was young for it, which meant that he was always competing with boys more mature than himself. He says that 'this situation has the unfortunate effect of reconciling a boy of lively temper and talents . . . to holding a subordinate station among his class-fellows—to which he would otherwise affix disgrace'. If Scott had been placed in the Rudiments class, as his age would have warranted, his master would have been Nicol, whose reputation for brutality was well known.[4] Scott's second criticism is that

[1] Cockburn, *op cit*, p 8.
[2] Mackenzie, *op cit*, p 34.
[3] Lockhart, *Life of Scott*, Edinburgh Edition, Jack, 1902, Vol 1, p 28.
[4] Nicol became the friend of Robert Burns; he was the 'Willie' who 'brew'd a peck o' maut'.

G

boys sat in their places according to merit, 'and it requires a long while, in general, before even a clever boy, if he falls behind the class, or is put into one for which he is not quite ready, can force his way to the situation which his abilities really entitle him to hold'. The system meant that boys like him, younger than the majority, were forced to be the associates of the less able spirits. 'A boy of good talents, therefore, placed even for a time among his inferiors, especially if they be also his elders, learns to participate in their pursuits and objects of ambition, which are usually very distinct from the acquisition of learning; and it will be well if he does not also imitate them in that in-difference which is contented with bustling over a lesson so as to avoid punishment, without affecting superiority or aiming at reward. It was probably owing to this circumstance, that, although at a more advanced period of life I have enjoyed considerable facility in acquiring languages, I did not make any great figure at the High School—or, at least, any exertions which I made were desultory and little to be depended on.' Lockhart, writing of this period of Scott's life, says: 'His quick apprehen-sion and powerful memory enabled him, at little cost of labour, to perform the usual routine of tasks, in such a manner as to keep him generally "in a decent place" (so he once expressed it to Mr Skene) "about the middle of the class; with which," he continued, "I was the better contented, that it chanced to be near the fire".' Lockhart adds in a footnote that according to a schoolfellow, Irving, Scott's place was usually between the 7th and the 15th from the top of the class. 'Dr James Buchan was always the *dux*; David Douglas (Lord Reston) *second*; and the present Lord Melville *third*.'[1]

Scott and his brothers had a tutor to assist them at home, 'a young man of an excellent disposition and a laborious student'.[2] He taught Scott writing, arithmetic, and heard him say his French lessons. This is an interesting reference because French was not then taught in the High School, and writing and arithmetic were optional subjects for which boys made separate arrangements with the Writing Master. Lockhart tells us that Scott took writing and arithmetic 'at a small

[1] Lockhart, *op cit*, p 98.
[2] Lockhart, *op cit*, p 31.

separate seminary of writing and arithmetic, kept by one
Morton, where, as was, and I suppose continues to be, the custom of Edinburgh, young girls came for instruction as well as
boys'.[1] It was possibly at this school that Scott learned French.[2]
Scott's tutor, the Rev James Mitchell, gave some reminiscences
to Lockhart. He says, for example, 'On my going into the family,
as far as I can judge, he might be in his twelfth or thirteenth
year, a boy in the Rector's class. However elevated above the
other boys in genius, though generally in the list of the duxes,
he was seldom, as far as I can recollect, the leader of the school;
nor need this be deemed surprising, as it has often been observed
that boys of original genius have been outstripped, by those
that were far inferior to themselves, in the acquisition of the
dead languages.'[3]

Another of Mr Mitchell's recollections gives us a glimpse of an
incident in Scott's schooldays. It was the custom of the
Rector to inspect the classes of the other masters at regular
intervals. Adam had been assaulted by Nicol and the boys of
Adam's class felt strongly against Nicol. 'The classes of those
masters the rector in rotation inspects, and in the mean time the
master, whose school is examined, goes in to take care of the
rector's. One of the masters, on account of some grudge, had
rudely assaulted and injured the venerable rector one night in
the High School Wynd. The rector's scholars, exasperated at
the outrage, at the instigation of Master Walter, determined
on revenge, which was to be executed when this obnoxious
master should again come to teach the class. When this
occurred, the task the class had prescribed to them was that
passage in the Aeneid of Virgil, where the Queen of Carthage
interrogates the court as to the stranger that had come to her
habitation—*Quis novus hic hospes successit sedibus nostris?*
Master Walter having taken a piece of paper, inscribed upon
it these words, substituting *vanus* for *novus*, and pinned it to
the tail of the master's coat, and turned him into ridicule by
raising the laugh of the whole school against him.'[4]

[1] Lockhart, *op cit*, p 110.
[2] Steven, *op cit*, p 251. French was introduced into the High School
curriculum only in 1834.
[3] Lockhart, *op cit*, p 119.
[4] Lockhart, *op cit*, p 119.

There is an interesting parallel to this story in the manuscript of Lord Charles Hope, later Lord Granton, now in Edinburgh University Library. He writes: 'Nicol, as you say, was a good Scholar, but I did not consider him a *better* Scholar than Adam or Fraser.—His passions were quite ungovernable & He was altogether a most unprincipled Savage.—He persecuted poor Adam by every means in his power; & at last was guilty of a brutal Assault on him, for which the Magistrates did not expell him as they ought to have done.—As a specimen of Nicols unprincipled disposition, & at the same time of his Selfish cunning, take the following Anecdote.—You know it was at that time the Custom for the Rector once a week to go & examine the Class of one of the other Masters, who, at the same time, came into the Rector's Class & examined it.—On one of those occasions, when I was Dux of the Rector's Class, Nicol came to examine us.—He seemed to be in particular good humour, anticipating, I have no doubt, the triumph he expected over the Rector.—He went on for some time in the usual way, hearing us translate & construe.—He then began to put some difficult questions, which Several of the Boys could not answer, but on putting them to me & other Boys at the Head of the Class, they were all answered.—At last, He put a question which neither I nor any other Boy could answer.—On which he turned to me & said, You are a pretty fellow, Sir, to be at the Head of this School—not to be able to answer this question—I'll show you that your Cousin John Hope (the late Lord Hopetoun) in my Class can answer it, & make you ashamed of yourself.—He then called the Janitor & desired Him to call John Hope to come to Him.—John came & the question was put to him, but John could not answer it. Nicol was evidently very angry, but He had the Selfish Cunning not to outrage the Son of Such a Man as Old Lord Hopetoun.—So He merely desired Hope to go away and send Elliott, the Heriotter, to Him.—Accordingly Elliott came, & the question was repeated to him, but He did not answer it either, on which the Savage lost all command of himself, flew at poor Elliott, seized & shook by both Ears, till He almost tore them off, & quite forgetting himself, exclaimed You Scoundrel, Have not I been dunning this into you for a week past—showing that He had been leading his Boys out of their depth, & attempting to make them get by rote things they did not understand, in hopes of having it to say, that His Boys only in the third class were further advanced than the Rectors.— This explosion operated like Electricity in the Class—There was a universal shout & Hiss, & we all ran out of the school, leaving Nicol frantic but stupefied with rage.'

Henry Mackenzie pictures the High School as following a narrow course, but says that the masters were with one exception not brutal. The exception was Rae, 'a severe harsh-tempered man, but an excellent scholar, a rigid disciplinarian and the only frequent flogger of the school, consequently very unpopular with the boys, tho' from the reputation of his superior learning he had more scholars than either of the above-mentioned masters'.[1] Cockburn speaks about the harshness of the High School in his day (1787). He calls it 'notorious for its severity and riotousness', and his master, Christison, he calls 'The person to whose uncontrolled discipline I was now subjected, though a good man, an intense student, and filled, but rather in the memory than in the head, with knowledge, was as bad a schoolmaster as it is possible to fancy. Un-acquainted with the nature of youth, ignorant even of the characters of his own boys, and with not a conception of the art or of the duty of alluring them, he had nothing for it but to drive them; and this he did by constant and indiscriminate harshness.'[2]

Cockburn is bitter when he talks of Christison's driving and beating ways. 'Out of the whole four years of my attendance there were probably not ten days in which I was not flogged, at least once.'[3] Yet he claimed he had done his homework, which was not difficult; 'Every one of the boys had to rhyme over the very same words, in the very same way. . . . But I was driven stupid. Oh! the bodily and mental weariness of sitting six hours a day, staring idly at a page, without motion and without thought, and trembling at the gradual approach of the merciless giant. I never got a single prize, and once sat *boobie* at the annual public examination. The beauty of no Roman word, or thought,

---

[1] Mackenzie, *op cit*, p 33. The two other masters referred to were Farquhar and Gilchrist.

[2] Cockburn, *op cit*, p 3.

[3] Cockburn, *op cit*, p 3.

or action, ever occurred to me; nor did I ever fancy that Latin was of any use except to torture boys.'[1] Cockburn's tendency in the *Memorials* is to dwell on past excesses and miseries, and there is an element of exaggeration in this account, just as there was in Charles Lamb's description of his schooldays at Christ's Hospital. And Cockburn is generous in his appreciation of Dr Adam.

Of the annual visitations we get a glimpse in Mackenzie, when he says: 'They wrote *Versions*, translations from Latin into English, and at the annual examination in August recited *Speeches*, as they were called, from some of the Roman poets. Mine at the Rector's class was the episode of Nisus and Euryalus in Virgil, and attracted much notice from the impassioned manner in which I spoke it, having early a turn for theatrical studies.'[2]

It is only fair when quoting the adverse opinions of Scott and Cockburn on masters like Nicol and Christison, also to quote what they said of the Rector, Dr Adam. 'It was from this respectable man that I first learned the value of the knowledge I had hitherto considered only as a burdensome task,' said Scott and explains how Adam encouraged him and his fellows to write verse, and how his words of praise stimulated his ambition.[3] Cockburn says: 'Never was a man more fortunate in the choice of a vocation. He was born to teach Latin, some Greek, and all virtue . . . a warm encourager by praise, play, and kindness; and constantly under the strongest sense of duty.'[4] When Cockburn's class left the High School, they presented a book to Dr Adam: 'It fell to Francis Horner as the dux to give it, and he never acquitted himself better. It was on the day of the public examination; and after the prizes were distributed, and the spectators thought that the business was over, he stood forth with one volume of the book in his hand, and in a distinct though tremulous voice, and firm but modest manner, addressed Adam in a Latin speech of his own composition, not exceeding three or four sentences, expressive of the gratitude and affection

[1] Cockburn, *op cit*, p 4.
[2] Mackenzie, *op cit*, p 34.
[3] Lockhart, *op cit*, p 32. One of Scott's early poems, found in Dr Adam's papers, is in the High School Library.
[4] Cockburn, *op cit*, p 4.

with which we all took leave of our master. The effect was
complete, on Adam, on the audience, and on the boys.'[1]

The general tone of the school, according to Cockburn, was
'Vulgar and harsh. Among the boys, coarseness of language
and manners was the only fashion. An English boy was so rare,
that his accent was openly laughed at.[2] No lady could be seen
within the walls. Nothing evidently civilised was safe. Two
of the masters, in particular, were so savage, that any master
doing now what they did every hour, would certainly be trans-
ported.'[3] Scott, on the other hand, talks of vigorous exercise
in the yards, of manning the Cowgate Port with snowballs, and
of telling tales to his fellows in winter, 'an admiring audience
round Lucky Brown's fireside, and happy was he that could sit
next to the inexhaustible narrator'.[4] Mackenzie has a curious
reference to a game played in the yards, Bowl and Ring. 'It
was played with a ring which moved on a pivot, through which
the bowl of the adversary was driven by a sort of mallet, which
counted, I think, one in the game; the bowl of the player,
passing through the ring, and afterwards, like a billiard ball,
driven into one of the holes made on the margin of the green
or arena, counted also for the player. There was considerable
skill, and I think rather more interest than even at billiards,
in these different evolutions of the game. When I was at the
High School, the then Dowager Lady Haddington, who had a
house very near our playground, and whose daughter, an invalid,
was frequently disturbed by the boys entering the court in
front of her house, bargained to make us a present of a compleat
apparatus for Bowl and Ring, and also for Nine Pins, on condition of our never entering this court, nor making any noise
near it. The capitulation was honourably and strictly observed
by the boys.'[5]

Mention has been made of Cockburn's criticisms of his old
master, Christison, and some confirmation of Cockburn's
statements is to be found in a manuscript in the Town Council

---

[1] Cockburn, *op cit*, p 9.
[2] The same attitude towards an English accent is reported by George
Borrow, in *Lavengro*: Borrow was a pupil at the High School.
[3] Cockburn, *op cit*, p 10.
[4] Scott, various references, including *Redgauntlet*, and Lockhart, *op cit*,
Vol 1, p 30.
[5] Mackenzie, *op cit*, p 86.

records. It is dated April 1787, and Cockburn joined the school in October 1787. The manuscript describes a fight between Robert Lockhart, son of Mr Lockhart of Castlehill, and Christopher Durward, son of Mr Durward, Watchmaker in the Canongate. Many in the class had been in the habit of calling Durward a Papist, and Lockhart was alleged to have called him a 'dirty Papist'. A fight followed in which Durward is said to have struck Lockhart on the eye and mouth with a stone. One boy said he thought it was a 'piry' (a top) that Christopher had held in his hand. The matter was referred back to the Rector and masters. A different kind of escapade is mentioned in a letter in the High School library from one of the masters to the Rector, enclosing a fish hook, and saying that a boy had been convicted of idleness in playing with it.

The records of the High School, and the various histories of the school, give the names of distinguished pupils, but it is rare to find a note of what became of the members of one class. The nearest account is a list in the papers of Lord Robertson, eldest son of Principal Robertson, of the 74 boys who were in Gilchrist's class between 1761 and 1765. From notes by Lord Robertson and information from other sources it has been possible to trace 26 of them. Of six, it is merely said that they were 'in India'. Three were in London, a Lord of Chancery, an attorney, and a physician. Three were in the army, a general and two colonels. In Edinburgh were a Lord of the Court of Session, two surgeons, two members of the WS Society, three merchants, a dyer, a house-painter, a seal-engraver, and an under-clerk. There were two members of the landed gentry, the Marquis of Tweeddale, and William Fullarton of Fullarton.[1]

[1] National Library of Scotland, MS 3948 f 106.

Chapter IV

THE HOSPITAL SCHOOLS

THERE were four Hospital schools in Edinburgh during the eighteenth century, George Heriot's Hospital, the Merchant Maiden Hospital, the Trades Maiden Hospital, and George Watson's Hospital. Heriot's had been opened as a hospital as early as 1659, and the Merchant Maiden Hospital was probably opened in 1695 or 1696. The Trades Maiden Hospital dates from 1704, and George Watson's from 1734. Surely it is remarkable that there should have been four schools of this type in a city of the size of Edinburgh, and that their influence should be strong enough to stimulate the foundation of hospitals in other towns (eg Hutcheson's in Glasgow and Robert Gordon's in Aberdeen), and of other hospitals in Edinburgh itself at a later date. No city in the United Kingdom, with the exception of London, has so many foundations of this kind as Edinburgh, and it is interesting to speculate why this should be.

According to Miss M G Jones,[1] Hospital schools had an unsavoury reputation in England and Wales, and were generally less common than Charity day schools. She mentions the difficulties of organisation, and says: 'To be well run, a hospital had to be very carefully supervised.' That this is true will be seen in the consideration in this chapter of the organisation and management of the Edinburgh Hospital schools. The record of George Heriot's has references to riots, expulsions, and bickerings, and there are similar exciting episodes in the histories of the other schools. Much depended on the wise judgment of the governing body, but even more on the character of the resident master or mistress, and for these exacting jobs it was always difficult to get the right person. Though it is perhaps unfair to judge at this distance of time, and from incomplete records, it nevertheless appears that the method of management developed by the Merchant Company in adminis-

---

[1] Jones, *op cit*, p 48.

tering the Merchant Maiden Hospital and George Watson's Hospital was less cumbrous than that of the Town Council and City Ministers over Heriot's.

The puritan and middle-class influences which inspired the movement towards the founding of Charity schools were also the forces behind the establishment of the Hospital schools. Charitable Christian people felt that it was a good thing to help the poor and fatherless children, and that for the good of their souls as well as the good of the state they should be trained in habits of religion and habits of industry. It pleased them to see the children, in their uniforms, attending church service, and many of them speak of being deeply moved by the sound of the children singing.[1] The children of the Edinburgh hospitals, like those of London,[2] attended church regularly, and it was a popular sight to see them marching there in uniform. The hospitals had also their daily religious services. As for training in habits of industry, the hospitals had very much in mind the future occupations of their boys and girls. They did not merely supply the basic training in reading, writing, and accounts, but aimed definitely towards apprenticeships or similar situations. Provision was made in Heriot's and Watson's for able boys to proceed eventually to the College, but the majority entered trades or crafts. In the girls' hospitals the stress was on all kinds of domestic work, and even girls who intended to be governesses had to learn all the household duties.

The popularity of Hospital schools in Edinburgh was due to the fame of George Heriot's Hospital at the end of the seven-

[1] Sir W Fraser, *The Melvilles*, Edinburgh 1890, p 266, letter from Alexander Belsches, Advocate, to Lord Balgonie: 'Apropos Monday being Heriot's day, I went to the church, where was the whole world, and heard the sermon and singing. Mr Brown of the New Gray Friars had a suitable sermon from I Kings, 6-12, "I fear the Lord from my youth". The singing was exceedingly good. They sung, after all, the 133rd Psalm as an anthem. Franks, the New Kirk precentor, led the boys, and our precentor led the girls of the 2 Maiden Hospitals, the other precentors sat by themselves singing the bass; but it was very agreeable to see so many young creatures in their new clothes, and hair dressed, and flowers in their hands, so happy and so contented.' The date was June 1768.

[2] Perhaps the best known of the many London references is Blake's poem, 'Holy Thursday' in *Songs of Innocence*:
' 'Twas on a Holy Thursday, their innocent faces clean,
The children walking two and two, in red and blue and green,
Grey-headed beadles walked before, with wands as white as snow,
Till into the high dome of Paul's they like Thames' waters flow.'

teenth and beginning of the eighteenth century. The fine building was pointed out to strangers with pride, and Heriot's generous gift was compared with its great original, Christ's Hospital in London. The link between the two is clearly expressed in the Disposition and Assignation of his property dated 3 September 1623, where the founder stated that he wished to 'found and erect ane publick, pious, and charitable worke within the said burgh of Edinburgh . . . and in imitatione of the publict, pious, and religious work foundat within the citie of London called Chrystis Hospital thair'.[1] Faint resemblances in the constitutions of the two hospitals suggest that Dr Balcanquall, Heriot's nephew and executor, who drew up the constitution of Heriot's, had studied the Christ's Hospital arrangements. He may well have done so, for, apart from the founder's express intention, Balcanquall, as Dean of the Savoy, may have had some official connexion with Christ's Hospital. Some of the Christ's Hospital funds came from the resources of the Savoy. Christ's Hospital was originally placed by Edward VI under the Lord Mayor, Aldermen, and Common Council of the City of London, and this may have suggested the placing of Heriot's under the Lord Provost, Magistrates, and Town Council of Edinburgh. But Balcanquall added to the Governors of Heriot's the city ministers for whom there is no direct counterpart in the Christ's Hospital constitution. Heriot's did not have the right enjoyed by Christ's Hospital, to co-opt as Governors those who gave large benefactions. The lists of officials of the two hospitals are similar, and in both the Treasurer occupied an important role. In both hospitals arrangements were made for suitable boys to enter apprentice-ships, and for able ones to proceed to the University. But the parallel should not be pressed far, for the two hospitals were in many ways different, and Christ's Hospital tended to recruit its boys from the clergy and the lesser professions, while Heriot's remained a hospital for the sons of tradesmen.

Mary Erskine wished to do for the daughters of merchant burgesses what George Heriot had done for the sons of freemen, and with that in view she approached the Merchant Company

---

[1] Steven, *History of George Heriot's Hospital*, p 20. *The Herioter*, June 1928, also quotes this passage.

of Edinburgh in 1694 with the offer of money to help in the founding of a Hospital school. The Company agreed, and raised a 'fund for the lasses' to supplement the bequest of 10,000 merks set aside by Mary Erskine.[1] The hospital may have been opened in 1695, and in 1696 was definitely installed in the Company's own halls in the Cowgate. In 1706, it moved to its own premises in Bristo, purchased as the result of another gift by Mary Erskine.[2] The same Mary Erskine helped in founding a parallel Hospital school under the auspices of the Incorporation of Trades, opened in 1704, and known as the Trades Maiden Hospital.[3] These two foundations are sometimes confused, and it is often particularly difficult to identify them in references in eighteenth-century newspapers where both are called 'the Maiden Hospital'.

George Watson was a successful businessman who had for most of his life been interested in philanthropic work. He had acted as Treasurer of the Merchant Maiden Hospital, and, though not a member of the Merchant Company, had been made a Governor of the Merchant Maiden Hospital in 1710.[4] By his will of February 1723, he left money to Heriot's, the Merchant Maiden and Trades Maiden Hospitals, the Society in Scotland for the Propagation of Christian Knowledge (with which he had been prominently connected), and the residue to the Merchant Company for a new hospital for boys. This was to be 'as near to the rules of the foundation and management of Heriot's Hospital and the Merchant Maiden Hospital as the nature of the thing will allow of'.[5] The boys to be admitted were to be children or grandchildren of 'decayed merchants' or ministers of the city.[6]

---

[1] Towill in *Book of the Old Edinburgh Club*, XXIX, p 4.

[2] Towill, *op cit*, p 12.

[3] Towill, *op cit*, XXVIII. The Trades Maiden Hospital still exists as a hospital in Edinburgh, though the girls attend day schools. It is the only survivor of the old eighteenth-century hospitals.

[4] Heron, *The Merchant Company of Edinburgh*, p 86.

[5] Heron, *op cit*, p 84.

[6] In Watson's Hospital Minutes for 29 Nov 1736, there is an interesting discussion on the siting of the hospital. It was agreed that it should not be placed between the High School and College as this would expose the boys to the insults of both 'as well as being let into their vices'. Then follows a statement that the vices of Heriot's were attributable to its neighbourhood with the Grassmarket, where there were 'mean and wicked boys' as in all populous cities.

The number of pupils in residence varied according to the financial state of the hospitals. Heriot's, the largest and wealthiest foundation, had never fewer than 100 boys. In 1742, there were 136.[1] In 1759 the total was 140 boys, which appears to have been regarded as the maximum.[2] Watson's was a smaller institution. It began with 12 boys and by 1746 there seem to have been—the records are not clear—24 in residence.[3] In 1755 the Governors decided to limit the number to 40.[4] There is no further detailed information, except that in 1797 the increasing expenses forced the Governors to reduce the numbers by accepting only half of those for whom there were vacancies.[5] The Merchant Maiden Hospital had 40 girls in the 1730s, but by 1781 the number was over 70.[6] The roll in 1791 was 70.[7] The Trades Maiden Hospital began, as its *Rules and Constitution* relates, with 23 girls; by 1791 the number had risen to 50.[8]

THE MANAGEMENT OF THE HOSPITAL SCHOOLS

Since Heriot's was the model for the other foundations, it will be well to describe its method of government first. The governing body consisted of the Lord Provost, Magistrates, and Town Council of Edinburgh, together with the city ministers. At the time when the Statutes were framed by Dr Balcanquall, nephew and executor of the founder, the church in Scotland was episcopalian. Indeed, provision was made, in the event of maladministration, for the affairs of the Hospital to be investigated by the Chancellor of Scotland, the President of the College of Justice, the Lord Advocate, and 'the two Archbishops'.[9] It seems doubtful whether, when the constitution was framed, the Town Council had the power over the city ministers which

[1] Minutes, 2 June 1742.
[2] *The Caledonian Mercury*, 4 June 1759.
[3] Minutes, 3 April 1744 and 3 April 1746.
[4] *ibid*, 3 April 1755.
[5] *ibid*, 11 May 1797.
[6] *ibid*, 28 May 1781.
[7] Brown, *op cit*.
[8] Towill, *op cit*, XXVIII.
[9] Steven, *Heriot's Hospital*, p 33.

it possessed after the Revolution of 1688.[1] In placing both Town Councillors and city ministers on the governing body, Balcanquall perhaps had in mind a more equitable balance than actually obtained. In an episcopal church, bishops and archbishops could have supported the action of the ministers if they differed on any point from the Town Council, but under the presbyterian system the Town Council appointed and paid the ministers. The ministers complained on occasions that in spite of the oath which all governors had to take,[2] the Councillors sold hospital property to the detriment of the Hospital, and the advantage of the Councillors or their friends. The Town Councillors might well have complained, and there is some ground for thinking that they did so, that the posts of schoolmaster and assistant schoolmaster were generally given to young men aspiring to the ministry. Such men, of course, held these posts for a short time only, as they left when they were called to charges as ministers.[3] A constantly changing staff is not a good thing.

There are other examples of differences of opinion in the governing body, in the course of which ministers and Town Councillors tended to take opposite sides. In 1737, the Governors agreed to grant a feu of the lands of Heriot's Crofts and St Leonard's to the town, an arrangement to which one at least of the ministers, the Rev Robert Wallace, objected. In

---

[1] See Chapter I.

[2] *Statutes* Cap III: 'I, A B, do faithfully swear and promise before God that to the best of my knowledge and power I shall carry and demean myself in all matters which concern the rents, the election of officers or scholars, or anything else belonging to George Heriot's Hospital and if I know any going about at any time to defraud or defeat the intention of the said pious founder, I shall reveal it to this assembly or their successors. So help me God and the contents of the Bible.'

It is interesting to compare this oath with that laid down for the Governors of George Watson's Hospital. This text is from 'Statutes and Rules of George Watson's Hospital', 1755:

'I, A B, do solemnly swear and demean myself faithfully and knowledge and power, I shall carry and demean myself faithfully and honestly in all matters which concern the election of the officers or children, or anything else belonging to George Watson's Hospital; and if I know any person going about to defraud or prejudge the said pious work, I shall obstruct it to my power, and reveal it to the governors.'

Similar oaths were taken by the Governors of the other hospitals.

[3] An advertisement for a schoolmaster for Heriot's Hospital which appeared in *The Edinburgh Evening Courant* for 26 April 1766, said: 'N.B. Those who are not prosecuting other studies, will, if found qualified, be preferred.'

1759, in the more important case of the feuing to the town of the lands of Broughton, needed in the development of the New Town, seven ministers all objected that the Hospital was being defrauded. A subsequent law-suit on the same matter went to the Court of Session, where the action of the Governors was upheld.[1] On this occasion the ministers listed their reasons for dissenting and published them in a pamphlet.[2] Another pamphlet, of 1773,[3] states quite bluntly that the funds have been diminished by improper administration and a bad choice of Governors. It was pointed out that there were 25 ·Town Councillors and 16 ministers on the governing body, and the ministers were always outvoted. The anonymous writer says that it was the ambition of rich citizens to enter and remain in the Town Council. As the Town Council had the presentation of ministers, every now and then there was to be found among the ministers a Judas or a Haman! This pamphlet probably overstates the case; Arnot's *History of Edinburgh*, which appeared seven years later, is much kinder to the administration of Heriot's Hospital and, indeed, praises the work of its Treasurer. Though, in a sense, the Town Council was the employer of the ministers, it is unsafe to assume that the ministers were deterred from speaking and acting as their consciences dictated. The evidence of the minutes is that in all matters relating to the appointment of teachers, and of the curriculum of the boys, the ministers generally had an important part. But it is clear enough that the balance of Town Councillors and ministers was unfortunate, and led to differences of opinion and some weakness in direction.

From the beginnings of the Merchant Maiden Hospital, the Merchant Company followed a policy which it has consistently pursued with subsequent foundations. It set up a Board of Governors,[4] and gave the Board powers to manage its own funds and properties. In this way, while being generally responsible

---

[1] Steven, *Heriot's Hospital*, p 121.
[2] Pamphlet in Edinburgh Public Library, '*Reasons of Dissent by city Ministers*', 1760.
[3] Pamphlet in National Library of Scotland, '*An Address to the Citizens of Edinburgh, Relative to the Management of George Heriot's Hospital*. By a Free Burgess of Edinburgh', 1773.
[4] Towill, *op cit*, XXIX, p 7.

for the Hospital schools, the Merchant Company did not directly manage any one of them. The governing body of the Merchant Maiden Hospital consisted of the Master of the Merchant Company, thirteen members chosen by the Company, five members chosen by the Town Council, three members chosen by the city ministers, two members of the name of Erskine,ᐧ and a Treasurer chosen by the Company. One of the early Treasurers of the Merchant Maiden Hospital was George Watson, though he was not himself a member of the Merchant Company. On the whole, this governing body appears better balanced than that of Heriot's Hospital.

The Trades Maiden Hospital was under the general control of the Incorporated Trades of the city. The governing body[2] consisted of the Deacons of the various incorporated trades, two Trades Councillors, two persons of the name of Erskine,[3] and the Convener of the Incorporated Trades who presided, the total number of Governors being 27. Provision was made for adding to the number of Governors persons who gave sums to the Hospital of not less than 2000 merks. This may seem a large governing body, a fact which was recognised from the earliest days, for from the beginning a committee of nine mem-

[1] Mary Erskine was proud of her connexion with the family of Mar. Among early members of the governing body was James Erskine, Lord Grange. The Rev Mr Towill quotes a letter of his (*op cit*, p 82), and there is an interesting entry in his *Diary of a Senator of the College of Justice*, ed Maidment, under the date of June 1717. 'I went first to visit that woman, with no other design but to get in a friend of my wife's to the Maiden Hospital, upon which our acquaintance began. She had then ane aversion (and justly) at me, having seen me during my lewdness very beastly drunk. Yet now desiring my assistance in her designs about the hospitalls, I gave it heartily, and did all I could, and with success, to carry them on, and never shew'd any desire after her money: nor even when I had reason to expect it, did lay it in the balance with her publick designs, (as she complained to me that others had done), but encouraged her to be liberal to them, and helped her forward. This made the woman take a kindness for me, which I allso endeavoured to improve. She died in the summer 1707.'

The letter quoted by Mr Towill is from Lord Grange to the Governor of the Merchant Maiden Hospital, about the presentation of a girl to the foundation, dated 10 Sept 1707; it mentions Mary Erskine and is therefore proof that she died after that date.

[2] *The Rules and Constitutions of the Trades Maiden Hospital*, 1734. Copy in Edinburgh Public Library and in the National Library of Scotland.

[3] Mary Erskine gave money to the Incorporated Trades on the same conditions as she gave it to the Merchant Company, and stipulated that two of the Governors should be of the name of Erskine. The persons nominated, according to the 1734 Rules, were Lord Grange and Mr David Erskine, who were also nominated to the Merchant Maiden Hospital.

bers of the Governors was appointed to act as a management committee. This arrangement stood the test of time, and the Committee of Nine, as it is known in the Minutes,[1] was functioning as late as 1862.

The governing body of George Watson's Hospital consisted of the Master and Treasurer of the Merchant Company and twelve members of the Company, with 'four Old Bailies and the Old Dean of Guild of Edinburgh, who serve in the Council of Edinburgh as such', the Minister or Ministers of the Old Church of Edinburgh, and the Treasurer of the Hospital. These twenty or twenty-one persons were presided over by the Master of the Merchant Company.[2] As in the case of the Merchant Maiden Hospital, this body of Governors, and not the Merchant Company, had control over the Hospital's income, could lend out money, and invest in land and other securities, besides all the daily business of regulating admissions, diet, staff, and curriculum.

Some general points emerge from a comparative study of these governing bodies. There is a broad similarity among them because they all, in some degree, are modelled on Heriot's. The two boys' hospitals and the Merchant Maiden Hospital had as statutory members of the governing body ministers of the Church of Scotland.[3] The Town Council was represented on the governing bodies of the boys' hospitals, but not on the governing bodies of the girls' hospitals. The one important way in which Heriot's was different from all the others was that the Master of Heriot's sat with the Governors and had a vote.[4] The Master of Watson's and the Governesses in charge of the girls' hospitals were considered as employees and as such did not vote as Governors, though they were in attendance at meetings.

[1] Towill, *op cit*, XXVIII, p 7.
[2] *The Statutes and Rules of George Watson's Hospital*, Edinburgh 1755. Copy in National Library of Scotland.
[3] All the hospitals were, of course, visited by members of the Presbytery. See also Edinburgh Presbytery Minutes for 28 May 1712 and 1 April 1713.
[4] Heriot's Statutes 1627. 'And because it is fitt that the Maister of the Hospitall schould be weill regairded in his plaice to breed the greatter respect unto him in all electiones and uther busines which in any way concerne the Hospitall he sall have a single suffrage and voyce as weill as any of the rest of the electors. . . .'

H

THE WORK OF THE GOVERNORS

In the administration of the Hospital schools a necessary part was the regular visitation by members of the governing body. In Heriot's the system was simple. In September of each year the newly constituted Governors appointed six visiting committees, one for each period of two months. Each committee had four or five members, usually from different representative bodies. One committee, for example, consisted of a Bailie, an ex-Bailie, a Merchant Councillor, and a Deacon Convener. The committees had to inspect the Hospital and the proficiency of the boys in the principles of religion, their diet, clothing, and living conditions. In addition there was a special committee, known as the Committee for Auditing the Treasurer's Accounts, to which all important policy matters were referred, which acted as a Finance Committee. For special occasions, such as the drawing up of a new curriculum, special Education committees were formed; these, however, were not standing but rather *ad hoc* committees.[1] The Governors met at least once a month, and their minutes show a detailed attention to administration. More time seems to have been spent, however, on matters affecting the Trust's property than on consideration of how the boys were fed and educated, but that is perhaps an unfair criticism arising from the fact that the buying, selling, and feuing of property has to be recorded accurately and at length. Nevertheless, many matters affecting education were referred to committees and are never mentioned again.[2]

In the Merchant Maiden Hospital, two Governors were appointed for each month in the year, to visit the Hospital weekly. No notice was given of these visits, and the visitors had to write their observations at least once a month in the visitors' book, on the management of the Hospital and the progress of the girls. These comments were read at the quarterly meetings of Governors. That the Governors took their duties seriously may be gathered from the rules laid down in 1776.[3]

[1] A special Education committee drew up a new scheme of education in 1780.
[2] For example the teaching of drawing, 20 April 1767.
[3] *Rules for the Government and Order of the Merchant Maiden Hospital, Edinburgh.* Printed by Balfour and Smellie, 1776. Copy in National Library of Scotland.

A list of questions is provided in these rules which the visitors could use or not as they wished. They were urged to be careful of detail, 'as a cursory visit will not answer this end'. Among the questions to be put to the Governess, for example, are the following:

> Do you correct those who offend, and maintain due authority in the house?
> Do you catechise the children and instruct them in the principles of religion and virtue?
> Does the master for teaching reading, writing, arithmetic, and singing regularly attend his hours?

As regards questioning the girls, the rules suggest that the Governors saw the wisdom of taking a lady with them:

> If any gentlewoman comes along with the visitors, let the girls bring their work, let her opinion be asked about their progress, and if she thinks them properly taught.   If she can suggest any improvement, or any other branch of education suitable to their station, and which might qualify them better for doing for themselves, let the same be marked in the visiting book.
> Ask for a sight of their writing, at different times, and see what improvement they have made.   Examine them in their knowledge of arithmetic, of weights and measures.   Inquire for a specimen of their making out an account.
> Let the visitors hear some of them read: and, as they see proper, examine them in their knowledge of the principles of religion.

It is clear that visitation was taken very seriously. The insistence on a weekly visit was a wise arrangement.[1]

THE TREASURER

The position of Treasurer was a most important one, for of all the officials he was the one who had to be in constant touch with the work of the Hospital. The Treasurer of Heriot's was elected yearly, but could be re-elected.[2] The Treasurer had to receive rents, keep stock and money, pay wages, attend

---

[1] That the Merchant Company have thought so may be proved by the fact that it is still the duty of vice-conveners to visit weekly the Merchant Company schools for which they are responsible.

[2] *The Edinburgh Evening Courant*, 9 Feb 1780, contains a letter praising the good work of the former Treasurer of Heriot's, Mr J(ohn) C(armichael), from 1762 to 1780. The letter says that the funds, embarrassed when he took over, had been brought 'to affluence'.

to building repairs, and give the master money for the food of the Hospital. He had to get the accounts weekly from the master and the caterer. His accounts had to be audited monthly by the special committee already referred to, and he had to make up all his accounts yearly for the Governors. There had been trouble with a Treasurer before 1762, and a committee reviewed the regulations for the post at about that time.[1] Stricter rules were made then about the amount of cash the Treasurer could have in his possession, and the Treasurer had to be able to produce a cautioner. In 1788, a further regulation laid down that money in the bank should be in the names of the Chairman of Governors and the Treasurer, and should be payable only to their joint order. Though it was an honorary post, the Treasurership was sought after, partly because it was important and probably also because the Treasurer had much to do with the allocation of contracts.

A source of difficulty in Heriot's was that by the very nature of its constitution, appointments in the Hospital or in its management were apt to be linked with local city politics, and it is generally accepted that Edinburgh, like other Scots towns in the eighteenth century, was from time to time in the hands of unscrupulous men. In 1763 there were complaints about the management of Heriot's, which ended in a suit taken by the Merchant Company and others against the Hospital Governors. The case for the Merchant Company included allegations such as that the Lord Provost (Drummond), knowing that Bailie Rochead was a declared competitor for the office of Lord Provost in 1758, caused the Treasurership of Heriot's to be laid before Rochead as a bait, to keep him away from the Provostship. Rochead was in straitened circumstances, did not make up the Heriot's accounts for three years, went bankrupt in 1763, and Heriot's was then over £900 in arrears.[2] This case

---

[1] Heriot's *Statutes*, 1818 ed. Copy in Edinburgh Public Library.
[2] See pamphlets in Edinburgh Public Library:
    (a) Memorial by a considerable number of the Burgesses of Edinburgh, Relative to the Management of Mr George Heriot's Hospital. 1763.
    (b) Summons of Reduction . . . The Merchant Company and Trades of Edinburgh against the Governors of Heriot's Hospital. 1763.
    (c) Information for Magistrates, Governors etc. 1764.
This presents the case for the Governors.

was not proved against the Governors, but it was unfortunate that the possibility of fraud should exist.

In the other hospitals the Treasurer held an equally powerful position; indeed, in some respects the position there was more important than in Heriot's. The Master of Watson's and the Mistresses of the Maiden Hospitals were employees of their Governors, and did not sit at Governors' meetings as the Master of Heriot's did; consequently, they took their orders from the Treasurer, who acted as the agent of the Governors. The Treasurer of Watsons' was expressly ordered to see that the Master was doing his job.[1] The girls of the Merchant Maiden Hospital, in the course of difficulties with the Mistress, appealed to the Treasurer.[2]

THE RESIDENT STAFF

The Master and Governess

The most important resident official was the Master in the boys' hospitals, the Mistress (or Governess) in the girls'. The post was not always held by a teacher; in fact, it was rather exceptional for the Master of Heriot's to be a schoolmaster. John Watson 'Merchant in Edinburgh' became Master of Heriot's in 1702; his successor in 1720 was David Christie, who had been schoolmaster in Kelso; Christie's successor in 1734 was William Matheson, Merchant in Edinburgh and, when he resigned in the following year, John Hunter, writer in Ayr, was appointed. Most of the other Masters in the eighteenth century were not schoolmasters. It was not easy to find suitable candidates for the post of Master, and in 1741 the position was unfilled for ten months. The Master was not called upon to teach, though he was expected to catechise the boys weekly. 'A man of respect and prudence' was what was wanted in 1735, 'unmarried, not under 40 years old, nor above 60'.[3] He had to be resident in the Hospital, and indeed was not supposed to

---

[1] *Statutes*, 1755. 'And as he will have frequent occasion to be in the Hospital, he may observe and superintend the Master and Officers and Servants in the Hospital, their conduct and due officiating in their several stations, and report to the Governors his observations of their misbehaviour or neglect of duty.'

[2] Towill, *op cit*, XXIX, 56.

[3] *The Caledonian Mercury*, 8 May 1735.

sleep out without the express consent of the Lord Provost or one
of the ministers.[1]   He was entitled to a new gown every year,
and was expected always to wear one.   He dined at a separate
table in hall with the schoolmaster.   He was responsible for the
discipline of the boys, staff, and servants, and for collecting all
accounts for submission to the Treasurer.

The terms of appointment of the Master of Watson's follow
very closely those of Heriot's; in fact many of the phrases are
exactly the same.   'There shall be an unmarried person, of
good respect, and free of the burden of children, chosen master
to the hospital, who shall have power to govern the children
and servants within the same.   His principal care shall be to see
that the children and servants be brought up and instructed in
the fear of Almighty God; and therefore he shall, every Lord's
Day and Thursday, some time in the afternoon, catechise and
instruct the children and servants in the common grounds and
principles of faith and Christian religion, contained in the
larger and shorter catechisms, approven by this national church.
And if any of the children or servants shall be guilty of mis-
demeanors, such as swearing, lying, fighting, spoiling of their
clothes or chambers, or the like, he shall take care that they
receive due correction and chastisement.'[2]   The statutes are
careful to insist that the Master be a Protestant, and 'well
affected to the Protestant succession'.   Like the Master of
Heriot's he had to collect the accounts and hand them to the
Treasurer.   'For the greater decency and distinction, he shall
always wear a gown within the precincts of the hospital.'   He
dined at a separate table in hall with the schoolmaster.

There were only four Masters of Watson's Hospital in the
eighteenth century, of whom two were ministers, the Rev
George Anderson (1741-52) and the Rev William McKay
(1752-55), one was a bookseller in Edinburgh, Alexander Duning
(1755-79), and the last, James Richardson (1779-85) had been
minister of a dissenting congregation in Newcastle.   Duning
lacked authority and from time to time the Governors decided
to dismiss him.   It was suggested that in view of his age he

---

[1] Steven, *Heriot's Hospital*, ed Bedford.   *Statutes*, p 339.
[2] *Statutes and Rules of George Watson's Hospital*, 1755.   Copy in National
Library of Scotland.

might be allowed to remain on the staff in the capacity of Steward, but he carried on as Master until 1779 when he retired on a pension of £20.[1] When Richardson left in 1785, the Governors asked the senior schoolmaster to act as Master, and Mrs Rannie, the mistress, to act as Steward. This arrangement continued until the end of the century, the senior schoolmaster and the mistress each receiving a special gratuity for their extra services.[2]

The position of Governess in the Maiden hospitals was similar to that of Master in the boys' hospitals; the regulations for the Trades Maiden Hospital were in fact modelled almost word for word on Heriot's.[3] The duty of examining the girls in the principles of religion is put down as the principal care of the Governess of the Merchant Maiden Hospital. She must frequently visit the classes and observe the behaviour, progress, and application of the girls, and keep a book for recording their diligence and behaviour, 'that when they are leaving the house, due regard may be had in distributing the profits of the work, according to the application and prudent behaviour of each girl while in the house'. This reminds us that the girls' hospitals differed from the boys' in that they carried out various kinds of work, the profit from the sales of which was available to be distributed among the girls when they left.[4] In 1791, girls leaving the Merchant Maiden Hospital received each the sum of £3 6s 8d, except a few who were allowed £8 6s 8d.[5] The Governess had the power to admonish and chastise where necessary. She (or a mistress) had to be present at all meals, and she could not leave the hospital for a night without the permission of the Governors. The Governesses were not always teachers; there is in fact only one who is definitely known to have been a teacher, Margaret Montgomery, Governess from 1765 to 1774. At the time of her appointment, Miss Montgomery is described as 'Doctrix to Miss Wylie all

[1] Minutes, 11 Dec 1779.
[2] Minutes, 10 May 1785, 12 Feb 1787, 3 April 1798.
[3] *Rules and Constitutions*, 1734.
[4] *The Caledonian Mercury*, 14 Nov 1759. A letter appealing for funds and clothing for French prisoners in Edinburgh Castle has the sentence: 'The city hospitals for young maidens have offered to make the shirts for 2d each.'
[5] Brown, *op cit*, 1791.

the time she kept a school, presently keeps school as mistress'.[1] The other three applicants are described as housekeepers.[2] Mr Towill is probably right when he describes the typical Governess of the Merchant Maiden Hospital at this time as a 'homely and simple eighteenth-century woman'.

In all the details of catechising, supervising the girls, staff, and servants, taking the accounts weekly to the Treasurer, and always sleeping in the Hospital, except by special arrangement with the Governors, the position of Governess in the Trades Maiden Hospital was similar. The rules and constitutions in this respect follow those of Heriot's closely; she was publicly presented to the Hospital by the Governors, and had to have her meals 'at a table cross at the head of the other'. A Governess who was infirm or old could be 'respectfully dismissed, but if she have served above ten years and not able to maintain herself, she is to be allowed lodging and maintainance in the hospital during her life'.[3] In 1776, the Governors decided that no one should be appointed Governess under the age of 30. The advertisement in 1786 summarises the duties: 'She must be a person of decent virtuous character, capable to conduct and manage the domestic business of the Hospital, to keep accompts, and a regular accompt-book, and to superintend the education and morals of the girls, and the conduct of the schoolmistress, assistant schoolmistress, and the servants.'[4]

THE TEACHING STAFF

The teaching staff of Heriot's Hospital consisted of a schoolmaster and two assistants called, as was the custom, 'doctors'. The schoolmaster's was an important post, next in authority to the Master's, and schoolmaster and Master had their meals together, at a table separate from the boys and the rest of the staff. The schoolmaster was expected to be able to teach English, writing, arithmetic, and the rudiments of Latin. The

---

[1] For Mrs Wylie, see *The Edinburgh Evening Courant*, 7 Jan 1754, where she is described as the relict of John Wylie, Teacher of English; she kept a school in Pearson's Close.
[2] Towill, *op cit*, XXIX, p 39.
[3] *Rules and Constitutions*, 1734.
[4] *The Caledonian Mercury*, 18 Oct 1786.

post was a resident one, and in addition to board and lodging, the schoolmaster was paid a salary of £21 13s 4d (1733), later raised to £25 (1766), sterling. Apart from teaching, the duties included supervision of the dormitories and of the boys' appearance. The schoolmaster was obliged to wear a gown in the Hospital, and was indeed provided with a new one each year. The assistants were also resident: their salaries in 1776 were £18 stg. Posts in Heriot's Hospital were frequently sought by men who intended to enter the ministry, which in part explains the rapid turnover of schoolmasters and assistants. The Governors made a regulation in 1754 that men should be appointed to these posts on condition that they would resign on being licensed to preach but this regulation was not strictly enforced.

George Watson's Hospital, smaller than Heriot's, had until 1768 only one schoolmaster on the staff. In that year a part-time assistant was appointed, and in October 1771, two full-time schoolmasters were appointed. As in Heriot's, however, none stayed long in these resident posts: the ten years that J McKay served from 1746 to 1756, and Richard Buchanan from 1781 to 1791, were exceptional, and the average stay was not more than two years. When McKay demitted office in 1756 on being ordained minister and appointed to Eddrachillis, the Governors of Watson's minuted that the office of schoolmaster had been neglected by former masters applying themselves to the study of Divinity, and that therefore they should not choose a Divinity student to succeed McKay.[1] The Heriot's regulation of a similar character had been made only two years earlier.

The Governors of George Watson's took the appointment of staff very seriously. The first schoolmaster, John Penman, was selected from three candidates after being examined in Latin, writing, and arithmetic, and he was appointed to teach English, Latin, writing, arithmetic, book-keeping, and the common church music. The report of the 'trials' of John Christieson, appointed in 1788, is as follows: 'The Committee then proceeded to examine Mr Christieson by making him read a passage of English Prose and another in Verse, and asking him some questions on English Grammar. On this part of his trial, the

---

[1] Minutes, 9 Jan 1756.

Committee were of opinion that he was not so much master of the just manner of pronunciation as could be wished but make no doubt that he will acquire it. They then examined him upon the Latin and Greek languages, with his knowledge of which they were perfectly satisfied. A question was given him in Arithmetic, which he solved, but did not appear to be thoroughly acquainted with Book-keeping. Upon the whole the Committee entertain a favourable opinion of his abilities and industry and hope he will prove an useful teacher'.[1] One of those who signed this report was Dr Adam, Rector of the High School, who had himself been schoolmaster in Watson's from 1760 to 1763.

The salary of the schoolmaster in Watson's was £15 stg in 1741, and had been raised to £20 in 1757. In 1791, by which time there were two schoolmasters, the senior had £40 and the second £30. On the whole the Watson's salaries were rather lower than those paid in Heriot's, but teaching in the smaller hospital may have had compensations. The schoolmasters, like the schoolmaster in Heriot's, was provided with a gown; in November 1742 there is a complaint that the gowns supplied were of 'slight Orkney stuff', and so threadbare that they could not be worn to church. The Treasurer was authorised to provide black cloth gowns at 15s a yard.[2]

In the girls' hospitals there was no question of even the rudiments of Latin, and the teachers aimed first of all to teach the girls to read, and then to 'work stockings, lace, coloured and white seam, spinning, carding, washing and dressing of linens, dressing of meat, cleaning of house and all sorts of needlework . . . and if they can to teach the girls also writing, arithmetic, and the common parts of vocal music'.[3] Men could be employed as visiting teachers, and the Merchant Maiden Hospital appointed a visiting writing-master, James Cumming, as early as 1734.[4] Andrew Lawrie was appointed in 1752 to the Merchant Maiden Hospital, and for many years was attached to both the girls'

[1] Minutes, 15 April.
[2] The Master of Watson's, Rev W McKay, was given a suit of clothes of value 10 guineas 'for his extraordinary care and diligence' in 1752. Minutes, 25 May 1752.
[3] *Trades Maiden Hospital Rules*, 1734.
[4] Minutes, 21 Oct 1734.

hospitals. In 1780, the Governors of the Merchant Maiden Hospital considered how to improve the teaching of reading, which had become an important problem since some young girls had been admitted who were 'wholly ignorant of the first principles'. More time was needed, and it was agreed that Lawrie and his son should be employed. In place of the 11 hours a week that Lawrie had been giving, father and son should give a total of 17 hours, at the existing salary. The additional one hour a day for six days was to be devoted to reading. James Mowat, who succeeded Lawrie in 1784, also taught reading, writing, arithmetic, and singing. The Lawries and Mowat taught in the Trades Maiden Hospital as well as in the Merchant Maiden Hospital. Though it is no doubt true that reading, writing, and some form of accounts were increasingly taught in the girls' hospitals from the 1770s, yet the general impression obtained from a study of the Minutes is that the main concern in both establishments was with 'work'. The mistresses were first and foremost practical housewives, and reading and writing were limited to what was severely utilitarian.

Other Members of Staff

The Statutes of Heriot's make provision for a large staff. In addition to the Treasurer, there was to be a clerk to do the legal work connected with the purchase of lands, etc; he had to work closely with the Treasurer. Then there was a butler, whose duty was to look after food, drink, laying of table-cloths, silver plate, spoons, salts, stoups, cups, and candlesticks. The cook, with a boy to assist him, did the preparation of food, and was responsible for utensils. According to the revised Statutes of 1795, he was not allowed to skim the broth. The caterer had to buy good wholesome meat at the best rates. The janitor had to be unmarried and of honest report, and, in the words of the 1627 original, 'He salbe a man of guid strength abill to keip out all sturdie beggeris and vagrant persones.' The gardener kept the kitchen garden and all walks and hedges. Six women servants were engaged to wash clothes, make beds, sweep rooms, and attend the sick. They were to be 'of guid and honest report, unmarried and who must nevir marie. They salbe of the aige of fourtie fyve yeiris at the least.' This rather formidable list of officials was in fact modified for the posts of butler and caterer were merged in that of steward. There was a mistress in charge of the women servants; among other duties, she had to see that the boys were neatly dressed. The serving women were responsible for combing the boys' hair.

The Watson's staff seems by comparison modest: it consisted, in addition to the Treasurer, of a steward, cook, janitor, and serving women. The terms of their employment were similar to those of Heriot's, and in some cases the same words and phrases are used. The janitor, for example, 'shall be one able to keep out all sturdy beggars and vagrant persons'.[1] An interesting variation is that 'he shall be of the employment of a taylor, and shall be obliged to bestow all his spare time in mending of the boys' cloaths'.

The girls' hospitals were in their organisation even simpler, for they were really what they called themselves, families. In the Merchant Maiden Hospital there lived a Governess and two schoolmistresses, and servant women helped in the housework. The Trades Maiden Hospital was smaller, and had a Governess and one schoolmistress, with women servants. The girls did a great deal of housework themselves, and most of the sewing and laundrywork.[2]

THE CURRICULUM

(a) *In the Boys' Hospitals*

The curriculum of Heriot's as outlined in the Statutes of 1627 is succinctly put thus: 'To teach the scholars to read and write Scots distinctly, to cypher and cast all manner of accounts, as also to teach them the Latin rudiments but no further.' Allowance was also, however, to be made for those who were considered 'hopeful scholars' to go to the High School and thereafter to the College of Edinburgh. The words are: 'But after the scholars have learned to read and write Scots distinctly

---

[1] Watson's *Statutes*, 1755. Copy in National Library of Scotland.
[2] *Merchant Maiden Hospital Rules*, 1776. Copy in National Library of Scotland. *Trades Maiden Hospital Rules and Constitutions*, 1734. Copy in National Library of Scotland.

and the Latin rudiments they shall be put out to the free grammar school of Edinburgh there to be taught until such time as they be either fit for the College or to be apprentices.'[1] This arrangement was a wise one; the few in any random selection of boys who were 'hopeful scholars' got their chance at the High School, and if they showed ability, at the University. The majority left Heriot's to become apprentices or enter other trades.

The basic course provided in Heriot's consisted of reading, writing, and arithmetic or 'accounts', and pupils were expected to be proficient in them before they went on to the High School. Boys entered at the age of 7 or 8 and went on to the High School at 10 or 11. In 1697 the Governors decided that only boys who were 11 should be allowed to go to the High School, and they were to stay there for the full five-year course.[2] In 1721, in conformity with tendencies in England, the Governors agreed that English grammar should be taught from Sir Richard Steele's book 'for the idiom and orthography of the language'.[3] Book-keeping seems to have been introduced, but in 1731 the Governors ruled that this subject should not be taught.[4] It would appear, however, that book-keeping was taught whenever there was a schoolmaster capable of teaching it, and by 1781 it was accepted as part of the course for all boys.[5]

In 1780, a committee of the Governors was set up to reconsider the plan of education in Heriot's, and that committee's recommendations give us some picture of what the Governors were aiming to achieve. All boys were expected to learn the reading and spelling of English, the principles of English grammar, 'writing in the way of copy pieces, or grammatical exercises', arithmetic, book-keeping, geography including the use of the globes, and the rudiments of Latin. In addition, 'For the encouragement of such boys as have made good progress in English, writing, and arithmetic, and who seem to have a genius that way, they may be taught some of the practical parts of Mathematics

[1] *Statutes*, Chap XII, XIII in Steven, *Heriot's Hospital*, p 341.
[2] Minutes, 11 Oct 1697.
[3] Brightland's *Grammar of the English Tongue*, 1711. Recommended by 'Isaac Bickerstaff'.
[4] Minutes, 19 April 1731.
[5] *ibid*, 21 Nov 1781.

and the art of Drawing or Designing.' This was to be done between 4 and 6 pm by a suitably qualified master, but if none was available on the staff, the boys should attend such a master in the town.[1] The interest in the practical applications of mathematics is in line with the development of the subject in in other Edinburgh schools at the time.

The teaching of the rudiments of Latin was necessary as a link with the High School. From time to time a Governor speaks in the minutes of the desirability of teaching more Latin in Heriot's,[2] but it was probably obvious enough to the teachers that Latin, especially in the stiff doses of the eighteenth century, was too much for the majority. The Governors felt that all Heriot's boys should receive a thorough training in reading, writing, and arithmetic; in 1695, it was reported to them that though a few of their boys attending the High School had a 'good hand of write', most of them were deficient in arithmetic. (In the rigid classical time-table of the High School there was a little time for writing but none for arithmetic.) The Governors then arranged that the Heriot's boys should return from the High School every day at 11 for training in writing and the four rules of arithmetic.[3] Insistence on the part of the Governors that all educational training should have a practical value crops up again and again; in 1738 several Heriot boys at the High School asked to be withdrawn, 'partly from a consciousness of their not making sufficient progress in their studies and possibly from an inclination to employ the remainder of their time in improving themselves in writing and arithmetic'.[4]

There are no exact figures of the numbers of Heriot's boys who went to the High School. Though it seems to have been thought by some of the Governors in 1763 that in time past all Heriot's boys had gone to the High School, there is no ground for this belief.[5] We know that there were 23 Heriot's boys at

---

[1] Minutes, 19 April 1780.

[2] *ibid*, 7 June 1742. The visiting committee reported that those boys who were learning Latin were doing so well that the committee thought it would be better for them to stay on in Heriot's than to go to the High School. See also Minutes, 15 Oct 1722.

[3] *ibid*, 9 Sept 1695 and 17 Oct 1709.

[4] *ibid*, 9 Oct 1738.

[5] Minutes, 10 Oct 1763. The visiting committee was asked to look into the records to discover the reason for altering the former method of sending all the boys in the Hospital to the High School.

the High School in 1665,[1] and 36 in 1678,[2] that 7 went in one year in 1738,[3] and that a total of 11 were in attendance in 1762.[4] The safest statement is that the numbers probably varied between 11 and about 35 in attendance at any one time, and that individuals regularly went on to the College, supported by grants from the Governors. The quotation given on page 100 is interesting in its reference to one Elliott, 'a Heriotter', in William Nicol's class in the High School in 1778-79.

Music was also taught at Heriot's. In 1757, Cornforth Gilson from Durham, who was appointed by the Town Council to organise the teaching of church music in the city churches, was appointed to teach music in Heriot's.[5] The appointment in Heriot's was probably an added inducement to Gilson. He was a man of some ability, an author and composer, and was engaged by the Musical Society of Edinburgh for their concerts. The Sederunt Book of the Society, now in the Edinburgh Public Library, records how Gilson brought a choir of boys from Heriot's to take part in the oratorios performed three times a year by the Society. Gilson must have had the artistic temperament, for by 1762 the Governors of Heriot's were warning him that unless he attended to his duties more regularly he would be dismissed; in reply he petitioned for arrears of salary which he said he had not claimed.[6] In 1776, his successor, Hamilton, was said to be so unsatisfactory that it was not likely that the boys would be able to sing an anthem on June Day, so Gilson was brought back, only to be finally dismissed in October.[7] In the plan of education adopted in 1780, the visiting music master was to attend not at the ordinary school hours, but at midday, late afternoon, or after evening prayers.[8]

The curriculum of George Watson's Hospital followed generally the lines of Heriot's. The schoolmaster's duty was, according to the Statutes,[9] 'to teach them to read English and

[1] Minutes, quoted by Rev Dr Lee.
[2] ibid, 21 Oct 1678.
[3] ibid, 9 Oct 1738.
[4] ibid, 11 Oct 1762.
[5] ibid, 14 Jan 1757.
[6] ibid, 19 April and 7 June 1762.
[7] ibid, 15 April and 7 Oct 1776.
[8] ibid, 19 April 1780.
[9] Statutes, 1755.

the Latin tongue, in so far as the Governors shall think fit they should be taught within the Hospital; and, if they can, likewise teach them writing, arithmetic in all its parts, and book-keeping, and all the common parts of vocal music'. Boys who showed 'an extraordinary genius for letters' should be given grants to enable them to proceed to the College. There is no suggestion here that Watson's boys went to the High School. An interesting feature of the Merchant Company's arrangement was that there had to be an annual review and examination of the boys, carried out by a minister or ministers of the Old Church of Edinburgh, two of the Governors, the Professor of Humanity in the College, and the Rector of the High School, 'if upon invitation they shall please to take the trouble'.

There was provision in the Statutes of Watson's for boys who were found 'to have an extraordinary genius for Letters', to be kept at school while in the Hospital, and to have the sum of £10 stg paid to them 'for prosecuting their studies at the College of Edinburgh for the space of five years,' after which time they would have to leave the Hospital. They had to pass an oral examination by a committee of the Governors every year. At the end of the five years, able boys might be granted £30 stg to prosecute their studies by themselves. It was stressed that this arrangement was intended only for those with a 'bright and pregnant genius for Letters', and that most of the boys would be bred as merchants or tradesmen. The first case of a boy with a 'genius for letters' occurred as late as 1772. He was allowed to attend the College classes in session 1772-73, 'the Governors being at no part of the University charge'. He was allowed to live in the Hospital.[1] The following year the boy's father requested the 'encouragement' allowed in the Statutes for boys with 'a genius for learning'. The ministers on the governing body examined the boy and recommended him, and the Governors agreed to meet his College expenses.[2] From this time there were generally two boys supported at Universities in this way.

---

[1] Minutes, 16 Nov 1772 and 10 Nov 1773.
[2] The boy who was first of what has become a very distinguished procession was James Orrock.

(b) *In the Girls' Hospitals*

In the girls' hospitals the curriculum was markedly vocational. Reading, writing, and arithmetic had from the beginning their places, but in the first half of the eighteenth century the real stress was on the domestic arts of sewing, mending, and making stockings. There is little mention of cooking, though the Governess of the Merchant Maiden Hospital put forward the suggestion in 1734 that the girls 'should be educate for some months at 'the Paistry School'.[1] The Governors did not accept this suggestion. Spinning was taught in both hospitals, being introduced in 1734 at a time when the Board of Trustees for Manufactures was endeavouring to develop spinning in Scotland.[2] In 1735, the Governors of the Merchant Maiden Hospital resolved 'to try both French and Scotch ways of spinning, to repair the old wheels and to get six French wheels'.[3] In 1744, the Governors agreed to a request from the Board of Trustees that they should employ a teacher for 'spinning yarn fit for Cambrick after the French method, so that they be taught a business by which they can never be in want of bread'. In 1743, the Governors of the Trades Maiden Hospital also bought the necessary wheels to encourage the teaching of spinning.

While training in the useful domestic arts was the principal aim of the Maiden Hospitals, the Governors did not neglect chances of profit. The making of shirts for French prisoners has already been noted. A balloon used by Lunardi in 1785 was made by the girls of the Merchant Maiden Hospital.[4] The Trades Maiden Hospital advertised regularly in terms like these: 'Gentlemen's vests and ruffles, as also handkerchiefs, aprons, and shoes for ladies, are drawn and sewn in tambour, and embroidered in the neatest manner and at the most reasonable rates; and all kinds of white and coloured seam are done as formerly.'[5] A note adds that the Governors had extended the education of the girls to include these manufactures, 'to make them more useful and in hope to improve the annual income of the hospital'. With changes in fashion came changes in training,

---

[1] Towill, *op cit*, XXIX, p 60.
[2] See Appendix IV.
[3] Towill, *op cit*, XXIX, p 60.
[4] *The Edinburgh Evening Courant*, 26 Dec 1785.
[5] *ibid*, 15 Jan 1777.

I

and the 'making of things in the millinery way', of aprons, and of various kinds of embroidery are added.   The Trades Maiden Hospital introduced hairdressing in 1790, and discontinued it in 1794; mantua-making in 1794, and stay-making in the same year.

The idea that the girls should help to run their own hospital, and should share in the profits was one that appealed profoundly to the charitably inclined middle class.   As has been mentioned, the profits in the Merchant Maiden Hospital were divided among the girls on leaving according to the Governess's estimate of their worth.[1]   The same writer, speaking of the Trades Maiden Hospital, says that girls paid by way of entry money £1 13s 4d and received when they left a bounty of £5 11s 1½d.   At this distance of time, one cannot help being sceptical about this profit-making self-help; one cannot help feeling that the work of young children was faulty and not worth much, and that they might well have been forced to attain unnaturally high standards.

The teaching of reading, writing, and arithmetic was considered to be a basic part of the course at both Maiden Hospitals. According to Towill,[2] 'In 1737, when they chose a new mistress, the governors of the Merchant Maiden Hospital decided to test her in reading an English book, and to get a report from one of the ministers as to her ability to teach the Christian religion.' Yet the advertisement for a mistress that appeared the following year makes no mention of reading and writing and merely invites applications from 'any unmarried gentlewoman, not under 25 years of age'.[3]   From the middle of the century, however, there is more interest in the teaching of academic subjects.   In 1758, the Governors of the Trades Maiden Hospital founded a library for the girls, financed partly from fines paid by deacons for non-attendance at meetings.   In 1763, they found that the standard of reading was not satisfactory, and arranged the girls into three classes, the lowest to study words of one syllable, the next words of two syllables and easy passages from scripture, and the third to read words up to seven syllables.   This class arrangement follows the method of spelling-books on the syllabic system.

[1] Brown, *op cit.*
[2] Towill, *op cit*, XXIX, p 61.
[3] *The Caledonian Mercury*, 2 May 1738.

The Governors of the Merchant Maiden Hospital received a report from their monthly visitors in 1776 criticising adversely the progress in English. The subject was then taught in both Maiden Hospitals by the same visiting master, James Lawrie. (Lawrie wrote a small book on the teaching of reading, writing, and spelling in the hospitals, copies of which are in the Edinburgh Public Library. In addition Lawrie also treats of moral and religious matters, and gives advice on making and cutting quill pens.) In 1777 the Governors of the Merchant Maiden Hospital had considered the appointment of a man as wholetime teacher and chaplain, but had then decided against this move. In 1784, the Governors' committee on education, being still perturbed about the state of education in the Hospital, recommended the following arrangements[1]:

1. That a new teacher attend, whose sole employment in the House shall be to teach English according to the present improved methods received in the established English schools of Edinburgh. That no candidate should be considered who is not either married or at least 40 years old.

2. That this English master should attend and teach six hours in summer and five in winter every lawful day except Saturday.

3. That the girls (about 80 in number) be divided equally into four classes.

4. That the hours, as well in sewing as in work, be—summer— 7-9 am; 10-12; 2-4.30; 5-7. Winter, 9-12 noon; 2-4.30; 5-7. That each of the four classes should attend the English master for one period each day.

5. On Saturdays the English master shall attend each class for one hour solely for explaining religion.

6. The Writing master, who is also to teach arithmetic and singing, shall attend three hours—the two senior classes to attend him, viz. the third for writing, the fourth for writing and arithmetic.

The first full-time English master, James Mowat, was appointed in 1784 to work on this programme. One of the mistresses, who had objected to the new arrangements, had to be dismissed. The records indicate that Mr Mowat was a successful teacher. The visiting master for writing introduced the study of geography in 1795.[2]

[1] Towill op cit, XXIX, p 62.
[2] Towill op cit, XXIX, p 63.

APPRENTICESHIP

Both boys' hospitals made provision for binding suitable boys as apprentices. In the early Statutes, after a statement that boys of academic promise should be encouraged to continue their studies, there appears the recommendation that those not fit for study should, if thought suitable, be apprenticed.[1] The Governors paid the apprenticeship fees, a sum of £20 in 1755[2] but raised to £30 in 1775.[3] The payment of apprenticeship fees in Heriot's was arranged in 1775 as follows:

£12 10s to the master two years after the signing of the indentures.
£12 10s two years later to the master.
£5 to the master at the expiry of the apprenticeship, but this last sum to be given by the master to the apprentice to purchase new clothes, providing he has faithfully served out his time and gets a certificate from his master to that effect. If no certificate is given, the £5 is not paid, either to master or apprentice.[4]

The Watson's arrangement was similar. The Governors of Watson's in addition to paying the apprenticeship fees, made a special grant to apprentices who, having behaved well, arrived at the age of 25 unmarried (or married with the consent of the Governors), and 'free of debt and every unworthy engagement'. This special grant was £50, to be used in setting the apprentice up in business.

From time to time the Governors of Heriot's discussed whether boys should be allowed to be apprentices while remaining resident in the Hospital, but this was not agreed. It was conceded, however, that boys could be apprenticed before they were 16, could live out, and be granted an allowance in lieu of board and lodging until they reached the age of 16.[5] Watson's took the opposite view, and the Statutes of 1755 record that boys may be apprenticed before 16 but continue to receive clothing, bed, board, and washing in the Hospital until the age of 16.

In Heriot's the tradition grew up under one Treasurer (John Carmichael, a man who gave devoted service to the Hos-

---

[1] Heriot's Statutes, 1627. Watson's Statutes, 1755.
[2] Watson's Statutes, 1755.
[3] Heriot's Minutes, 17 April 1775.
[4] *ibid*, 17 April 1775.
[5] *ibid*, 16 April 1739.

pital) that he was the person responsible for arranging apprenticeships and settling disputes about them, but in 1779 it was pointed out that this was really a function of the Governors. A committee was set up to look after the problems of apprenticeships, consisting of three groups of two members each, who would meet in the Hospital at least every two months to hear and determine all such matters. The Treasurer was, notwithstanding, to continue to help to find masters for boys who sought apprenticeships.[1]

Some interesting details about apprenticeships are to be found in the Watson's Minutes. There was, for example, an agreement made in 1747 with the Edinburgh Shipping Company about the taking of Watson's boys as apprentices. The fee payable by the Governors was to be not less than 100 pounds Scots, and boys were to be bound for four years. They were to be maintained by the Hospital in clothing and washing, 'and taught the theory of navigation by a master at home, at the Hospital's expense, the masters allowing them leisure hours for that purpose'. The Shipping Company refused to be burdened with responsibility for the boys in sickness or death. The Shipping Company did agree to cause the masters of its ships to teach the boys the practical part of navigation, and to keep the boys in bed and board during their apprenticeship. On first entering the service, boys had to bring their own bed and bedding. Boys so apprenticed were not to be under 15 years of age. Three boys went as apprentices under this scheme in 1747.[2] Other boys were apprenticed to surgeons, timbermerchants, saddlers, haberdashers, printers, and to 'merchant shoemaker and merchant apprentice in Philadelphia'. By 1748, 14 boys were in properly arranged apprentices. The special grant of £50, payable when a successful apprentice became 25 years of age, was withheld if the Governors had any doubts about a boy's worth. An apprentice in Leith who had been found guilty of theft was decreed to have forfeited claim to the grant.[3] Another boy was refused the grant because he had inherited an estate of £300.

[1] Heriot's Minutes, 18 Oct 1779.
[2] Minutes, 16 Feb 1747.
[3] ibid, 15 Feb 1748.

LIFE IN THE HOSPITAL SCHOOLS

The daily life in Heriot's began with morning prayers, at 7. Breakfast was at 8, and morning school was from 9 to 12 in the winter months, and 10 to 12 in the summer. Afternoon school was held from 2 to 5 on Monday, Wednesday, and Friday, and from 2 to 4 on Tuesday and Thursday.[1] This arrangement was slightly altered in 1780, and the day was arranged as follows: 7 Prayers and thereafter classes until 9; 9-10 breakfast; 10-12 schools; 12-2 dinner and recreation; 2-4 schools; 4-8 recreation except for prayers (6 pm) and special classes for selected boys; 8 pm supper; by 10 pm all in bed.[2] This programme was altered again in 1795 by the addition of schools and preparation after Chapel and before 8 pm, and it was also agreed that the boys could be allowed out to visit friends on Saturday afternoons and on Thursday afternoons once a fortnight.[3] At Chapel and at meals the boys were under the supervision of the schoolmasters, and the Master or a schoolmaster with the porter visited all the dormitories after 10 o'clock each night.[4]

The hours in Watson's were the same as those mentioned in the Heriot's records; those laid down for Watson's in 1772 are precisely those mentioned in Heriot's minutes for 1780.[5] The Watson's minutes, however, add this interesting sentence: 'Each boy shall have a task prescribed to him before dismissing of the school for the day which he is to give an account of next morning according to the different classes.' Is this the first specific reference in Scottish schools to homework?

The hours of the Merchant Maiden Hospital which have already been quoted, are similar to Heriot's. There was 'work' from 7 to 9 in the morning, before breakfast, but this was probably the domestic work of the house. 'Work' was also the routine between 5 and 7.[6]

---

[1] Minutes, 1 Sept 1735.
[2] *ibid*, 1 April 1780.
[3] *Regulations*, 1795. Copy in Edinburgh Public Library.
[4] Minutes, 1 April 1780.
[5] Watson's Minutes, 3 April 1772.
[6] Towill, *op cit*, XXIX, p 62. See also *supra*, p 131.

Diet

Such references as are made to the diet of the Hospital schools indicate that it was monotonous, limited, and particularly lacking in fruit and vegetables. In the Heriot minutes of the early part of the century there are more discussions on ale than on food. In 1700, the Governors forbade the selling of ale by the servants,[1] and in 1703, presumably in a further effort to stop the traffic in ale, the allowance to the women servants was cut from one pint daily to three mutchkins.[2] Further mention of this retailing of ale is made in 1715,[3] and in 1744 the Governors made an enquiry into whether it would be possible for the Hospital to brew its own ale, but came to the conclusion that it was cheaper to give the ale contract to the brewers who bought the Hospital's barley crop.[4] Ale formed part of the diet of the Merchant Maiden Hospital also, being supplied along with porridge or bread for supper each day[5]. The most detailed description of the meals in Heriot's is provided in the Regulations made by the Governors in 1795.[6] For breakfast the boys had a mutchkin of porridge and a half mutchkin of milk (butter milk in the summer and sweet milk in the winter). For dinner there was beef and broth on Sundays and Thursdays, mutton and broth on Tuesdays, and bread and milk on the other days, except Saturday when there was broth and a mutchkin of table beer. At four o'clock they had a 'four hours' piece' consisting of 5 ounces of bread. Supper was the same as breakfast in the winter, but consisted of bread and milk in the summer. The Watson's meals were similar.[7] The Merchant Maiden Hospital followed exactly the same menu for breakfast and supper except for Sunday when there was a 'flesh supper'. For dinner, the girls had on Sundays an egg; Mondays and Fridays, boiled meat and broth; Tuesdays and Thursdays, roast meat; Wednesdays,

---

[1] Minutes, 2 Sept 1700.
[2] *ibid*, 13 Sept 1703.
[3] *ibid*, 2 Aug 1715.
[4] *ibid*, 31 Dec 1744.
[5] Towill, *op cit*, XXIX, p 34, quoting minute of 1733.
[6] Regulations, 1795. Copy in Edinburgh Public Library.
[7] Minutes, 25 May 1752. Some of the details are interesting. Mutton was supplied in August, September and October, 'One shoulder or jigget among six', and the loin, breast and back ribs were to be boiled with broth.

two eggs; Saturdays, bread and butter. There is a slightly greater variety about the menus for the Merchant Maiden Hospital, but both there and in Heriot's more meat was provided than in the Town's Hospital of Glasgow in 1733.[1] By modern standard the diet was lacking in vegetables, and it is not surprising to find that the boys and girls suffered from time to time from scurvy and similar deficiency diseases. When they did so, they were sent to take the water at Corstorphine.[2] Heriot boys sent to Corstorphine were taught in the parish school, the Governors paying the master at the rate of 2s a quarter for each boy for English, writing, and arithmetic. A Watson's boy who had undergone an operation was sent by the Governors to St. Bernard's Well and was maintained there while he recuperated.[3]

During the Napoleonic wars a standard loaf was introduced and used in all the Edinburgh hospitals. The first reference is in the Watson's Minutes of 31 December 1795, when a joint meeting of the Governors of Watson's and the Merchant Maiden Hospitals agreed to introduce a new wheaten bread as recommended by 'a Member of the Legislature'. This was known as Privy Council or Portland Bread. The bakers agreed to supply it at one-eighth part cheaper than ordinary household bread. At about the same time the Treasurer and Mistress of Watson's were asked to consider a substitute for potatoes 'when that vegetable is not in season'.[4]

Dress

The public liked to see boys and girls of the Hospital schools in uniform, and the staff probably found that uniforms helped discipline, and aided the identification of wrongdoers, or runaways. The uniform for Heriot's was described by Dr

---

[1] Ferguson, *op cit*, p 33. Breakfast in the Town's Hospital consisted of porridge with milk or ale; dinner, bread and butter on Sunday, bread and broth without meat on the other days; supper, broth with bread and cheese or butter on Sundays, porridge with ale or milk on the other days. This was the diet for all persons under 15 years of age.

[2] Towill, *op cit*, XXIX, p 35. Heriot Minutes, 19 April 1756.

[3] Minutes, 3 April 1769.

[4] Minutes, 31 Dec 1795 and 18 Feb 1796.

Balcanquall in the Statutes as of 'sad russet cloth, and to consist of doublets, breeches, stockings of hose, and gowns, all of this colour, with black hats and strings'.[1] The wearing of the uniform had not been strictly enforced towards the end of the seventeenth century, and in 1703 the Governors insisted that all boys be dressed in sad russet.[2] The two pairs of trousers found in the school when alterations were being made in 1952 probably date from this period; they are well patched and are a credit to the women servants who looked after them. The Governors rule that each boy should have two pairs of breeches and three shirts, 'and that their britches should be lyned with leather skinns'.[3] Much later in the century there were complaints that the boys appeared on the streets in a shabby and dirty condition, and the Governors agreed that their clothes 'ought to be as fine as those of any other Charity Boys in the city'. (This is an oblique reference to Watson's.) The Master and the Mistress were enjoined to see that the boys went out neatly dressed.[4] In 1789, a committee of the Governors recommended that it would be better if the clothes were of a lighter colour and the stockings were grey, and that leather caps should be worn instead of hats, 'as this would give them a better appearance when abroad'.[5] The boys of Watson's Hospital 'should be decently apparelled in Cinnamon-coloured Cloaths made after such fashion as the Governors may think fit'.[6]

The girls' hospitals made most of their own clothes, and there are many references in the minutes of the governing bodies to the details of uniform, on which these entirely masculine committees did not hesitate to pronounce. Neither of the girls' hospitals, however, had only one prescribed colour for uniform; in this they were unlike the many blue-coat or grey-

---

[1] There is a pathetic advertisement in the *The Caledonian Mercury* of 10 Nov 1762, which says: 'There are two boys in Heriot's hospital cloathing, wandering about in the country these fifteen days, one of them has red hair, of nine years old. . . . NB. They are not to be trusted to, if they say they will go home themselves.'
[2] Minutes, 7 June 1703.
[3] *ibid*, 17 April 1704.
[4] *ibid*, 16 Oct 1786.
[5] *ibid*, 8 Jan 1789.
[6] Statutes George Watson's Hospital, 1755.

coat schools in England. The Merchant Maiden Hospital in early days had gowns 'of Orkney stuff', to be dyed 'blue or green or any other colour'. At a later date, the gowns were coloured green only, but in 1782 white frieze coats were introduced as uniform. Five years later white was dropped in favour of cotton drugget 'of a different colour to the Trades Maidens'.[1] In 1791, the girls had been attending church in coloured bonnets given them by friends; at the request of the Governess, they were given uniform black silk bonnets, and, later, beaver hats.[2]

Behaviour

Since in all the Hospital schools cases of serious disciplinary trouble had to be reported to the Governors, it is inevitable that there are more references in the Minutes to bad behaviour than to good. Bad behaviour is to be noted in the records of the girls' as well as the boys' schools, and the most that can be said about its incidence is that under some masters and mistresses the outbreaks are commoner than under others. Weak discipline and lack of understanding were probably the cause of a good deal of the trouble. In Heriot's—and very likely in the other Hospital schools also—the rigid discipline, the narrow course of instruction, the lack of organised games or other spare-time pursuits, all tended to foster a kind of gang spirit. At its best this spirit represented loyalty and comradeship; at its worst, conspiracy. A similar spirit is to be found in the girls' hospitals.[3]

The commonest offence was staying out of the Hospital overnight. The Governors of Heriot's decided that the punishment for this would be expulsion,[4] and in 1731 three boys were whipped for sleeping out and were then expelled.[5] In the fol-

---

[1] Towill, *op cit*, XXIX, p 33.

[2] Towill, *op cit*, XXIX, p 33. Mr Towill also quotes many interesting details about the provision of stays and scarves and nightgowns. In 1740 some of the girls had to stay away from church because their shoes were worn out.

[3] Towill, *op cit*, XXIX, p 56. The case described is of three girls who climbed the garden wall to meet three young men, and refused to give each other away.

[4] Minutes, 2 June 1729.

[5] *ibid*, 19 April 1731.

lowing year three more were whipped and put in the stocks for
the same offence, and the Governors had their rule of 1729
'put up in the Chapel in Capital Letters'.[1] Expulsion was the
greatest punishment in the hospitals, serious because it meant
the loss of apprenticeship or other grants as well as board and
lodging. The stocks and solitary confinement were lesser
punishments in Heriot's; solitary confinement and a diet of
bread and water, with possibly the cutting off of hair, were the
punishments in the Merchant Maiden Hospital. Sometimes
a public rebuke was administered.[2]

In the later part of the eighteenth century there are frequent
mentions of indiscipline in the Merchant Maiden Hospital,
and one cannot help agreeing with Mr Towill that the cause was
to be found in the larger number of older girls—of sixteen and
seventeen—who were then resident. Naturally they resented
rules made for younger girls, and naturally, too, they sought
the company of men and boys when they could get it. There
are many cases of girls climbing the garden wall to get out, and
of boys climbing the wall to get in.[3]

In Heriot's there was a fagging system known as the 'Garring
Law', under which the younger boys had to do what they were
told by the older boys. Those boys who were in their fifth
year in the house were known as 'Garrers', from the Scots
verb 'gar', meaning to force or compel. The Minute of the
Governors in which first reference is made to this system in
1751 records that it was the practice for all boys at their first
entering the Hospital to be put under oath not to reveal to the
masters or to anyone in authority any injuries they received or
any adventures or crimes in which they might be involved.[4] The
Governors decided that if they found any boys trying to enforce
engagements of this kind, they would expel them. In spite of
this threat, 'garring' continued. Stamping it out was difficult
in such a closed society. The Master made a detailed report

---

[1] Minutes, 17 April 1732.
[2] Towill, *op cit*, XXIX, p 53. The reference is to 1757: 'The Governess
complained of diverse misdemeanours of Jean Meggat who was called in and
rebuked by the Rev George Hay in presence of the Governors.'
[3] Towill, *op cit*, XXIX, p 54.
[4] Minutes, 14 Oct 1751.

on the Garring Law in 1793.[1] According to him, the older boys forced the younger to clean their shoes, to insult their companions, to buy or sell, to tell falsehoods, and to steal. Punishment was inflicted if the little boys disobeyed. In the words of one of the women servants: 'If they are desired by these Garring boys to do the blackest action on earth, they must do it or hazard their lives.'[2] This must have been the background for an episode reported to the Governors in 1793, when a number of boys refused to eat their 'pottage'. When a master reprimanded them, one boy threw his 'pottage' on the table, and the rest, on the command 'No sup' from one of their number, refused to eat their pottage.[3] Indiscipline also took the form of 'bickerings' with the boys of George Watson's Hospital. On one occasion the City Guard had to be summoned.[4] After another fight with the Watson's boys, twenty-two Heriot boys stayed out all night and went to Portobello.[5]

The conception of self-discipline, or of the boys assisting in the organisation of the Hospital on the lines of the modern prefect system, is alien to the ideas of the eighteenth century. Nevertheless there are hints in the records that suggest that the boys were able when they wished to assist authority by ordering themselves. In 1775, for example, when two boys had been expelled for sleeping out, the other Heriot boys sent a petition to the Governors saying that they would obey rules if the offenders were allowed back, and offering to report all cases of misdemeanour to the masters. This sounds as much like a threat as an offer of help, but the Governors agreed, and it is later recorded in their minutes that at least for a time the boys strictly kept the terms of their agreement.[6] It is indicative of a changed attitude that, in the Statutes drawn up in 1809, it is stated that the Master should appoint one or more of the older

---

[1] Minutes, 17 Jan 1793.
[2] *ibid*, 8 Feb 1793.
[3] *ibid*, 11 Nov 1793.
[4] *ibid*, 4 Nov 1783. Eight boys were expelled 'for going in a hostile manner to Watson's Hospital and attacking it, cursing the servants, and abusing the Governor and Master of said hospital, breaking the windows and committing other matters of abuse . . .'.
[5] *ibid*, 11 Nov 1793.
[6] *ibid*, 9 Oct 1775. See also the pamphlet on the Alves Morrison case in Edinburgh Public Library.

boys every week to be Censors in wards, schools, and church, and be accountable for any misbehaviour.[1]

Occasions

June Day, when the Founder's birthday was celebrated, was an occasion of festivity in Heriot's Hospital. The Founder's statue was decorated with flowers, and from time to time painted. This was a pious duty generally undertaken by the boys, but sometimes when they were alleged to have stolen flowers for the 'buskin o' Geordie', the work was put in the hands of a gardener.[2] David Crawford, who was Steward in Heriot's from 1791 to 1810, published a volume of poems, *Poems Chiefly in the Scottish Dialect*, one of which describes the decoration of the statue.[3]

> George Heriot's statue steeve does stand,
> Aboon the gate wi' heart an' hand,
> Ay waiting ready to receive
> The freemen's sons, his help who crave.
> They gie him naething late or soon,
> Except about the first o' June,
> They mend his coat, or mak it new,
> An' gie him roses not a few.

There is mention of a Decorating Club, founded as early as 1712, which was concerned with the elaborate arrangement of flowers in thistle, shield, lover's knots, cornucopias, etc, and also arranged a dinner for old boys.[4] This must be one of the oldest former pupils' clubs in Scotland; the minutes date from 1792.

The order of the annual service in commemoration of George Heriot was laid down in the Statutes drawn up by Dr Balcanquall. The Lord Provost, Magistrates, and Ministers were to

---

[1] Statutes, 1809. Copy in Edinburgh Public Library.

[2] *The Caledonian Mercury*, 5 June 1739. 'The boys educated on the foundation, who on that day usually dress up the effigy of their benefactor with flowers, being hindered from so doing on account of reiterated complaints of their robbing gentlemen's gardens for implements, took it so ill, that when the Psalm was raised they would not so much as open a lip, but hanged their heads as if inclined to tune up *Miserere*.' See also *The Edinburgh Evening Courant*, 15 May 1780.

[3] Copy in National Library of Scotland. Second edition is of 1798.

[4] Supplement to *The Herioter*, June 1928.

assemble and proceed to Greyfriars Church where a sermon was to be preached by one of the city ministers. Ministers were to undertake this duty in order of seniority. The discourse should include an exhortation to others to follow the example of the pious founder. A fee should be given to the preacher for the purchase of books.[1] The church service was attended by pupils from the other hospitals; the girls of the Merchant Maiden and Trades Maiden Hospitals are specially mentioned, but no reference is made to the boys of George Watson's.[2]

At the weekly church services there was rivalry between the two girls' hospitals. 'At one point', says Mr Towill, 'the rivalry grew so acute that when one hospital sang, the other girls stopped, and remarks were passed about their faces and figures.'[3] The Governors of the Merchant Maiden Hospital suggested that, in order to end the difficulty, the Merchant Maidens and the boys of Watson's should attend Old Greyfriars, and the Trades Maidens and boys of Heriot's should worship at New Greyfriars, but nothing came of this proposal.[4]

The Governors of the hospitals on the whole took their duties very seriously, and there is seldom any hint of pleasure or enjoyment in the minutes of their proceedings. Yet in 1771 the Governors of Heriot's authorised their Treasurer to give the boys an 'Entertainment' yearly, on the first Monday in June.[5] Interesting, too, was the annual meeting, begun in 1762, which the Governors of the Trades Maiden Hospital had with the girls, at which the girls read and sang.[6] The same Governors in 1758 formed a library for the Trades Maidens partly from the fines levied on deacons who failed to attend meetings.[7] Heriot's had formed a library before 1756; in that year an inventory was made of its contents.[8] Prizes in writing and arithmetic were instituted in Heriot's in 1751, under the

---

[1] Minutes, 7 June 1762, record that the Rev Mr Erskine, the preacher that year, handed over the honorarium of 100 merks to the Hospital for the purchase of religious and moral treatises for the use of the boys.
[2] *The Caledonian Mercury*, 3 June 1776. See also the letter quoted above, page 106.
[3] Towill, *op cit*, XXIX, p 42.
[4] Minutes, Merchant Maiden Hospital, 1805, quoted by Towill, *op cit*.
[5] Minutes, 3 June 1771.
[6] Towill, *op cit*, XXVIII, p 9.
[7] Towill, *op cit*, p 12.
[8] Minutes, 19 April 1756.

will of Dean of Guild Heriot; that in writing was won in 1771 by Henry Raeburn, probably the most distinguished pupil of the school in the course of the century.[1]

CONCLUSION

The place of the Hospital schools in education in Edinburgh is not easy to define. In numbers their contribution was not large: in the later years of the century about 170 boys and 120 girls were being cared for and educated in the four hospitals. Their existence was at once in the city, and yet not entirely of it. The inhabitants of Edinburgh were proud of these schools, and liked to see the young people in their uniforms. Yet they were always slightly apart from the other schools, though Heriot's maintained its long connection with the High School. The hospitals gave to Edinburgh, however, something of a distinctive character, at its worst a clannishness, but at its best a pride in the old and respectable tradition of residential schools.

[1] Minutes, 3 June 1771.

Chapter V

PRIVATE SCHOOLS AND PRIVATE TEACHERS

MOST of the histories of Scottish education have been concerned with the growth of the public system, and accordingly have described the parish schools and the burgh schools, and have tended to neglect the private schools or to treat them as of little importance. Even the standard work of Grant, *The History of the Burgh Schools of Scotland*, regards the private schools mainly as rivals to the officially established schools, though Grant admits that towards the end of the eighteenth century the demand for schools had increased so much that in many parts of Scotland town councils actually encouraged private schools by giving grants to private teachers. This, as we have seen, was no new thing in Edinburgh, where Porterfield was given a salary as early as 1694. In fact, in this as in other educational developments, Edinburgh was different from other parts of Scotland. A study of the advertisements and references in newspapers, of the titles and authors of textbooks, of references in literature, and of the Edinburgh Directories, makes clear that private teachers of many subjects worked in Edinburgh at all times during the century, and that their numbers increased very markedly later when the population too increased. Edinburgh contained many more private schools and private teachers than any other Scottish city, and they made an interesting contribution to education in Edinburgh, and through Edinburgh to Scotland.

Under the heading of 'private schools' we have to consider an extraordinary variety of establishments. There were schools where little children were taught the elements of reading and writing, schools where boys—and sometimes girls too—were taught Latin, schools for writing and arithmetic, for all the practical branches of mathematics, and schools for the learning of foreign languages. Some teachers held public

144

classes in the forenoons and gave private tuition in special subjects at other times. Alexander Masson, for example, one of the town's English teachers, kept on his private classes at other hours.[1] There were also lecture courses on subjects like experimental science, or elocution. Special classes were arranged in church music. Art, dancing, instrumental music were all catered for in Edinburgh, and these subjects were important in a city which attracted pupils to its boarding schools. There were boarding schools for girls, and also boarding arrangements for boys whose homes were outwith the city. It is unlikely that there was such a variety and scope of private schools in any other city in the United Kingdom, apart from London. Surely this had some influence on the social life of the city, and the development of literature. Where teachers were available, there grew up interested groups of adults, from whom some individuals of genius gained impetus and encouragement.

The education of Walter Scott illustrates the great part played in Edinburgh by private teachers. Before he went to the High School, he learned to read and write at the private schools of Leechman and Morton. While he was a pupil at the High School, he had as tutor the Rev Mr Mitchell, who supervised his reading and heard him his French. He was sent to learn music from Alexander Campbell, author of *Scotish Poetry*. As a young man, Scott learned geography and fortification from old Dr MacFait, and took two classes in drawing and painting, one from Mr Burrell and one from Mr Walker. It was a class in German, taught by Dr Willich, that turned his mind towards German romantic poetry, and his first published work, the translation of ballads after Bürger, was published by Manners and Miller, Manners having been a fellow-student with Scott under Dr Willich.

One of the fascinating developments in Scottish education in the eighteenth century was the foundation of the academies, beginning with Perth Academy in 1760. These schools aimed at teaching modern literature and science, and were modelled on the dissenting academies of England.[2] Students from the

[1] See page 52.
[2] See Appendix V.

K

English dissenting academies were in the habit of coming to the Scottish Universities rather than Oxford and Cambridge for religious reasons, and they came in large numbers especially to Glasgow and Edinburgh. At a first glance it seems odd that, in spite of so many obvious links between them and England, there was no academy set up in either Edinburgh or Glasgow. Stirling, Dundee, Dumfries, Elgin, all set up academies on the Perth model. In Edinburgh, however, modern science and languages were already taught in the many flourishing private schools as well as in the College. These private schools and tutors provided in themselves all the facilities of a polytechnic. It may be mentioned that a number of the private schools in Edinburgh used the name 'academy', though they were in no way under public control as Scottish academies like Perth Academy were.[1]

The Town Council looked, in the main, with a lenient eye on the private schools and private teachers. After about 1724 the Town Council did not insist at any time that all private teachers should be licensed. Licensing of this kind was approved of by the Church in the seventeenth and early eighteenth century, and was proposed from time to time by the Presbytery even later, but the Town Council did not endorse this course of action, and when the Presbytery protested about the existence of private teachers who were not officially licensed, the Town Council replied with delaying tactics. It is true that after the survey of private English schools made in 1758, the Town Council established its own four schools, but no other action was taken against private teachers. Indeed, the Town's teachers were allowed to retain their private pupils. It might be thought that masters of the High School would object to this general toleration, for in earlier centuries they had successfully held that private teachers of 'grammar' were invading the privileges of the High School. The High School masters did protest in 1724 against the increase in private schools where 'grammar' was taught. The Town Council then approved the suggestions that none be allowed to teach grammar in the city without the authority of the Council and that, in addition to

[1] Wm Perry and Wm Gordon, for example, referred to their schools as academies, no doubt because 'academy' sounds more impressive than 'school'.

the five High School masters, five private teachers of grammar (ie of Latin) properly licensed would be sufficient for the needs of the city. These private teachers should work under the same rules (ie of textbooks) and hours as the High School, and their schools should be inspected by a committee consisting of a city minister, the Professor of Humanity, and the Rector of the High School.[1] This kind of arrangement to protect the monopoly of the High School masters does not appear to have been enforced, and there is no other record of action either to safeguard the position of the High School or to enforce the licensing of private teachers. The number of private teachers increased and included distinguished men like Mr Mundell, whose practice was almost entirely with the sons of the nobility. No doubt it would have been unwise to try to put men like Mundell out of business. Another point that must be remembered, too, is that the prestige of the High School grew with the century, and its masters attracted so many pupils that they had no need to be jealous of the private schools.[2] The 1724 decision of the Town Council is interesting in another way. It recognised that there was room for private teaching of Latin in Edinburgh, and that the High School by itself was unable to meet the needs of the city. This is an early recognition of a fact that became more obvious as the city grew in area and numbers, that there was room for a second High School. Though the possibility of a second High School in the New Town was mooted from time to time, it was not until the early nineteenth century that the subject became one of heated public discussion, one outcome of which was the establishment of the independent Edinburgh Academy.

To give some idea of the number and variety of private schools and the scope of the instruction provided in them, it will be convenient to consider them in groups, but the divisions made for this purpose are arbitrary. In those days a private teacher taught what he was interested in, or what he thought would pay him. Sometimes these teachers taught groups of related subjects like arithmetic, accounts, and book-keeping; or English

---

[1] Minutes of the Town Council of Edinburgh, 5 Aug 1724. Quoted in Steven, *op cit.*
[2] See Chapter III.

(that is, reading) and writing; or modern languages; or practical mathematics; there is no rule, but an interesting diversity.

The principal sources of information about private schools are the advertisements in the Edinburgh newspapers, and, after 1773, the Edinburgh Directories. The evidence of advertisements must be accepted with caution. The newspapers at the beginning of the century were small, and the practice of advertising increased as the century progressed and the size of the newspapers grew. Some teachers advertised much more often than others; some, like Mundell who was the most distinguished private teacher of his day, never advertised at all. It is clear, therefore, that while the list of names from this source provides interesting, it does not give conclusive, evidence. It is interesting and may even be illuminating, for example, to note that only 5 teachers of the elementary subjects of reading, writing, and arithmetic advertised between 1705 and 1709, that 5 are known to have practised in 1725, 8 in 1750, and no fewer than 44 in 1775. A similar increase can be observed in the number of teachers of languages and other more advanced studies. The advertisements often yield genuine information about the individual teachers, their methods of teaching, and what they felt the public ought to know about their successes.

ENGLISH

The commonest and simplest form of education was the learning of reading. That there were schools in Edinburgh like the 'Dame Schools' mentioned in the histories of education in England is certain, and there is a reference to them in the Town Council minute of 1758 which was quoted in Chapter II.[1] What is said about them is disappointingly brief: 'five or six more schools taught by women at different prices. The number of scholars at each of them does not exceed fifteen.' These were probably for children of the middle classes, for children from wealthy homes were taught the elements of reading and writing at home, and the poor, if they went to school at all, went to the Charity schools. Many of the private teachers who taught

[1] See Appendix III.

other subjects held classes for beginners as well. James Porterfield, for example, who was a private teacher as well as an
officially licensed one, claimed that he could teach the elements
of reading to a child of normal capacity in eight or nine months.[1]
John Warden in 1751 undertook to teach children 'from 5 to
7 years of age, to read English according to the best pronunciation, within 4 months from the day of their entrance; those from
7 to 10 or 12, within three months'. Warden's advertisement
continues: 'Others who are come to years of maturity, and have
not arrived to even a tolerable degree of reading, and (which
is likewise an infinite loss and too frequent in both sexes,
especially in the female sex) who cannot spell even the most
common words, I will perfect such in three months at farthest.'[2]
Arthur Masson, before he established himself as a teacher of
languages, taught young children, and says in his advertisement
that such classes were limited to twenty pupils.[3] His brother
Alexander Masson in 1766 opened a school for beginners under
6 years of age, for whom he charged 5s a quarter; for those who
could not attend school regularly, he was prepared to give
private lessons twice a week in their own homes.[4] Cortes
Telfair (or Telfer), an Englishman from London, set up school
in 1772 for young children 'beginning the spelling book'. No
doubt in these, as in his more advanced classes on elocution, Mr
Telfer insisted, as he said in his advertisements, that 'great care
is taken that no Scotch may be spoken'.[5] The age at which
children learned to read varied considerably, but 5 or 6 seems
to have been usual. Boys started on the rudiments of Latin at
the High School normally at the age of 9 years, and it was
assumed that they could read and write in English by that time.

The teaching of English increased in importance in the United
Kingdom in the course of the eighteenth century, partly
because of the influence of the vigorous essays of Addison,
Swift, and Steele, and partly because English was beginning to
be used as the medium of education in place of Latin. In

---

[1] See his advertisement on page 195. He probably referred only to the
recognition of letters and a knowledge of very easy words.
[2] *The Caledonian Mercury*, 24 Dec 1751.
[3] *The Edinburgh Evening Courant*, 23 Oct 1755.
[4] *ibid*, 27 June 1767.
[5] *ibid*, 16 Sept 1772.

Edinburgh, the old practice of reading lectures in Latin gradually went out of favour in the College, and English took its place. At the same time interest in English grammar, English speech, English pronunciation, and English composition grew in the schools and in the city. We can accept the word of authorities like Boswell and Smollett that the natives of Edinburgh were particularly sensitive about the way they spoke and wrote the English language.

What is called 'the new method' of teaching English is first found in Edinburgh in the advertisement of a book by John Warden, in 1737. This was a collection of passages from the *Spectator*, *Tatler*, and *Guardian*, and Warden claimed to follow 'Mr Rollin's Method of teaching and studying the belles lettres, and his ancient history'. Passages are included from Latin as well as English, in which connection Warden makes this interesting comment: 'the publisher (ie Mr Warden) has constantly used both boys and girls to read Latin in his school, and has taught them to distinguish between the pronunciation of that language and English, for which practice he has the approbation of the first-rate Latin and French masters in this kingdom'.[1] Rollin's method, to which Warden refers, advocated the reading of English extracts and the study of English grammar, the teaching of English, in fact, in the way in which Latin had traditionally been taught. Other books followed Warden's, like *The Edinburgh New Method of Teaching English*, by R Godskirk and J Hume of 1750, and '*A New Grammar for the Speaking and Writing English properly and correctly: with Exercises of bad English, in the manner of Clark and Bailey's Exercises in the Latin*', of the same period. Warden's son, also called John, held strong views on the importance of teaching English grammar. Ladies, he said, did not normally learn grammar in any other tongue, for the grammars of French or Italian were of little use in explaining English, and therefore they should be taught a sensible form of English grammar.[2]

Arthur Masson is a good example of the popular teacher of English and modern languages in the second half of the century. Fortunately he advertised his private school frequently, and

[1] *The Caledonian Mercury*, 23 June 1737.
[2] *ibid*, 21 Nov 1751.

gave personal details in his advertisements; as a result it is possible to learn something of his life and attitude to teaching. He had been educated at Aberdeen Grammar School and Marischal College, Aberdeen and, after teaching in Aberdeen and Glasgow, came to Edinburgh 'with some persons of quality, in order to instruct them in the French', and advertised that he intended to open a class in French and one in English grammar. He hoped also to teach his pupils 'how to read with propriety our English poets'.[1] In 1755, he announced classes in Italian as well as French and English. His pupils gave public performances of reading and reciting English in 1756 and subsequent years, from which we can gather that Masson was quick to sense the interest of Edinburgh people in elocution. A charge was made for admission, and Masson said that the profits would be used for fitting up a genteel and convenient room for teaching, and for buying such books as were useful for English. His advertisement in 1761 is dated from London, and announced that he had learned Spanish and Portuguese there and proposed to teach them in Edinburgh on his return, but that his principal business in London was 'his improvement in the English Language, which above all others ought to be the study of every Briton'. He had engaged a young Englishman 'of excellent pronunciation' to be his assistant. His schoolroom in the first turnpike below the Tron Church was very large, fit for 100 scholars and, as there were 'two chimnies', there could be two classes, one for young ladies and one for young gentlemen. He offered private tuition in the proper pronunciation of English to young gentlemen of the College, High School, and other schools.[2] In a later advertisement of the same year, he stated that he had decided to charge fees on the same basis as the High School where, he said, 'a minimum is fixed and something is left to the discretion and generosity of the employers'.[3] Masson was in France in 1765, where he carried a letter from Hugh Blair to David Hume.[4] He returned with certificates attesting his knowledge of French from Duclos, Secretary to

[1] *The Edinburgh Evening Courant*, 23 Oct 1755; *The Caledonian Mercury*, 26 Feb 1757.
[2] *The Caledonian Mercury*, 2 Nov 1761.
[3] *ibid*, 21 Nov 1761.
[4] *Letters of David Hume*, ed J Y T Greig, Oxford, Vol I, p 517.

the French Academy, Diderot, Alembert, and the Abbé Vailli, and announced that he was starting classes in French for young ladies and gentlemen not above 12 years of age at half a guinea a quarter. His pupils would get practice in French from a young Frenchman who had come to stay with Masson in order to learn English.[1] These pupils later gave a public performance of reading, speaking, and explaining French prose and verse in the Assembly Hall, and the young Frenchman read a passage from *Paradise Lost*. Up to this time, Arthur Masson had been assisted by his brother Alexander, and Alexander had looked after the classes during his brother's absence in France, but they separated after this time. From 1769 Arthur Masson professed the teaching of English, French, and Italian, stressing in particular English pronunciation based on the style taught by Sheridan. He gave 'practical' lectures to advanced scholars in English and French, and his assistant took the beginners in an adjoining room. The highest class read a part of the Bible each Friday, and the advanced scholars were taught English grammar.[2] His advertisement in 1771 mentioned his textbook in Italian, in which he claimed to have reduced the study of that language to such easy principles that his pupils could be able to read and understand it in three months. The advertisement of the following year has a carping tone. Of his *French Collection* he says that it is widely used in England and in Scottish towns other than Edinburgh, and adds darkly that he thought he knew the reason for this. In spite of rumours to the contrary, he says, he has not given up his English classes, and he mentions a possible confusion with others of the same name.[3] Later he says bluntly: 'There is another person of the name of Masson (with whom he has no connection) who professes to teach English.'[4] He made an innovation in 1778, when he advertised a 'Literary Mischianza' on the day of the races. 'About one o'clock, or immediately after the company return from the race, Specimens

---

[1] *The Edinburgh Evening Courant*, 16 Nov 1765. Diderot wrote: 'Je ne pense pas qu'on puisse trouver en Angleterre quelqu'un qui soit plus capable d'instruire dans la connaissance du François et de la bonne littérature Françoise.'

[2] *The Caledonian Mercury*, 21 Oct 1769.

[3] *The Edinburgh Evening Courant*, 4 July 1772.

[4] *ibid*, 19 June 1773.

of Reading Choice Pieces in English, French, Italian, Spanish, and Portuguese in prose and verse, with an English translation. By Arthur Masson, MA, Teacher of Languages. After which there will be some favourite Italian songs, by a gentlewoman from Italy, accompanied on the guitar by a gentleman of the same country, who have engaged to favour him on this particular occasion. There will likewise be played some airs on the mandoline, an instrument but little known in this country. Tickets of admission at 2s 6d each. . . . Mr Masson has several times given literary exhibitions *gratis*, but as some of his brethren have taken money for their tickets of admission, he hopes the ladies and gentlemen to whom he has the honour to be known, will not be offended at his attempting, for once, the same method; and that they will excuse him for not making a personal application, which he declines only from a point of delicacy. He flatters himself that his attempt to cultivate the *Belles Lettres* in Scotland will meet with some encouragement.'[1] In the following year he retired and went to live in Aberdeen. He was a scholar of some standing, author of a number of popular textbooks, one of which, his *English Collection*, is mentioned by Burns in his fragment of autobiography as a book which delighted him. Masson was also a friend of Robert Fergusson, according to a reference in A B Grosart's edition of the poet's works. Masson was proud to refer to Thomas Sheridan as his mentor in English pronunciation. That opinionative and hot-headed Irishman, father of Richard Brinsley Sheridan, lives for us in the pages of Boswell's *Johnson*. His lectures on language, to be mentioned later in this chapter, were popular in Edinburgh. There is something comic in the thought of the Aberdonian Masson teaching English pronunciation in Edinburgh on the model of Sheridan's Irish brogue.

William Perry was an enterprising Englishman who, after teaching for some time in Kelso, set up an academy in the Tailors' Hall, Cowgate. While at Kelso, he had published *The Man of Business and Gentleman's Assistant*, a book intended for apprentices, shopkeepers, and others whose main interest lay in commerce, as well as landed gentry. His academy in Edinburgh was a private school where Perry taught English,

[1] *The Caledonian Mercury*, 25 July 1778.

writing, arithmetic, and book-keeping. He was a lexicographer, and also a publisher. His *Royal Standard Dictionary* of 1775, and *Only Sure Guide to the English Tongue; or New Pronouncing Spelling-book* of 1776 were reprinted frequently in the United Kingdom and in America. Perry took over a small printing business in Edinburgh for the purpose of printing and publishing his own works, and the complications of running this business at the same time as he was teaching and writing were too much for him, and he was imprisoned for bankruptcy in 1778. He raised an action against his creditors, and in the course of proceedings, an inventory was made of his effects at Tailors' Hall. The contents of the schoolroom were as follows:

> A chimney grate
> Two school tables
> A pulpit and stool
> A small table
> 4 long stools
> A paper rase (for cutting paper)
> 2 sconces or hanging candlesticks
> A sliding rule
> A case of mathematical instruments.

It is rare to find any list of schoolroom equipment, and this is interesting because it is so meagre. There are no books, but none is mentioned in the rest of Perry's house, and it looks as if he had disposed of them in a safe place before he was arrested.[1]

Perry had advertised for boarders when he came to Edinburgh, young gentlemen and noblemen at 28 to 40 guineas a year according to age, and one guinea entrance money. He was also willing to board students attending the College, at 10 guineas a quarter. English language was his main preoccupation, and he meant to teach his pupils to read 'with gracefulness and propriety'. In the advertisement of a course of public lectures on the art of reading and speaking in January 1776, occurs the following: 'In the course of these lectures will be occasionally introduced the following characters, viz The Schoolboy, Schoolmaster, Common Reader, Monotonist,

[1] Bill Chamber Processes, Nos 20, 120; 20, 143; 26, 843; 76, 298. All are to be found in HM Register House, Edinburgh.

Jingler, Stammerer, Word-monger, Clipper, Coiner, and Distorter; also Orations on Bar, Physical, Clerical, Scotch, Irish, and English Oratory—specimens of the dialects of several counties of England remarkable for their barbarism and corruption of speech—Causes of Stammering, etc.'[1]

The papers about Perry in the Register House contain a statement of his annual earnings. He said that 'with unremitting industry and application' he had been 'engaged in the business of his Academy from 8 in the morning till 9 at night in private and public classes to very great advantage'. He claimed to have 'the reputation of an able teacher' and 'an income of no less than £220 per annum accruing therefrom'. He also made £200 a year from the sale of his books. Even if these figures are exaggerated, it is obvious, when the salaries of £15 a year paid to the town's English teachers are borne in mind, that a private schoolmaster could make a good living in Edinburgh.[2] No doubt this was because of the presence in Edinburgh of members of the nobility and gentry; Perry adduced as his friends the Earl of Erroll and Sir John Anstruther, and said he was attending many other families of distinction up to the time of his imprisonment.

Perry lost no opportunity for advertising. In May 1776, he conducted a public examination of the scholars of Mr Ogilvie's school in Leith, and the newspaper account of the occasion includes this sentence: 'What is very remarkable is that the youngest class, some of whom are not four years of age, repeated the different sounds of the vowels and diphthongs from Mr Perry's *New Pronouncing Spelling Book* to an astonishing degree of accuracy.'[3]

William Scott first appears as a teacher of English in Edinburgh in 1774. Before that time he was, as he was proud to point out in the preface to his *Dictionary*, assistant to his uncle, James Burgh, master of an academy at Newington Green, near London.[4] Burgh was a Scotsman, cousin of Principal Robert-

[1] *The Caledonian Mercury*, 10 Jan 1776.
[2] Minutes of the Town Council of Edinburgh, 4 Sept 1782.
[3] *The Caledonian Mercury*, 6 May 1776.
[4] William Scott, *A New Spelling, Pronouncing, and Explanatory Dictionary of the English Language.* Edinburgh. The edition in National Library of Scotland is of 1802.

son, and was a successful schoolmaster.[1] It is significant to note in Scott's case, as in those of Masson and Perry, how powerful was the influence of England on Scottish private schools.

The school which Scott proposed to open in Edinburgh was for writing, arithmetic and 'the art of reading English with propriety' to groups of ladies and gentlemen not exceeding six in number.[2] He also intended to give private tuition. In order to make himself known in Edinburgh he gave public readings of prose and verse, and a course of lectures on reading.[3] He announced a class on elocution in 1779, for the five winter months from 7 to 8 in the evenings, restricted to eight students, each paying two guineas for the course of 10s 6d a month.[4] These ventures being successful, he was able to give up his writing school in 1781, though he continued private tuition in English, writing, and accounts.[5] In English language he advertised three classes, one for University students, one for 'young gentlemen attending the High School', and one for young ladies.[6] He also gave a course of lectures on elocution in St Mary's Chapel, the charge being 5s for the course, or 2s for each lecture. In 1784, his classes for young gentlemen cost 15s a quarter, and for those described as 'of more advanced years', that is, over 16 years of age, £1 1s a quarter.[7] In 1785 he advertised for boys at 40 guineas a year including instruction in English, writing, arithmetic, algebra, geography, and book-keeping.[8] His public readings continued, the series for December 1786 including passages from *Richard III*, *The Apprentice*, and Smollett's *Ode to Independence*. This advertisement ends with the significant words: 'NB. The room will be sufficiently warmed.'[9]

---

[1] *Dictionary of National Biography*. His academy was at Stoke Newington, where 'he remained until 1771, publishing many works and making money'.
[2] *The Edinburgh Evening Courant*, 11 Jan 1774.
[3] *The Caledonian Mercury*, 4 Jan 1777.
[4] *ibid*, 8 Nov 1779.
[5] *The Edinburgh Evening Courant*, 12 May 1781.
[6] *ibid*, 10 Nov 1781.
[7] *The Caledonian Mercury*, 8 Dec 1784.
[8] *The Edinburgh Evening Courant*, 12 Oct 1785.
[9] *The Caledonian Mercury*, 9 Dec 1786.

ELOCUTION

Mention has been made of the courses of lectures which various teachers delivered on elocution, the pronunciation of English, and the reading of specimen passages. This is a fascinating feature of life in Edinburgh after the middle of the century, and no account of education in the city would be complete without consideration of it.

The earliest reference to such lectures is in 1748, when Mr Davies, one of the managers of the new concert hall, and an actor, gave a number of lectures on reading and speaking English.[1] In the same year, Adam Smith, at the instigation of Lord Kames, gave a series of lectures on Taste and Composition.[2] Mr Watson gave a series of lectures on similar subjects in the following years.[3] Adam Smith became Professor of Logic in Glasgow in 1751, and Mr Watson became Professor of Logic at St Andrews in 1758. In 1759, Hugh Blair read lectures in the College of Edinburgh on Rhetoric and Belles Lettres, and was made professor, at first without salary, but in 1762 at a salary of £70 a year as the first Regius Professor of Rhetoric. This was the first chair in the Scottish Universities devoted to Rhetoric and English Literature.

At about this time there was concern among educated Scotsmen about correctness in writing English, and particularly the avoidance of Scotticisms. The first collection of Scotticisms was compiled by James Elphinstone, and published as an appendix to David Hume's *Political Discourses* in 1752. Elphinstone published another list in the *Scots Magazine* in 1764. James Beattie's well-known collection appeared in 1779. Many examples of the sensitiveness of the Scot abroad on the subject of Scotticisms are to be found in Boswell. He took lessons from Mr Love, an actor from London who was playing in Edinburgh, and from old Mr Sheridan.[4] Edinburgh was a place where lectures on oratory or English pronunciation could be sure of an audience, and accordingly many lecturers visited it.

[1] *The Edinburgh Evening Courant*, 3 Mar 1748.
[2] Grant, *History of the University of Edinburgh*.
[3] Grant, *op cit*.
[4] Boswell, *Life of Johnson*, Everyman edn, Vol II, p 417. *Boswell's London Journal*, Heinemann, p 9.

Thomas Sheridan is the most important of the early lecturers. His first course began on 30 June 1761, for four days a week and for four weeks. These lectures were attended by more than 300 gentlemen, 'the most eminent in this country for their rank and abilities'.[1] A second course intended for ladies and those gentlemen who could not attend the first followed a month later, a simpler course but equally popular, for the report in the *Scots Magazine* says the house was crowded. The first course dealt with the following heads: Articulation, Pronunciation, Accent, Emphasis, Pauses or Stops, Pitch and Management of the Voice, Tones, and Gestures.[2] The second course began with the 'very first elements of speech, and thence proceeding through syllables and words to sentences and verses'. It was a simpler course, for the first could be understood only by those who 'were acquainted with the learned languages'.[3] It was presumably Sheridan's success that encouraged William Noble to open a school for the reading of English, 'taking all imaginable care of the quantity, accent, and manner of expression, by which he hopes that the barbarisms, so often and so justly complained of here, will be properly guarded against'.[4] Sheridan returned in 1764, and again delighted his audiences. A list of the poems he read aloud includes several passages from Milton, of which Belial's reply from *Paradise Lost* was rendered by Master Sheridan.[5] Other poems read by Thomas Sheridan were Pope's *Unfortunate Lady*, Gray's *Elegy*, some parts of Macpherson's *Ossian*, and Dryden's *Ode on the Power of Music*. All of these, like the scenes from *The Provok'd Husband* which were also given, are declamatory in type and well suited to be spoken. One wonders whether the interest in the spoken word, common in England as well as Scotland in the eighteenth century, did not have an influence on the kind of poem written.

[1] *Scots Magazine*, July 1761, Aug 1762, and Vol 24, pp 372, 481, and 593.
[2] *The Edinburgh Evening Courant*, 17 June 1761.
[3] *The Caledonian Mercury*, 22 July 1761. *Boswell Papers*, Vol 1, p 129. 'Mr Sheridan's lectures are vastly too enthusiastic. He is to do everything by oratory. It is like the verse in the Song extolling Drunkenness:
    Alexander hated thinking
    Drank about at Council-board
    He subdued the world by drinking
    More than by his conqu'ring sword.
[4] *The Caledonian Mercury*, 19 Sept 1761.
[5] *The Edinburgh Evening Courant*, 10 June and 14 July 1764.

There was one very definite result of Sheridan's lectures, the formation of a Society for the English Language. 'Tomorrow the plan of a new establishment for carrying on, in this country, the study of the English tongue, in a regular and proper manner, is to be laid before the *Select Society*. As this is a matter of great importance, and there are obvious reasons for considering it immediately, it is expected that all the members will attend at the usual place and hour of meeting.'[1] The Select Society, founded in 1754 by a group in which Allan Ramsay junior, the painter, was a moving spirit, consisted of some of the ablest men in the city. The Society for the English Language was formed, and engaged Mr Leigh, 'a person well qualified to teach the pronunciation of the English tongue with propriety and grace', to instruct groups or individuals.[2]

A number of those who gave lectures and demonstrations on English language and literature were actors and actresses, some of whom were, as the phrase is, 'resting'. Their efforts, according to Dibdin, the historian of the Edinburgh Stage, were so popular that they were able to make a living out of them. Writing of the year 1776, he says: 'For several years previous to this a number of actors and actresses, notably Mr Stayley and Mrs Baker, had made a livelihood by giving lectures on and teaching elocution, the pronunciation of the English language, etc.' Dibdin says that the practice was overdone, and led to the following curious advertisement in the press: 'At a period when the attention of the public is so laudably engaged in the study of the language of our sister kingdom; it is hoped it will not be deemed improper to pay some regard to that of our own; and that an effort to keep alive some of the first pieces of poetry that can adorn any language will meet with the approbation of those possessed in any degree of the *Amor Patriae*, or who do not wish the Scotch name to sink into utter oblivion. Therefore on Friday next, 15th March, in St Mary's Chapel, Mr Young will deliver a lecture on the Scottish language.' The point of this advertisement is that Mr Young was the prompter at the Theatre Royal.

[1] *The Edinburgh Evening Courant*, 27 July 1761.
[2] *The Caledonian Mercury*, 28 July 1762. See also McElroy, L, and McElroy, D, *The Literary Clubs and Societies of the Eighteenth Century in Scotland*, an unpublished thesis in the University of Edinburgh.

The year 1776 saw many lecturers on elocution in Edinburgh. Mr Scott, teacher of English, read prose and verse in St Mary's Chapel.[1] Mrs Baker gave a public class on reading English, at 10s 6d for twenty lectures: 'Any gentleman may read for 10 minutes each evening in rotation, if they propose the author the evening before.'[2] Mr Perry gave a course of lectures on the art of reading and speaking, at 2s each lecture.[3] Mr Melmoth gave a course of lectures on correct pronunciation and elegant delivery of English in St Mary's Chapel, at £1 1s for twelve lectures, in which he was critical of Sheridan. 'Proper care will be taken to keep the Chapel warm.'[4] Walker, author of the famous *Rhyming and Pronouncing Dictionary*, repeated his 1775 lectures in 1776.[5] An epigram on a Lecturer of the English Language appeared in the *Caledonian Mercury*[6]:

> A pedantic strange cook is arrived here of late,
> Who has hash'd up cold English, Scotch palates to cheer.
> Bills of fare he has given, and with art high disguised;
> But our critical cooks have each dish analysed
> And declare the ingredients that make up his olio
> Are extracted from quarto, octavo, and folio;
> When they're dressed and dished up, 'tis the most can be said
> That instead of true turtle, he gives us calf's head.
>
> Epicurus.

Melmoth had given elaborate accounts of his lectures in the press, and the epigram may refer to him. Even in the Theatre Royal, the lecturers were portrayed, for between the play and the farce was performed 'a favourite scene taken from *The Orators*, written by Samuel Foote, called "The Lecturer", Lecturer, Mr Smith, and Donald McGregor the Scots Pupil, Mr Mills'.[7] Mr John Herries, Lecturer in the Old Jewry, London, gave a course of six lectures for 10s 6d in June.[8] All of these activities in six months indicate a remarkable public appetite for lectures on elocution.

---

[1] *The Caledonian Mercury*, 6 Jan 1776.
[2] *ibid*, 6 Jan 1776.
[3] *ibid*, 10 Jan 1776.
[4] *ibid*, 9 March 1776.
[5] *ibid*, 3 Feb 1776.
[6] *ibi*, 13 March 1776.
[7] *ibid*, 3 April 1776.
[8] *ibid*, 17 June 1776.

Many of these lecturers repeated their courses in the following years, and they were joined by distinguished scholars like James Elphinstone, who gave what he called a 'scientific course' on the English language in 1779; one of his nine lectures was on Scotticisms 'and other provinciality'.[1] Elphinstone also formed a private class. Robert Hamilton, MA, opened a class for young gentlemen in the art of reading English with propriety, and mentioned that he had twice gained a prize for elocution in the University of Glasgow.[2] Actors who gave courses on elocution included C Charteris 'of the Theatre Royal', and Francis Waldron of the same theatre.[3] There was also 'an English lady', who, being 'totally disengaged from any other employment', was happy to teach young ladies the proper pronunciation of English. Clergymen like the Rev Rest Knipe and the Rev Mr Cleeve also delivered courses.[4]

Some of these lectures could be classed as entertainments, and Waldron referred to his lectures as 'A new species of literary entertainment'; he read Milton, and passages from *Tristram Shandy*, and imitated Garrick in *King Lear*. William Scott's series in 1781 had as aim 'to facilitate the study of elocution' and provide 'an agreeable and rational amusement to persons of both sexes'.[5]

CLASSICS

Since a knowledge of Latin was a necessary part of a gentleman's education, and essential to any kind of University training, it is not surprising to find that there were at all times in the eighteenth century a number of private teachers of that subject. The High Schools of Edinburgh and Canongate were not large enough to meet all needs, and there was a tendency for the sons of the nobility and gentry to attend private schools or have private tuition. A number of the sons of men of rank certainly went to the High School, but it is safe to say that the

[1] *The Caledonian Mercury*, 3 March 1779.
[2] *The Edinburgh Evening Courant*, 10 Jan 1780.
[3] *ibid*, 24 April and 11 Nov 1780.
[4] *ibid*, 19 March 1783, and *The Caledonian Mercury*, 5 Jan 1784.
[5] *The Edinburgh Evening Courant*, 24 Nov 1781.

L

private schools would not have been so large or so profitable had it not been for the presence in Edinburgh of so many wealthy and titled families. At the beginning of the century, for example, the well-known schoolmaster, James Kirkwood, formerly master of the Grammar School of Linlithgow, and author of a celebrated little book, *The Twenty Seven Gods of Linlithgow*, set up a private school for Latin in Edinburgh. He said himself that it was 'the greatest that ever was in Edinburgh, and by far the most gainful . . . having about 140 scholars, almost all noblemen's and gentlemen's sons'.[1]

The most distinguished private teacher of classics in the course of the century was James Mundell, whose pupils were drawn from many aristocratic families. A pamphlet in the Library of the University of Glasgow is entitled, '*List of the Scholars educated by the late Mr James Mundell, Edinburgh*: Printed by Mundell and Wilson. MDCCLXXXIX.'[2] The names are listed under the years from 1735 to 1761 inclusive. The numbers for each year are not high, the greatest being 33 in 1753, and the smallest 6 in the fateful year of 1745. The names of Islay Campbell, Sir John Whiteford, James Boswell, Patrick Heron, Lord Cardross, the Hon Stuart Erskine, Alexander Murray (later Lord Henderland), and Luke Fraser (Walter Scott's master at the High School), appear among the 567 boys on the list. There were also girls, the 94 names including those of Many Boswell and Lady Anne Agnes Erskine. Little is known about Mundell. He became a Burgess and Guild Brother of Edinburgh in 1740, by right of his wife Agnes Bennett. His school was in the West Bow.[3] There is a reference to him in the Town Council minutes of a date some time after his death, which however indicates the esteem in which he had been held. In 1795, in the course of the quarrel between Nicol, the friend of Burns and a master in the High School, and Dr Adam, the rector of the High School, Nicol announced that he proposed to resign and open a private school. A subcommittee of the Town Council then reported: 'If he [Mr

---

[1] Kirkwood, *The History of the Twenty Seven Gods of Linlithgow*, 1711. The twenty-seven gods were the members of Linlithgow Town Council, with whom Kirkwood had quarrelled.
[2] Glasgow University Library Pamphlets, Y4, h, 27.
[3] *The Edinburgh Evening Courant*, 10 March 1764.

Nicol] chooses to give up his public class he will be in precisely
the situation Mr Mundell was in, whom he quotes in his
answers, and then Dr Adam will be in the situation of his predecessors in office, Messrs Lee and Matheson, and they per-
suade themselves that in this case Dr Adam will no more apply
the hand of power to oppress Mr Nicol than Mr Lee and Mr
Matheson did oppress Mr Mundell who never was a master of
the High School.'[1]   James Mundell died in 1762, but his old
pupils met annually from 1764 onwards.[2]   Much of the
information about other teachers is gained from their many
advertisements in the press, but Mundell did not advertise at
all—he was probably very well known, and did not need to—
but if one dare judge him by the success of his old pupils, he
must have been a great teacher.

Another well-known teacher of classics was James Moir,
who settled in Leith Wynd in 1761, having previously been in
charge of an academy at Alloa.[3]   The subjects he wished to
teach were Latin, Greek, arithmetic, geography, geometry,
and navigation, but when he moved in 1762 to Forrester's Wynd,
he specialised mainly in Latin and Greek.[4]   His Latin class met
between 10 and 12, and 3 and 5 each week day, and for two
hours on Saturday, and he professed to keep the numbers
small in order to give individual attention.   The following
report of a public examination of his school is in a way a modest
advertisement.   'On Thursday last, Mr Moir's private class in
this place was publicly examined before several gentlemen of
taste and learning when the boys in their several stations explained some of the choicest of the Roman classics, and performed other scholastic exercises with an accuracy and precision
which did honour to their master.   Several of the gentlemen
who were present thought proper to cause insert the above
article in this and the other public papers as a piece of justice
due to Mr Moir's merit.'[5]   Moir wished to give Greek a more
prominent place than it usually held in Scotland at that time,
and proposed to begin teaching it after boys had completed

[1] Minutes of the Town Council of Edinburgh, 18 March 1795.
[2] The Edinburgh Evening Courant, 10 March 1764.
[3] The Caledonian Mercury, 23 Nov 1761.
[4] Edinburgh Directory, 1786-88.
[5] The Edinburgh Evening Courant, 20 Aug 1763.

three years of Latin. Both languages would then be taught for two years, and then there would be a sixth year where the drudgery would be over and a boy would be able in Latin and Greek, 'to discover their analogy and beauties, together with the use of the classic maps'.[1] It was usual for teachers to postpone the teaching of Latin until boys could read the mother tongue, but Moir felt that he did not need to wait so long.[2]

From his advertisements, it is possible to picture what Moir's school was like. In 1764, he was holding classes in Latin, Greek, and Euclid, and boys were moved up and down the classes 'according to their genius'. An hour a week was set aside for arithmetic and book-keeping, and two hours on Wednesdays and Saturdays for the study of globes and maps. His advertisement for this year concludes: 'NB. There is a large garden belonging to the house in which scholars may walk at leisure hours.'[3] In 1766, he had two Greek classes, one reading Homer and Xenophon, and the other Anacreon; and two Latin classes, one reading Livy and the other Caesar's *Civil War*. He proposed to start a Greek class for beginners.[4] By 1775 he had added Italian and Spanish to the subjects he taught privately, and his classes in Latin and in English grammar were restricted in numbers to thirty in each. His Latin class read Latin only, 'except that once a week he makes his scholars apply to the grammar of their native tongue and the maps—he attends particularly to etymology and syntax'.[5] He provided private tuition in Longinus, Xenophon's *Memorabilia*, Aristotle's *Poetics*, Sophocles' *Oedipus*, Euripides' *Orestes* and *Medea*.[6] Moir was a good scholar, and published a *Latin-English Dictionary*, a Latin translation of Aesop, *The Scholar's Vademecum*, and an edition of Ruddiman's *Grammar*. In 1786, at the end of a list of his publications which Moir included in his advertisement, he added the following letter from Dr Adam: 'Mr Adam presents his compliments to Mr Moir and begs his acceptance of a copy of this new edition of his Grammar, and of his thanks

---

1 *The Edinburgh Evening Courant*, 6 Sept 1763.
2 *ibid*, 28 Aug 1764.
3 *ibid*, 29 Aug 1764.
4 *ibid*, 21 June 1766.
5 *ibid*, 21 Oct 1775.
6 *ibid*, 7 Nov 1781.

for the benefit he derived from Mr Moir's accurate publications in composing it.'[1]

MODERN LANGUAGES

There have been teachers of French in Edinburgh for many years, and it would be strange if this were not the case, when the French influences in the Scottish court are remembered. There are references to teachers of French in the Town Council minutes as early as 1574, and the names of Nicolas Anglois (1580), Jean Beaugrand (1616), William Cowdone (1634), and William Destenbruix (1672) indicate a continuous tradition of teaching the language in Edinburgh.[2] The Town Council granted a sum of money for a schoolhouse, and sometimes supplemented this with a small annual salary; the teachers were allowed to charge fees. On one occasion at least the Town Council employed the French schoolmaster to write a letter to the town of Campvere, and paid him 40 shillings as a fee.[3]

In the early part of the eighteenth century there was also some instruction in French in the College. French was not a subject of the normal course, and there was no chair in the subject, but Guillaume Ker in 1734, and John Murdoch in 1737 were allowed by the Town Council to hold classes in French in the College buildings, in addition to the private classes they held outside.[4] The Town Council minutes of 7 December 1737 note a petition from John Murdoch, Teacher of French, and record the decision to grant him 'the use and possession of that vacant room in the Colledge No. 37 . . . for teaching of French therein', on condition that he fit up and repair the room at his own expense and keep it in good repair.

'Jupiter' Carlyle had attended the French class of Guillaume Ker, of whom he writes: 'It was in this year (1736) that I attended the French master, one Kerr, who, for leave given him to teach in a College room, taught his scholars the whole session for a

---

[1] *The Caledonian Mercury*, 12 Aug 1786.
[2] Minutes of the Town Council of Edinburgh, 20 Aug 1574, 8 July 1580, 12 July 1616, 19 Feb 1634, and 24 May 1672.
[3] *ibid*, 12 Oct 1599.
[4] *The Caledonian Mercury*, 24 Oct 1734 and 27 Oct 1737; Minutes of the Town Council of Edinburgh, 7 Dec 1737.

guinea, which was then all that the regents could demand for a session of the College, from the 1st of November to the 1st of June. During that course we were made sufficiently masters of French to be able to read any book. To improve our pronunciation, he made us get one of Molière's plays by heart, which we were to have acted, but never did. It was the *Médecin malgré lui*, in which I had the part of Sganarelle.'[1] It is an indication of how different Edinburgh was from the rest of Scotland in the provision of private schools, that Carlyle found when he transferred to Glasgow College, that at that time there was no teacher of French in the whole of Glasgow.[2]

There was also some teaching of French outside the College. A Frenchman advertised in 1720 to teach the language 'at a reasonable price'.[3] In 1731, James Freebairn gave a series of lectures in French in the Magdalen Chapel on the subject of 'Tragedy and Epic'. His introductory lecture, dedicated to the Earl of Eglinton, was printed, and a copy exists in the National Library. Clearly, these lectures were addressed to an aristocratic audience, for the author begins with, 'My Lords and Messieurs' and expresses a hope that the French language should become familiar to the 'jeune Noblesse de notre Pais'. These lectures were given twice a week, at midday on Mondays and Wednesdays, at one guinea for the course, or 'un Cheling' for each lecture. Freebairn claimed that this was the first time that a series of public lectures of the kind had ever been delivered in Scotland: he hoped by means of his lectures to encourage the arts in general, and belles lettres in particular.

In the period between 1700 and 1750, it is true to say that there are relatively few advertisements for the teaching of French: Ker, Murdoch, Freebairn, and Francis Archibald (1739), are the only names. But after 1750, and increasingly after 1760, the advertisements are numerous, and some of the teachers

---

[1] *Autobiography*, p 49.
[2] *ibid*, p 83. Carlyle was referring to the town of Glasgow, and not the University. The University of Glasgow made an arrangement some time in the 1730s, similar to that in the College of Edinburgh. See Coutts, *History of the University of Glasgow*. In 1714, John Grandpré, a Frenchman who had taught for some years in Edinburgh, was invited by the Town Council of Glasgow to set up school there, with an annual salary of £12 10s. Grandpré went to Glasgow, but returned to Edinburgh in the autumn of 1714.
[3] *The Edinburgh Evening Courant*, 5 Jan 1720.

profess Italian, Spanish, and Portuguese. Between 1770 and 1779, for example, the following teachers are known to have practised in Edinburgh: F Bottarelli (Fr, Ital), J Brown, Louis Cauvin, Sen, and Louis Cauvin, Jun, M Le Brun, M de la Chappelle, Mr Duguid (It), Mr Lawrie, Mr Pepper, W Perry, Stephano Puppo (It, Sp, Port), Arthur Masson (Fr, It, Sp).[1] From 1770 to the end of the century there were always seven or eight teachers of French, and at least one teacher of the other Romance languages, in Edinburgh. In 1786, there were readings of French plays during Race Week. This is an interesting parallel to the readings of English which were popular ways of teaching elocution.[2] It is not surprising that in 1790 the number of people professing to teach French was increased by émigrés.[3] Of German, on the other hand, there is no record before Mr D'Asti in 1786. It was in 1788 that Henry Mackenzie delivered a lecture on German literature that excited the interest of Scott, and led to the formation of a German class under Dr Willich in 1792.

French was a fashionable subject in the girls' boarding schools after the year 1750. Before that time, it is mentioned in the curriculum of only one school, Mrs Ainslie's in 1748. After 1750, it appears in practically all the girls' schools except those concerned only with cookery. Usually, it was taught by visiting masters, but occasionally the proprietrix or a resident governess was responsible for the instruction. In some of these schools Italian was also professed, and in one, Spanish.

Some of the teachers of modern languages were also teachers of English, like Masson and Perry. There were also foreigners like M Remon, a Spaniard, Baron Ricci, an Italian, and Puppo and Olivieri, Italian musicians, who may have stayed only for short periods in Edinburgh. The Cauvins, father and son, became respected citizens, and Louis Cauvin's Hospital commemorates them to this day.

---

[1] In the National Museum of Antiquities, Queen Street, there is an oval medal of silver. The obverse is inscribed: 'Académie Françoise de Le Brun, Edinbourg. 1780'. The reverse is inscribed: 'Au Plus Habile'.
[2] *The Caledonian Mercury*, 22 July 1786.
[3] *ibid*, 13 and 27 May 1790.

ARITHMETIC, MATHEMATICS, BOOK-KEEPING, AND WRITING

While it is true to say that the teaching of these subjects developed during the eighteenth century to something like their modern importance, it would be wrong to imagine that they were unknown in Edinburgh before that time.[1] James Corse was granted permission by the Town Council in 1658 to teach 'arithmetic, geometry, astronomy, and all other arts and sciences belonging thereto, as horometry, planimetry, geography, trigonometry'.[2] He moved to Glasgow in 1660 to teach the same range of subjects. The publication in Edinburgh of Robert Colinson's *Idea Rationaria or The Perfect Accomptant* in 1680, and of James Paterson's *Scots Arithmetician* in 1685 indicates that these subjects were known and probably therefore taught in Edinburgh at that time.[3]

Of the mathematical subjects, only arithmetic was usually taught in the English schools and charity schools of the seventeenth century, and it is only in the eighteenth century that mathematics, theoretical and practical, assumes a really important place. In the seventeenth century, young children learned the relatively easy processes of addition and subtraction, but multiplication and division presented difficulties, especially 'long' multiplication and 'long' division. In those days, these processes were usually carried out by means of 'Napier's Bones' or 'Napier's Rods'. In this device of the great mathematician, ten rods 'served the purpose of a multiplication table written on wood', which could be so manipulated that the learner had only to do addition instead of multiplication.[4] Cumbrous

---

[1] Macphail, *A History of Scotland for Schools*, 1956, says: 'With the growth of trade and industry, some Writing Schools and Commercial Schools were set up for the teaching of book-keeping, arithmetic, etc., the first at Dumfries in 1723; and in 1746, Ayr Town Council added book-keeping, navigation, surveying, mathematics, and science to the curriculum of Ayr Grammar School.' The details given in the text show that Dumfries and Ayr came after Edinburgh, as one would indeed expect, and probably also after Glasgow and Aberdeen.

[2] Minutes of the Town Council of Edinburgh, 30 April 1658.

[3] D K Wilson, *The History of Mathematical Teaching in Scotland*, University of London Press, 1935. *Publications of the Scottish Council for Research in Education*, VIII. Dr Wilson states that Colinson and Paterson had schools in Edinburgh (p 27), but gives no proof of this statement. No other references to such schools have been found.

[4] D K Wilson, *op cit.*

methods of this kind were possible in small businesses, and with the few problems of measurement to be found in a relatively simple community, but as soon as commerce and trade began to be regarded as of first-rate importance, quicker and neater methods of computation and recording were needed. The links between the teaching of arithmetic and trade, and between the teaching of mathematics and scientific subjects like navigation are so strong during the eighteenth century that it would be fair to call arithmetic and mathematics vocational subjects. Their bread and butter value was obvious, and private teachers could make a profitable living from them. Most of the teaching of these subjects in Edinburgh was in fact carried out by private teachers, a considerable number of whom brought their knowledge from England. Simple number was taught in the English schools, consisting of addition, subtraction and as much multiplication and division as the teacher could manage. A teacher of writing was attached to the High School, and possibly taught some book-keeping there, but was not considered important enough to be called a High School master. One or two teachers were officially approved by the Town Council as teachers of book-keeping. But generally most of the teaching of arithmetic, writing, and book-keeping, and all the teaching of mathematics and allied subjects except what was done in the College, was carried out by private teachers.

In 1705, the Town Council appointed John Dickson, merchant and then accountant to the 'good town of Edinburgh', to be master and Professor of Book-keeping in the city.[1] He advertised in the press that he was willing to teach the subject to all who wished instruction, and gave the following details: 'The said John Dickson having finished his two sets of book-holding, as a form and rule to teach the said science in a clear compendious method, conform to the Italian rule, wherein is included a stated account of draw-back, conform to the late Act of Parliament: any who desires to be taught the said science of book-holding they may apply themselves to the said John Dickson at his lodging in the Parliament Close the entry to the Mealmarket, where he will agree with the persons.'[2] This is a

[1] Minutes of the Town Council of Edinburgh, 15 June 1705.
[2] *The Edinburgh Evening Courant*, 15-17 Oct 1705.

very early reference to the teaching of book-keeping, for, according to the *Encyclopaedia Britannica*, the earliest example of modern book-keeping is probably a ledger dated 1697, one of the books of the Company of Scotland, now in the National Library of Scotland. In 1706, another teacher of book-keeping, Alexander Heriot, advertised that he, 'now book-keeper to the New Milns manufactory at Edinburgh, who hath these many years taught book-keeping still continues to do the same'.[1] Dickson and Heriot were businessmen who taught book-keeping because they understood that little-known science, and because there was a demand for it. Like their contemporary, George Watson, that well-known benefactor to Edinburgh, they had probably learned book-keeping abroad. Their pupils were likely to be businessmen and their apprentices.

In 1708, the Town Council gave permission to William Beatt to keep a public school for the teaching of writing and arithmetic.[2] In 1709, there was advertised a copybook published by Robert (*sic*) Morton, 'a London Penman', and in the following September, the following notice appeared: 'Ralph Morton has come to Edinburgh . . . where all the usual hands with accounts are exactly taught. And for expedition youth may be boarded. Persons may be taught abroad (ie in their own homes) . . . arithmetic vulgar and decimal are carefully taught (with writing) at 10s per quarter. Book-keeping also in the true Italian manner.'[3] Beatt and Morton appear to have been teachers of children, though they probably conducted classes for adults as well. Unlike Dickson and Heriot, they were professional teachers.

Nor was pure mathematics neglected at this time. Mr Sandars, 'late Professor of Mathematics in the University of St Andrews, now dwelling at the foot of Barringer's Close, there teaches the mathematical arts, and amongst the rest, navigation, fortification, and gunnery'. He also sold a textbook on geometry, logarithms, and trigonometry.[4] William Smart, Minister of the Gospel, was another private teacher of mathematics at

---

[1] *The Edinburgh Evening Courant*, 28-30 Aug 1706.
[2] Minutes of the Town Council of Edinburgh, 23 July 1708.
[3] *The Edinburgh Evening Courant*, 13-16 May and 9-12 Sept 1709, and 6-9 Feb 1713.
[4] *ibid*, 26-28 Dec 1705 and 22-24 Dec 1708.

this time, who also gave instruction in surveying, astronomy, navigation, and 'the use of the globes celestial and terrestrial'.[1]

By 1716 there were teachers of all branches of mathematics in Edinburgh, and in that year Messrs Lundin and Humfrey announced that they taught shorthand as well as writing and book-keeping.[2]

The Town Council continued to appoint teachers of book-keeping. In 1730 or 1731, William Stevenson, who had been a merchant in Rotterdam, returned to Edinburgh and was appointed teacher. He advertised a course of public lectures in 1731 at a fee of 10s 6d, to which his private pupils were admitted free.[3] In an advertisement in 1756, he claimed to have been teaching his subject for more than thirty years.[4] He says that his fee was 10s 6d for the summer and £1 1s for the winter session, and that he set his class an examination every Friday. In 1766, a note of criticism of other teachers creeps into his advertisement: 'NB. His being authorised, as public teacher of Book-keeping, by act of the Town Council of the city of Edinburgh several years ago, together with his long experience, both in real business and in teaching, he apprehends makes all other flourishes unnecessary.'[5] Two years later he moved to the Canongate, 'finding the city now over-stocked with young teachers of that branch of education'.[6] In 1785, the Town Council's teacher of book-keeping was James Anderson. Unlike Stevenson, he was a teacher, not a merchant, having begun as a teacher of writing 'after the new London method', and he professed arithmetic and French as well as book-keeping.[7]

It is interesting to record at this point how the teaching of mathematics in its practical application to navigation was developed in Leith. As early as 1680, the Trinity House of Leith appointed a Professor of Mathematics. His hours were six hours a day in the summer months and four hours in winter, and for this he was paid 120 pounds Scots a year. Each ship-

---

[1] *The Edinburgh Evening Courant*, 31 March-2 April 1708.
[2] *ibid*, 8-11 June 1716.
[3] Murray, *History of Book-keeping and Accountancy*.
[4] *The Edinburgh Evening Courant*, 10 June 1756.
[5] *ibid*, 19 Nov 1766.
[6] *The Caledonian Mercury*, 2 July 1768.
[7] *The Edinburgh Evening Courant*, 26 Oct 1785.

master in Leith paid 5s a year towards this salary, and each scholar and apprentice had to pay one pound ten shillings Scots for food every month. 'Foreigners' had to pay fees as might be arranged with the teacher. George Drennan was appointed in 1680. His successor was John Man, teacher of mathematics, who received a grant of £40 Scots for house rent.[1] In 1717, Robert Cook taught navigation and plain sailing, and was given £24 for house rent. Robert Lauchlan followed in 1719, and in 1741 was made a member of Trinity House because of his 'usefulness' as a teacher. Alexander Wood succeeded him, and was in turn succeeded by Alexander Ingram in 1783. Ingram's appointment, however, was to teach writing, arithmetic, and mathematics in the town of Leith, and he became a member of the staff of the new High School of Leith when it was opened at the beginning of the nineteenth century.[2]

Alexander Ewing in his early days was a teacher of writing, arithmetic, and book-keeping, and wrote a popular textbook on arithmetic for schools.[3] By 1759, he was concentrating more on surveying, navigation, and the use of an orrery, globes, and maps.[4] He advertised that his school was well furnished with instruments for practical work, and said: 'Such as employ him may depend on being conducted thro' those parts of learning in the most easy, expeditious and agreeable manner and at a moderate expense.'[5] In 1768 he advertised a course of forty lectures in geography on Mondays, Wednesday, and Fridays for gentlemen, and on the other three days for ladies, at a fee of £1 1s for the course. Similar courses were held annually for the next fifteen years.[6]

Robert Darling described himself in his early advertisements as a teacher of mathematics, geography, and architecture. The

---

[1] In the list of books published by James Watson there appears the following: '*Leith's True Almanack . . .*' by John Man, Teacher of Navigation to the Fraternity House of Leith'. A copy dated 1704 is in the National Library of Scotland. See List of Watson's publications, made by G P Johnston, and in the possession of the Edinburgh Bibliographical Society.

[2] For all these details, see John Mason, *History of Trinity House of Leith.* Glasgow, 1957.

[3] *The Edinburgh Evening Courant*, 10 Feb 1756.

[4] *The Caledonian Mercury*, 15 Oct 1759.

[5] *ibid*, 16 June 1762.

[6] *ibid*, 17 Dec 1768; *The Edinburgh Evening Courant*, 3 May 1783.

mathematics consisted of Euclid, Books I to VI, mensuration, trigonometry, and surveying; geography was the study of the globes and navigation; architecture consisted of the orders of architecture. Darling's advertisement is quite explicit about the kind of pupils he sought to attract. To merchants and landed gentlemen he taught writing, arithmetic, and book-keeping, and to sea-going men he taught mathematics, geography, use of the globes and maps, navigation, and keeping a journal at sea. He also professed fortification, gunnery, land-surveying, and estate planning, and prepared boys to enter the army or the navy.[1]

Some private teachers made a specialty of writing, among whom two deserve mention. William Swanson had come from London to succeed another teacher of writing, Walter Cossar.[2] Of Swanson's school Cockburn wrote this famous passage: 'Creech's shop was the natural resort of lawyers, authors, and all sorts of literary idlers, who were always buzzing about the convenient hive. All who wished to see a poet or a stranger, or to hear the public news, the last joke by Erskine, or yesterday's occurrence in the Parliament House, or to get the publications of the day, congregated there; lawyers, doctors, clergymen, and authors. I attended the writing school of William Swanson, the great handspoiler of the time, whose crowded classroom was on the south side of the High Street, close by the Cross; and I always tried to get a seat next a window, that I might see the men I heard so much talked of moving in and out of this bower of the muses, or loitering about its entrance.'[3]

The other and perhaps more deservedly known teacher of writing was Edmund Butterworth. He was writing master to the High School, not, that is, a member of the staff, but merely the teacher to whom boys were sent who wished to learn writing and accounts. He also taught these subjects privately. A beautiful scribe of the highly ornate style popular in England, Butterworth published several books on penmanship in collaboration with his son, and was employed on occasion by the Town Council to write out loyal addresses and burgess tickets.[4]

[1] *The Caledonian Mercury*, 30 Oct 1779.
[2] *The Edinburgh Evening Courant*, 10 Oct 1763 and 23 Oct 1765.
[3] Cockburn, *op cit*.
[4] Minutes of the Town Council of Edinburgh, 29 Oct 1783, 19 May 1790.

MUSIC

In serious music the most important force in Edinburgh, and indeed in Scotland, was the Musical Society of Edinburgh, founded in 1728. This select body was established for the performance of music, and at its concerts the works of Handel and his successors were heard in Scotland for the first time. To supplement the efforts of its playing members, the Society engaged professional musicians, many of them Italians, who were induced to stay in Edinburgh by the possibility of making good incomes from teaching. Niccolo Pasquali, for example, was invited to perform for the Musical Society after his arrival at the Theatre Royal, and the Sederunt Book of the Society says: 'Pasquali was engaged to come from Dublin here by the managers of the playhouse, and continued here for six or eight months without any scholar, but no sooner did he appear in the Musical room than he had every hour employed and continued so till his dying day.'[1] Pasquali was a private teacher of music in the city from 1740 to 1757, when he died. Among other musicians employed by the Musical Society who were also private teachers were Olivieri, a violinist; William Bates, a performer on and teacher of the harpsichord; Domenico Corri, Thomas Pinto, Giuseppe Puppo, and Stabilini. The choral items of the Musical Society's concerts were sung by choirs which included boys from George Heriot's Hospital, who were paid at the rate of 2s 6d each for each performance. The influence of these visiting professional musicians, even when their stay was short, must have been considerable, in teaching the technique of their instruments and in raising the standard of musical taste. Their audiences were, however, for the most part wealthy and aristocratic, as were their pupils, and these professional musicians had little influence on the lives and interests of ordinary people. What did have an effect on the musical taste of the mass of Edinburgh citizens was the movement for reform of church singing.

The story of the change in church singing in Scotland has been told by Dr Millar Patrick, and in it the musicians played an important, though not always an inaugurating part.[2] After

---

[1] W Forbes Gray in *Book of the Old Edinburgh Club*. XIX, p 205.
[2] Millar Patrick, *Four Centuries of Scottish Psalmody*.

the publication of the *New Psalter* in Aberdeen in 1666, which contained only twelve tunes, Scottish church singing was restricted to these twelve, and some churches never sang all twelve. This must have been very monotonous. A book by an Edinburgh schoolmaster, Thomas Bruce, *The Common Tunes, or Scotland's Church Music made plain*, added some more tunes to the standard twelve, and even included some secular songs, which suggests that the volume was intended for use in the home. But the real development of church singing came from Monymusk in Aberdeenshire, where the laird, Sir Archibald Grant, had induced Thomas Channon, a soldier of General Wolfe's regiment then in Aberdeen, to teach a choir to sing the psalms. Channon's methods were so successful in Aberdeenshire and Aberdeen that news of them spread to Edinburgh. A series of advertisements and notices in the newspapers from the the end of 1755 indicates how public interest was stimulated. One teacher advertised: 'That those who are inclined to learn the tunes that are sung in the churches of Scotland and presbyterian meetings in England may be taught them, from seven to nine o'clock at night in the Baxters' Hall, Bell's Wynd, by Archibald Letham for the small expense of one penny per hour. NB. As this undertaking is for the good of the public, the owners of the hall have granted it at these hours gratis, which is the reason why he teaches so low.'[1] An advertisement by a Mr Hutton at about the same time proposes a similar course, and begins: 'As there is a proposal for singing with propriety the psalm tunes commonly used . . .'.[2] Such a proposal was indeed before the Town Council, which passed an act in the same month which is significant as showing the council's concern for the church services, its control over the churches, and its consideration for the poorer classes of the population.[3] This act of the Town Council, which begins: 'Whereas the teaching of church music in private has of late years been very much neglected and the manner in which it has been performed in public very indecent and offensive', proceeds to announce that the council will appoint a teacher of church music, publish a collection of tunes,

---

[1] *The Edinburgh Evening Courant*, 4 Nov 1755.
[2] *ibid*, 20 Nov 1755.
[3] Minutes of the Town Council of Edinburgh, 26 Nov 1755.

and open schools for the teaching of these tunes under the city precentors, which the poor could attend without payment. Cornforth Gilson, a musician from Durham, was appointed to the new post, and a collection of tunes on the lines approved was published by Robert Bremner.[1] A scheme of instruction was drawn up by a meeting of the Town Council and the general kirk sessions of the city.[2] The arrangements for the new singing schools were intimated from the pulpits. These schools were conducted by six men and one woman, and were open every day except Saturday at a fee of 1s 8d a month. Poor people unable to meet this fee could have free tuition if they were able to produce the following certificates: 'That the bearer hereof . . . though desirous to be taught Church Music, is not able to pay for it, is attested by . . . (Elder or deacon)', and 'I have tried the bearer's ear and voice, and find him capable to be taught' (to be signed by Cornforth Gilson). According to the newspaper reports, this scheme was immediately successful, one stating: 'Most of the congregations of this city are now brought to sing in a regular and decent manner at least in comparison to what they did formerly.'[3] 'Some hundreds' had been taught to sing. In order to provide a fund for paying the teachers of those who could not afford to pay the fees, the gentlemen of the Musical Society organised a concert mainly of church music, of which the announcement in the press said: 'Some of the parts will be accompanied with a grand chorus of scholars who have been lately taught.'

Cornforth Gilson, the Englishmen who carried out this scheme, was precentor in the New Church and taught music in George Heriot's Hospital. He had engagements from time to time with the Musical Society.

By encouraging this scheme, the Town Council may claim to have stimulated an interest in music among ordinary people, and in a church which had tended to discourage music. The English schools founded by the Town Council in 1759 professed the teaching of church music as a fundamental part of their curriculum; in this, the Town Council maintained an old tradi-

[1] *The Edinburgh Evening Courant*, 10 April 1756.
[2] *ibid*, 21 Dec 1756.
[3] *The Caledonian Mercury*, 12 April 1757.

tion, for the Charity school of George Clark in 1699 included church music in its course.

DRAWING AND PAINTING

The first reference to a school for the teaching of drawing and painting in the city is to be found in the constitution of the Edinburgh School of St Luke 'for the encouragement of these excelent arts of Painting, Sculpture, Architecture etc. and Improvement of the Students'. This document, dated 1729, records the foundation of the school, but no very accurate information exists about its later history.[1] Among the twenty-nine names of artists and gentlemen interested in art who sponsored the new school, were those of Allan Ramsay and his son, Allan, the portrait painter, the Nories, father and son, and Richard Cooper, the engraver. George Marshall, a portrait painter, was president, Richard Cooper was treasurer, and Roderick Chalmers, secretary. The Town Council granted the use of rooms in the College.[2]

This school has been called ambitious by Brydall, in his *History of Art in Scotland*, but the arrangement of meetings on four evenings a week from 5 to 7, from November to the end of February, and in the mornings between 6 and 8 o'clock in the months of June and July, seems, on the contrary, to be modest. Before the school was established, the usual training for an artist in Edinburgh was, like that for a house-painter, by way of an apprenticeship to one of the masons and wrights who belonged to the Incorporated Trades. Roderick Chalmers, the secretary of the new school, was a heraldic painter, and James Norie and his son James were house-painters. The school of St Luke was intended to bring some of the width of artistic interest to Edinburgh that had been found by many generations of Scottish painters in the original School of St Luke in Rome. How long the Edinburgh School of St Luke lasted is difficult to say. Brydall says that the last mention of it occurs in June 1731, 'when a room in the University was

---

[1] The original document is in the archives of the Royal Scottish Academy. For full details, see Appendix VI.
[2] Minutes of the Town Council of Edinburgh, 30 Dec 1730, 6 Jan 1731.

M

granted for its use, soon after which it seems to have expired'. But there is a later reference in the Town Council Minutes for 10 December 1733, where it is recorded in 'the Town Council Minutes for 10 December 1733, that 'the Academy for Painting' occupied Thomson's Chambers within the College. It is also quite possible—though neither Brydall nor David Laing thought so[1]—that the school was functioning later and was the 'winter's academy' which Sir Robert Strange attended in 1735-37. Strange was apprentice to Richard Cooper, who was treasurer of the School of St Luke in 1729. Whether the school Cooper supervised six years later was the same St Luke's or a private establishment of his own, the following extract from Sir Robert Strange's Memoirs is interesting as illustrating the training of artists in these days:

'Mr Cooper encouraged me as much as possible in the study of drawing, well knowing its tendency towards forming an engraver. He was exceedingly communicative, and on all occasions opened to me his portfolios. In short, I soon became of consequence, and of real utility to him, and of course a favourite with him. Amongst other advantages to a young artist, we had winter's academy at Edinburgh. It was super-intended by Mr Cooper, who was well qualified for it, and was supported, at the easy subscription of half a guinea, amongst the few artists of that city, and a number of gentlemen who were solicitous of promoting the arts. I became a constant attender on this academy, after being in some measure qualified for it.'[2]

An attempt to encourage drawing and design was made by the Select Society for the Encouragement of Arts, Sciences, and Manufactures in 1755. This Edinburgh club included among its members many distinguished intellectuals and aristocrats. David Hume, who was one of them, wrote to Allan Ramsay, junior, who was also a member: 'Advertisements have been published to inform the public of our intention. A premium, I remember, is promised to the best discourse on taste and the principles of vegetation. This regards the *belles lettres* and the sciences, but we have not neglected porter, strong ales,

---

[1] *Proceedings of the Society of Antiquaries*, Vol VIII.
[2] Dennistoun, *Memoirs of Sir Robert Strange . . . and Andrew Lumisden.* London, 1855.

and wrought ruffles, even down to linen rags.'[1] Prizes were offered for the best drawings of flowers, fruit, and foliage, and for patterns incorporating the Doric, Ionic, and Corinthian columns. These competitions ended in 1759, and the Select Society transferred its interests to other subjects, one of which was the Society for the English Language, to which reference has been made.

It was in 1760 that the teaching of drawing and painting was at last established in a settled way. The Board of Trustees for Manufactures and Fisheries in Scotland had been set up in 1727 to administer some of the moneys of 'the Equivalent'. The funds from this source were later supplemented from the sale of forfeited estates after the Rebellion of 1745 and, with this money at its disposal, the Board established in Edinburgh an Academy of Design.[2] The first master of what became known as the Trustees' Academy was William de la Cour. The course was intended principally for the training of tradesmen as house-painters and designers, but de la Cour also taught drawing and painting privately.[3] The public classes met on three days a week, from 3 to 7 pm. The fees were one guinea a quarter, except for certain students nominated by the Trustees as showing promise, but too poor to pay. The course was of four years' duration. On de la Cour's death in 1767, he was succeeded by another Frenchman, Charles Pavillon, from the Royal Academy of Paris.[4] He died in 1772, and his place was taken by Alexander Runciman, the friend of the poet, Robert Fergusson.[5] Runciman was primarily an artist, and seems to have been more interested in encouraging the art of painting than in training house-painters and designers. There were complaints that students were admitted who made 'drawing only an amusement'. When David Allan succeeded Runciman in 1786, the Trustees drafted new regulations for the conduct of the Academy.[6] It was to be open on three days a week from 4 to 6, and students presented by the Trustees, but not more than 20

[1] Brydall, *History of Art in Scotland*.
[2] *Book of the Old Edinburgh Club*, XXVII.
[3] *The Edinburgh Evening Courant*, 14 July 1764.
[4] *The Caledonian Mercury*, 22 March 1769.
[5] *ibid*, 9 Dec 1772.
[6] *ibid*, 11 Nov 1786.

in number, would be taught free for two years. The object of the instruction was to be the improvement of taste, and students were to be admitted only if they followed or intended to follow the trades of ornamental manufacturer, house decorator, and furniture manufacturer, or if they meant to become designers for these trades. Instruction in drawing and painting, we may conclude, was given for the most part in private classes.[1] When Allan died in 1796, there was trouble for the Trustees, for the man they selected to succeed him, John Wood, had, it was alleged, submitted another's work as his own. Edward Graham, the rival candidate for the post, opened a private academy in which his pupils were six coach-painters, three engravers, and three boys who wished to become artists. One of these three was destined to become famous as Sir David Wilkie. Edward Graham appears to have been a good teacher, and there was satisfaction when Wood was dismissed in 1800 and Graham succeeded him as master of the Trustees' Academy.[2]

There were other artists who conducted private classes. Francis Laime offered to teach the art of drawing to ladies, gentlemen, 'and such youths as are inclined'.[3] An architect, Robert Robinson, gave lectures on the principles of perspective, 'more especially as regards the art of design relating to building and planting'.[4] He may have had in mind 'improving lairds,' and landscape gardening. George Walker was an artist whose classes Walter Scott attended, and of whom he wrote: 'I took lessons from Walker whom we used to call *Blue Beard*. He was one of the most conceited persons in the world, but a good teacher; one of the ugliest countenances he had that need be exhibited—enough, as we say, to *spean weans*. The man was always extremely precise in the quality of every thing about him; his dress, accommodations, and everything else.'[5] From his advertisements it appears that Walker charged one guinea a month for private tuition, or one guinea a quarter for his public class.[6] Scott also mentions attending the classes in oil-painting

---

[1] *The Caledonian Mercury*, 12 Nov 1789.
[2] *Book of the Old Edinburgh Club*, XXVII.
[3] *The Edinburgh Evening Courant*, 8 June 1756.
[4] *The Caledonian Mercury*, 15 Feb 1757.
[5] Lockhart, *Life of Scott*.
[6] *The Edinburgh Evening Courant*, 17 Feb 1781.

of a Mr Burrell; characteristically, though he admits he had little skill in drawing, and so could not learn much from Mr Burrell, yet he managed to get from Burrell, a Prussian, 'many a long story of the battles of Frederick, in whose armies his father had been a commissary, or perhaps a spy!'

BOARDING SCHOOLS FOR GIRLS

That Edinburgh was a centre to which young ladies were sent from different parts of Scotland for their education is known from a few references in literature, and from some scraps of information from lawyers' papers and family letters, as well as from contemporary newspapers.

The account for board and tuition for a thirteen-year-old girl at an Edinburgh boarding school in 1700 has fortunately been preserved.[1] The girl was Margaret Rose, daughter of Hugh Rose of Kilravock, and the mistress of the boarding school was Elisabeth Stratoun. Margaret had dancing, singing, playing the virginals, writing, fine sewing and embroidery, a course which appears to be typical of that given to girls of the upper classes. She had already learned to read, and Mrs Stratoun's was a 'finishing' school.

Lockhart recorded some information about the education of Sir Walter Scott's mother, the daughter of a Professor of Medicine. She attended the school of Mrs Euphemia Sinclair. "'She had received,' he says, 'as became the daughter of an eminently learned physician, the best sort of education then bestowed on young gentlewomen in Scotland.' The poet, speaking of Mrs Euphemia Sinclair, the mistress of the school at which his mother was reared, to the ingenious local antiquary, Mr Robert Chambers, said that 'she must have been possessed of uncommon talents for education, as all her young ladies were, in after life, fond of reading, wrote and spelled admirably, were well acquainted with history and the belles lettres, without neglecting the more homely duties of the needle and accompt book; and perfectly well bred in society'. Mr Chambers adds, 'Sir W further communicated that his mother, and many others of Mrs Sinclair's pupils, were sent afterwards *to be finished off* by the

[1] W Croft Dickinson and Gordon Donaldson, *A Source Book of Scottish History*, Vol III, p 407.

Honourable Mrs Ogilvie, a lady who trained her young friends to a style of manners which would now be considered intolerably stiff. Such was the effect of this early training upon the mind of Mrs Scott, that even when she approached her eightieth year, she took as much care to avoid touching her chair with her back, as if she had still been under the stern eye of Mrs Ogilvie.'" In his *Traditions of Edinburgh*, Chambers adds a little information about Mrs Sinclair. She was the granddaughter of Sir Robert Sinclair, Bart, of Longformacus, and had many pupils drawn from the nobility, including 'the beautiful Miss Duff', who became Countess of Dumfries and Stair, and the Misses Hume of Linthill. The Hon Mrs Ogilvie was wife of the Hon Patrick Ogilvie, of Longmay and Inchmartin, younger brother of the Earl of Findlater.

Mrs Sinclair's advertisement in 1752 is modest: 'Mrs Eupham Sinclair having given up the millinery business at Whitsunday last, still continues to board young ladies, and has for that purpose a good, well air'd house, in Swinton's Land, Middle of Forrester's Wynd, where she can conveniently lodge six or eight boarders, which is the utmost number she designs to take. They may be taught any sort of needlework, white or coloured, mending, joining, or dressing laces, clear starching etc.'[1]

Advertisements for boarding schools for girls appear in the Edinburgh papers throughout the eighteenth century, and, while the evidence of the numbers of such advertisements does not prove anything, it is at least a pointer to the popularity of this type of school. Before 1750 there are only four advertisements for these schools; between 1751 and 1760, seventeen; between 1761 and 1770, nineteen; and between 1771 and 1780, fifteen. These figures suggest that the numbers of private schools increased after the mid-century, when the city itself was growing in size and prosperity. The subjects mentioned in these advertisements are of some interest. Of 68 schools which give details, no fewer than 42 mentioned specifically needlework or millinery or fancy work in lace, or gum flowers. Nineteen schools professed French, in 11 of which either the proprietor or an assistant was French or had lived in France.

[1] *The Caledonian Mercury*, 2 July 1752.

(Some may have been the daughters of exiled Jacobites. A Miss Barclay said in 1784 that she had been educated in France from infancy, and a Mrs Johnstone said in 1766 that she had been nine years in France.) Only 8 schools mentioned cookery as a subject of instruction, and of these 5 were purely cookery or pastry schools. English, writing, and arithmetic are sometimes mentioned, but so seldom as to suggest that the boarding schools were intended for girls who could already read and write. Book-keeping appears three times, drawing four times, geography four times, music nine times, and dancing three times. A considerable number of the schools say no more than 'Masters will call in all subjects'.

The boarding schools accommodated relatively small numbers. Mrs Sinclair had room, as we have seen, for six or eight. The Misses Wightman, who advertised in 1748, took 14 boarders in their house in Bailie Fyfe's Close. Mrs Tremamondo in 1763 took eight. Mrs Benevent in 1784 restricted her numbers to six. Mrs Hamilton, who had moved in 1782 from Chessel's Court to a larger house in Argyle Square, says she had twelve rooms, but that her classes were kept small. She adds, rather severely: 'As education is the only object she has in view, she takes charge of no young ladies who come to town for public amusement.'

The fees for boarding show an increase as the century wears on. In 1748, they are at £5 a quarter, and remain on an average at about that figure until 1761. Thereafter they range between £7 and £11 a quarter. The Misses Lythgoe in 1779 charged for girls under 14 £22 a year for board, and for those over 14 £28 a year. Day boarders in this school were charged £14 a year. For these sums the Misses Lythgoe gave instruction in all kinds of needlework, writing, arithmetic, music, and French, and Miss Jean Lythgoe accompanied her pupils to dancing schools.

The teachers in the boarding schools were sometimes the wives of private schoolmasters, like Mrs Mitchell of Covenant Close, whose husband taught French to his wife's young ladies, but in his advertisement is careful to point out that his class for gentlemen was kept separate.[1] Mrs Le Picq, who ran a boarding

[1] *The Caledonian Mercury*, 3 June 1761.

school from 1762 onwards, was the wife of a popular teacher of dancing. A considerable number of the mistresses of boarding schools were widows, and if they could claim a noble or other respectable connection, so much the better. Mrs Boston of Mint Close was a minister's widow, and was assisted by her daughters. Mrs Campbell was the widow of a Customs Collector. Some were Frenchwomen or Italians, and a few were ex-governesses.

The most popular subject of the usual curriculum was needlework. The Misses Wightman—they generally refer to themselves in advertisements as 'the two Swedish Mistress Wightmans'—who received both boarders and day girls, professed in 1749, 'all manner of coloured work, such as Fire-screens, China Stitch, Sattin stitch; the colours shaded according to nature, likewise embroidery in gold and silver, true Dresden work, with Italian vests done upon cambricks; as also white seam, drawing, washing, dressing, pletting and washing coloured work; such of my boarders that inclines, may be taught to work watch and cane strings, straps for ladies' jumps with gold and silver, silk fringes for ladies' cloaks or capuchines, hacking beds etc.'. Examples of the embroidery that produced fire screens, and of the Tonder (or Dresden) needlework on muslin, done by ladies of the time, may be seen in the Royal Scottish Museum. More elaborate decorative work was taught by Mrs Gibson, who advertised in 1758 'flower painting after the Indian and English taste, japanning (ie lacquer work), shell flowers, gum flowers, enamelled flowers, and silver flowers. She also mentions 'sea-weed properly prepared for pictures'. Mrs Mitchell, in 1756, also mentions shell work, and 'filligram' work, which is understood to be filigree work with coiled paper. Lace work and the joining and mending of lace figure frequently. Sometimes a resident assistant, called a 'doctrix', taught reading, writing, or French. Visiting masters attended for music, French, writing, and dancing. In 1777, Mrs Hamilton in Chessel's Buildings in the Canongate had a resident mistress to teach French 'practically and grammatically', and a visiting master for French as well. Mrs Hamilton herself undertook music, and there was a resident governess for needlework and millinery.

There is an account of the life of a young lady at one of the
Edinburgh boarding schools that gives not only some idea of the
school, but a hint of the social life that attending these schools
often involved. It is from an article, 'Eighteenth Century
Scotland: Some Gleanings from Family Papers', by M J C
Meiklejohn, and it appeared in the *Glasgow Herald* in 1929.[1]
The writer is talking of the school bill of a young lady at a girls'
school in Edinburgh from 14 February to 11 August 1788.

'She goes to the play house (tickets 3s each) on no fewer than
ten occasions; she hires a coach or sedan-chair (total 14s 7½d)
to be carried to those dancing parties, for which "To 3 Month
Dancing £1 10s" (the fiddler being charged extra at 1s) had no
doubt prepared her. She goes riding or takes riding-lessons
(if an entry "To Horsemanship" 1s means that), and this enterprising young woman is even permitted by an indulgent schoolmistress to take "A Chaise for the race" at the cost of 4s.

'She wore a new "Printed Gown" (£1 8s) for the occasion and
a blue sash (4s), and had her hair waved for 5d, which was the
price of 'rollers for the hair'. That hair was also elaborately
dressed on a high-pitched frame of 'Catgut and wire' for which
a charge occurs twice in the bill, and the whole was finished off
by a "Black Mode Cloak" at 2½ guineas. The daughter of a
distinguished Forfarshire family, it was incumbent on her to go
smart on all public occasions, and accordingly there are items
on her bill for "Mussline for a breast ruffel", numbers of pairs
of gloves, "7½ yards Checkt Mussline for a gown" (£1 13s 6d),
three feathers and a dress-hat (6s 6d each), many yards of ribbon
and several pairs of stays at 21s a pair. Once an aunt came
through to Edinburgh to visit her niece—somewhat dowdy and
had to be smartened up, as the entry "Mussline for her Aunt's
frills 6s" seems to indicate.

'Nor was the culture of her mind neglected. She studied
"writing and counting" for two quarters for 30s; 35s worth of
French was acquired (or so one hopes); geography cost £1 2s 9d;
and there was "2 months music Mr Corri", at £3 3s 0d: also

---

[1] 21 Sept 1929. I have tried to trace the original papers, but though I have
had kind assistance of the *Glasgow Herald*, and generous help from Mr A N
Bartholomew of Meiklejohn and Sons, Publishers, I have failed. It is possible that the original papers were destroyed in an air-raid on London.

she played the guitar, for its strings cost half a crown. Board and washing for the period came to £15, and the total bill amounted to £47 3s 9d, which included an item of "Doctor's Accompts, £2 16s 8d"—possibly the lamentable result of too much gaiety . . . or of the injudicious spending of 17s charged as pocket-money.'

DAY SCHOOLS FOR GIRLS

Some of the boarding schools for girls took day-boarders, but there were also day schools providing a range of classes for young ladies from reading and writing to cookery, languages, music, and dancing. For example, Peggy Young of Castleyards in Orkney came in 1749 to live at the house of James Steuart, an Edinburgh lawyer, while she attended the schools, and Steuart's correspondence with her father has been preserved. He writes: 'You may believe my wife and I will spare no trouble in making her a compleat woman, and as easie to you as possible.' They sent her first to the writing, dancing, and singing schools. In the following year, however, Steuart writes that Peggy "is improving herself as fast as possible at the singing, pastry, and sewing, which is all the schools my wife thinks she need attend'.[1]

The cookery schools were popular, and fortunately we can discover a little about them from textbooks written by well-known teachers. *A New and Easy Method of Cookery*, by Elizabeth Cleland, was intended for the benefit 'of the young ladies who attend her school'. The second edition (1759) has the following chapter headings, illustrating how comprehensive Mrs Cleland's course must have been:

1 Of Gravies, Soups, Broths, etc.
2 Of fish and their sauces.
3 Of potting and making hams.
4 Of pyes, pasties, etc.
5 Of pickling and preserving.
6 Of made wines, distilling, and brewing.

The appendix gives 'fifty-three new and useful receipts, and directions for carving'.

[1] Steuart in *Viking Society for Northern Research*. London, 1913.

Another well-known teacher was Mrs McIver, who taught first in Peebles Wynd and later (1779 to 1786) in Stevenlaw's Close. For 15s a quarter Mrs McIver taught cookery, preserving, and pickling. In her earlier and possibly less profitable days in Peebles Wynd, she sold preserved cherries and raspberries, and also 'plumb-cake.' The fourth edition of her book, *Cookery and Pastry*, is in the British Museum, and contains a number of what appear to be distinctively Scottish recipes. There is one, 'To make parton pies', and one, 'To dress a sea-cat', which begins, 'Wash it very clean and skin it; turn the tail into the mouth'. There is also a recipe for 'A good Scots Haggies'. The British Museum copy has many manuscript additions, like 'Admiral Elliot's recipe for preserving salt beef always used at Wilton Lodge', and 'A Common Dram', which runs as follows: 'To one gallon of whisky put one dozen of lemons and sweeten it to your taste. Put on some of the whisky on the parings of the lemons and let it stand one day. Then add it to the rest, letting it stand a few days in a barrel till clear. Then bottle it for use.'

Private teachers in all the usual subjects were in attendance at day and boarding schools. It has been shown that there were many such teachers in Edinburgh, covering a great variety of subjects. Girls with special interests could find suitable teachers: not all were as fortunate or as learned as Agnes Steuart of Goodtrees, who studied mathematics under Professor Maclaurin. She married the 10th Earl of Buchan in 1739, and became the mother of Henry and Thomas Erskine.[1] Cookery, needlework, dancing, music, and perhaps a little French were the subjects that attracted most; since they probably looked forward to marriage and the management of a house, such a training was a practical one.

HANDICAPPED CHILDREN

Edinburgh had the first school in the United Kingdom for the teaching of deaf and dumb children. This was Mr Braidwood's school, which was visited by Johnson and Boswell in 1773.

---

[1] *Letters and Journals of Mrs Calderwood of Polton*. Ed Ferguson, Edinburgh, 1884.

Thomas Braidwood (1715-1806) began his school in Edinburgh in 1764 with one pupil, a boy of 13 who had lost his hearing at the age of 3, called Charles Sherriff, son of Alexander Sherriff of Craigleith. According to Braidwood's advertisement, this boy 'reads any English book distinctly, and understands both the meaning and the grammatical construction of the passages which he reads. He answers the questions put to him with great readiness, and his manner of pronouncing is articulate and distinct. He understands what is spoken by persons with whom he is familiar (and even by anyone that speaks distinct and slow), from the motion of their lips. Strangers also propose questions to him by writing with their fingers on a table and, as he can follow the most rapid motion of that sort, there is little difficulty in holding conversation with him. He writes with elegance, is thoroughly master of arithmetic, book-keeping, and geography etc.'[1]

Arnot says that Braidwood had a number of pupils by 1779, mostly from England, but some from America.[2] The article on Braidwood in the *Dictionary of National Biography* states that he had about 20 pupils in 1783. His school was then in Craigside House (now 93 and 95 Dumbiedykes Road), and no doubt it gave its name to Dumbiedykes and the laird immortalised in *The Heart of Midlothian*.[3] Braidwood moved to London in 1783, where he died in 1806.

His method was to begin by teaching the deaf to use the vocal organs, the writing of letters, and the composing of words. 'He next shows them the use of words in expressing visible objects, and their qualities. After this he proceeds to instruct them in the proper arrangement of words, or grammatical construction of language.' He liked to have pupils in his charge for from three to six years, and taught them the sign language and lip-reading.[4] The *DNB* article says that 'His only mechanical appliance was a small silver rod, about the size of a tobacco pipe, flattened at one end, and having a bulb at the other.' This he used to place the pupil's tongue in the right position.

---

[1] *The Edinburgh Evening Courant*, 12 March 1766.
[2] Arnot, *History of Edinburgh*.
[3] Edinburgh Room, Edinburgh Public Library.   Notes by Mr C Boog-Watson.
[4] Arnot, *History of Edinburgh*.

We are fortunate in having records by both Johnson and Bos-well of their visit to Braidwood's school. Johnson writes as follows:

'There is one subject of philosophical curiosity to be found in Edinburgh, which no other city has to shew; a college of the deaf and dumb, who are taught to speak, to read, to write, and to practice arithmetick, by a gentleman, whose name is Braidwood. The number which attends him is, I think, about twelve, which he brings together into a little school, and instructs according to their several degrees of proficiency. . . .

'This school I visited, and found some of the scholars waiting for their master, whom they are said to receive at his entrance with smiling countenances and sparkling eyes, delighted with the hope of new ideas. One of the young Ladies had her slate before her, on which I wrote a question consisting of three figures, to be multiplied by two figures. She looked upon it, and quivering her fingers in a manner which I thought very pretty, but of which I know not whether it was art or play, multiplied the sum regularly in two lines, observing the decimal place; but did not add the two lines together, probably disdaining so easy an operation. I pointed at the place where the sum total should stand, and she noted it with such expedition as seemed to shew that she had it only to write.

'It was pleasing to see one of the most desperate of human calamities capable of so much help: whatever enlarges hope, will exalt courage; after having seen the deaf taught arithmetick, who would be afraid to cultivate the Hebrides?'

Boswell adds a characteristic story: 'Dr Johnson has given liberal praise to Mr Braidwood's academy for the deaf and dumb. When he visited it, a circumstance occurred which was truly characteristical of our great Lexicographer. "Pray," (said he) "can they pronounce any *long* words?' Mr Braidwood informed him they could. Upon which Dr Johnson wrote one of his *sesquipedalia verba*, which was pronounced by the scholars, and he was satisfied.—My readers may perhaps wish to know what the word was; but I cannot gratify their curiosity. Mr Braid-wood told me, it remained long in his school, but it had been lost before I made my inquiry.'

In 1773, the governors of Heriot's Hospital had accepted to

the foundation a boy who was deaf and dumb. A committee of the Governors decided that it would not be wise to admit this boy to residence, and agreed to an 'outhouse' payment of £10 stg yearly to Mr Braidwood 'who has shown so extraordinary a skill in that way', and who had agreed to teach the boy to read and write gratis. The payment was to be made in lieu of board and lodging until the boy was bound apprentice.

After Braidwood's departure for London, John Johnston, a writing-master, advertised that he hoped to start classes for the deaf and dumb.[1] By 1790 these classes had begun in Richmond Place, and in 1799 his school, transferred to Reid's Court was described as an Academy for the dumb and defective in speech.[2]

Other private teachers professed to cure speech defects, like Mr Angier from London, who, in 1762, undertook to cure stuttering and stammering, 'speaking in the nose, lisping, a low, rough, hoarse, thick, mumbling, or squeaking voice'.[3] In 1789, Angier advertised with recommendations from Professor Cullen and Adam Smith.[4]

Cortes Telfair, who taught reading and writing and insisted that no 'Scotch' be spoken in his school, also offered to cure dumbness, stammering, and other impediments, but the teaching of the handicapped in speech was only incidental to his work.[5] A number of the lecturers and teachers who, as described already in this chapter, dealt with elocution, also professed to treat speech defects. The Rev Rest Knipe, for example, in 1784 taught pupils privately for these defects for one hour each evening, for 10s 6d a month.[6]

There is no mention of teaching the blind.

CONCLUSION

In this chapter only a few of the many private teachers of Edinburgh have been considered, but perhaps enough has been said to substantiate the claim that a great variety of subjects

[1] *The Caledonian Mercury*, 1 July 1786.
[2] *Edinburgh Directory*, 1799-1800.
[3] *The Caledonian Mercury*, 9 Oct 1762.
[4] *ibid*, 3 Aug and 2 Nov 1789.
[5] *The Edinburgh Evening Courant*, 16 Oct 1773.
[6] *The Caledonian Mercury*, 13 Nov 1784.

was available for those who could pay for instruction. There were many other lecturers and teachers, some associated with or attracted by the College. It is not surprising, for example, that Edinburgh should encourage lectures on Experimental Science, for the College was one of the foremost centres of scientific training in the world. There were lectures by Dr Buchan on 'Experimental Philosophy and Astronomy', whose aim was 'to impress the mind with the proper ideas of the great Creator and his works; to explain the nature of the Mechanical Powers, and to illustrate their use by a variety of working models ... in fine, to make philosophy an useful instead of a speculative science is the design of these lectures'.[1] Buchan had been left the apparatus of Mr James Ferguson, 'the most complete ever known in these parts'.

There were other and less serious subjects, such as dancing. Goldsmith and Cockburn have testified in well-known passages to the popularity of dancing in Edinburgh, and Topham went so far as to say that there were more dancing masters in Edinburgh than in any other city, having regard to its population.[2] It required a good deal of instruction to take a confident part in the formal dances described by these writers, and in the article on 'Social Assemblies of the Eighteenth Century' in the Old Edinburgh Club series.[3] There were native teachers like Downie, Macqueen, Strange, Barnard, and Martin, and foreigners like Signora Volanti, Charles Le Picq, and Monsieur D'Egville.

In the advertisement columns of the Edinburgh newspapers the only references, as far as can be found, to sport or games are to fencing. There was, for example, the fencing school run by Harry Fergusson, brother of the poet. His modest advertisement is as follows: 'Mr Fergusson continues to teach the art of the small sword for the ensuing season at his hall in Warriston's Close. He expects therefore that the gentlemen belonging to the town and University will encourage his undertaking; and in particular that those who are already acquainted with the principles of this art will continue to practise them.

---

[1] *The Caledonian Mercury*, 16 May 1778.
[2] Topham, *Letters from Edinburgh* 1774-75.
[3] *Book of the Old Edinburgh Club*, XIX.

As to his own abilities, it would be improper to say anything concerning them in this place: he chooses rather to submit to the judgment of the impartial spectators.'[1]   A better-known instructor was Francis Picard, who taught fencing in Don's Close, Luckenbooths, from 1753 to 1769.[2]

[1] *The Edinburgh Evening Courant*, 25 Nov 1767.
[2] *ibid*, 19 Nov 1753; *The Caledonian Mercury*, 30 Sept 1769.

Chapter VI

TEXTBOOKS

SINCE Edinburgh was in the eighteenth century the largest city in Scotland and also a centre of the printing trade, it is natural that many schoolbooks were published there, and that many of them were by Edinburgh teachers. The publication of schoolbooks was frequently advertised in the Edinburgh newspapers, and it has been possible to trace some of them. Many have not been found at all, but this is not surprising, for such books have always been 'expendable'. Not all of the books were written by teachers, but most of them were, and the authors who were not themselves schoolmasters were usually, like Thomas Ruddiman, men closely connected with the profession.[1] The textbooks are of value to the student of educational history as indicating the kind of instruction common at the time, but they must be studied with some caution and perhaps not always taken at their face value. Some authors were in advance of their fellows, and their ideas were therefore not typical. It is possible only to guess at what was typical, for no reliable information exists as to the popularity and circulations of the various books. All that can be claimed, indeed, is that while most textbooks may not be entirely reliable as guides to school conditions, at least they provide an interesting indication of general tendencies. More can be claimed for such well-known books as Ruddiman's and Adam's Grammars, which take their place in the development of educational method.

Some well-defined trends can be discerned. Many of the books to be described in this chapter are concerned much with facts—'dry facts, like biscuits'—lists of words for spelling and pronunciation, vocabulary lists in Latin and other languages, arithmetical tables, and grammatical rules. Yet though, throughout the century, the emphasis is on instruction and the imparting

---

[1] He was in constant demand as a 'visitor' or inspector of schools.

of facts, there is perceptible also a considerable change in method. The texts of the early years of the century made few, if any, concessions to their readers' youth; those at the end of the period show at least some attempt to suit the tastes of children, though still rather serious and moralising for our later times.

A complete study of all the textbooks produced by Edinburgh teachers at this time is probably now impossible. Schoolbooks are seldom preserved even in libraries, and it is often only chance that has led to their survival. Edinburgh is fortunate in having a fair number of such books in the National Library of Scotland, the Edinburgh Public Library, and the Grindlay Collection in The Royal High School. The David Murray Collection in the University of Glasgow includes a large number of schoolbooks. Of a number of books mentioned in the advertisement columns of the Edinburgh newspapers, copies are only to be found in the British Museum. The scope of this study is therefore limited primarily by the availability of material. It is further restricted in that it is concerned only with schoolbooks. A wider knowledge of children's lives, tastes, and manners in the eighteenth century may be acquired from such interesting books as Adam Petrie's *Rules of Good Deportment*,[1] or from the many children's story-books that appeared after the success of John Newbery's famous little books. No account is taken here of books on subjects of primarily adult interest, such as books on cookery, or fencing, or textbooks of university standard. A few of the textbooks written by Edinburgh schoolmasters and known to have been used in Edinburgh schools in the eighteenth century are selected for consideration. It is hoped that the details of subject-matter, approach, and method that can be elicited will help to give some impression of what schools in those days were like.

LEARNING TO READ

One of the earliest textbooks on reading published in Edinburgh was that of James Porterfield of 1706. The title gives some indication of its purpose: *Edinburgh's English School-*

[1] Published in Edinburgh, 1720. Copy in British Museum.

master, or Magnum in Parvo, Containing in few Lessons an Easy Way to Spell, or Read either Latin or English, Examined and Approved by the Colleges of Edinburgh and Glasgow. . . . By James Porterfield. Edinburgh. Printed for the Author and sold by him, on the North side of the High Street a little above the Weigh house.[1] An advertisement tells Porterfield's intentions: 'Any person of quality, or others desirous to have their children taught to read Latin being altogether ignorant of their mother tongue, and being six years old, may be taught in James Porterfield's School, a little above the weigh-house, on the North of the High Street, in eight or nine months time, provided they be of ordinary capacity; also those of my own scholars, having the true English pronunciation may be forthwith taught in six weeks, or two months at most, to read Latin without any hesitation.' A testimonial at the end of the book says that Porterfield had taught for many years with success in Glasgow 'by laying down in a new way, solid grounds for reading, and distinct dividing of words by syllables, which is of no small use'. The book begins with lists of the vowels and syllables, which were to be learned by heart and then tested by what are called 'Proof passages', containing arrangements of letters like 'Cr, fm, eth, live, gift, fp, dw, wr'. The idea was to teach simple words and parts of larger words, and then to proceed to more difficult words, including Biblical names. The method was that of rote-learning, but it includes an analytical approach to language, the method of syllabication, which was developed as the century wore on.[2] Among the books listed by James Watson, the Edinburgh publisher, is one of 1709 which mentions the same method of syllabication. It is *The Child's Tutor; or The Shorter Catechism, . . . having before it all the words thereof, ranked in the most convenient order, as to the accent, sound of the vowels, and division of syllables, for the benefit of young children, and direction of such as are commonly entrusted with their educa-*

---

[1] The edition examined is the third, of 1711. The copy is in the British Museum.

[2] For more about Porterfield, who was licensed by the Town Council in 1694, see page 34. He wrote a poem, *'God's Judgements against Sin; or a relation of three dreadful fires happening in the city of Edinburgh. . . .* Printed by James Watson, MDCCII'. This commemorated fires in the Canongate, Parliament Close, and 'Land Mercat'. It is verse full of religious wrath.

tion. This was probably a reprint of a book published in England, and no copy has been found.[1] It reminds us, however, that the Shorter Catechism and the Bible were common texts in the schools.

The Shorter Catechism was an important feature of the daily training of young children. The edition of *The A.B.C. or a Catechisme for Yong Children*, which was published in 1644, was authorised by the Church of Scotland and 'to be learned in all Families and Lector Schooles . . .'. This little volume includes the ABC in capitals, lower-case, and gothic type, with illustrations of vowels and consonants like 'ab, eb, ib, ob, ub'. Then follow the Shorter Catechism and some prayers and graces. The volume published by Freebairn in 1708 follows the same pattern, but adds the numbers up to a thousand in letters and figures, arabic and Roman. Editions like these were commonly sold in the eighteenth century, and many are to be found in libraries.[2]

In 1753, appeared *A Spelling Book . . . by John Warden, Teacher of English in Edinburgh.* The fact that he called it a spelling book, when it was really a primer in reading, indicates that Warden's approach to reading, like that of all the authors of textbooks on the subject in his time, was through spelling. In the preface he stipulates an orderly learning of sounds and spelling, for the meaning is, according to him, of no importance at the early stage. He begins with the alphabet, and then discusses vowels and consonants, tied letters (eg st), and exercises on syllables, diphthongs, unsounded letters, terminations, and the silent -e. There are lists of words to be learned, some of them curious; those on tied letters, for example, including the following: philo, azimuth, ishtaroth, affix, phasis. Then come tables of words grouped according to their pronunciation; for example a table 'wherein two vowels commonly a diphthong, are divided', including, 'Ain, dial, laish, proem, Alpheus, being, dier, lais, rhea, ambient, bier, lea, real, ammiel'. The author states that he disapproved of the common practice of teaching

---

[1] Information from the notes by G P Johnston on James Watson, in the records of the Edinburgh Bibliographical Society.

[2] There are some very good examples in the Murray Collection in Glasgow University Library.

reading from the Bible, and recommends rather lists of words of the kind quoted. One cannot help feeling that he made the process of learning unnecessarily difficult.[1]

The career of Arthur Masson has already been outlined. His first publication was *A Spelling Book*, which probably appeared before 1757.[2] The preface contains criticism of the so-called 'new method' of teaching a child to read. According to Masson, this method had been made to appear by some of its advocates to be a kind of hidden mystery. For his own part this true son of Aberdeen knows 'no better recipe for teaching a child to read than that of indefatigable industry and diligence'. 'The foundation of all reading is the thorough knowledge of the letters'. At first, there need be no book at all: he himself had used four small cubes with success, with the six vowels pasted on the sides of one, and the consonants on the other three. Then he 'made the child throw the cube of the vowels, till he should cast up an *a*, *i*, or *o* etc, and so with the consonants. When he hits on the letter proposed, he draws the stake, which may be whatever the teacher shall judge proper.'[3] The method can also be used for syllables, and possibly also for words, but, 'with greater success in private families than in a public school'. Masson's spelling book follows the general lines of Warden's in proceeding from letters to syllables, and then to one-syllable, two-syllable, and multi-syllable words. He recommends that the teacher should read aloud to his pupils and make them watch the stops and pauses. 'In order to make the scholars more attentive to these directions, it may be proper, at first to use the method of beating time as is practised in music. This may be done by knocking on the table as many times as the stop requires. If the stop be a comma, you are to give one knock; if it be a semi-colon you give two knocks; at a colon you give three; and at a full point or period you give four.' There

[1] Copy in National Library of Scotland. This bears the name 'Lady Betty Carnagy, 1756'.

[2] The second edition was advertised in 1757, and a copy of the third edition, dated 1761, is in the British Museum.

[3] Masson's method recalls John Newbery's charming *Little Lottery Book* (1768), in which the learners had to learn their letters by pricking pictures with a pin. Newbery's earlier works (some appeared about 1752) no doubt influenced the authors of spelling books.

In the Museum of Childhood, Edinburgh, there is a box of wooden blocks used by the Ruddiman children for learning their letters.

is an interesting reference to what he calls 'recent innovations' in spelling, like the use of *Honor* and *Favor* instead of *Honour* and *Favour*. Masson approved of the new forms as omitting silent letters, but rejected the reason put forward for the change, the returning to the Latin originals; he felt that the traditional spelling derived not from Latin but French.

Another who taught reading by the fashionable method of syllabication was John Drummond, who in 1767 brought out *An Introduction to the Modern Pronunciation of the English Tongue*.[1] Though he claims not to believe in elaborate syllabication, but rather in teaching and practising the vowels and consonants, Drummond follows much the same lines as Masson. One of his early exercises is a list of nonsense words like the following: 'lamenirovuzy, fusebedigo, cukyqu, patehux, ojuchyshaphethowhy'. Presumably the pupils spelt out these words aloud to practise letter recognition. He deals at some length with what he terms the 'powers' of the various vowels. For example, the vowel 'a' has three powers, as in *same*, as in *man*, and as in *fall*. These he numbers 1, 2, and 3, and the lists of practice words have the numbers corresponding to their powers marked above them. The practice is similar to that of some modern dictionaries. The lists of words are graded according to difficulty, and the last list includes *corpulency*, *sacerdotal*, *circumambient*, *interjacent*, and at least one word that it is surprising to find in a school book—*whore*. Drummond's book does not stop at lists of words, but proceeds to simple stories and fables, and a long section on behaviour at home, in the streets, in public appearances, and at school. Similar advice appears in Telfer's *Spelling Book*, and possibly both may be copied from an earlier source so far not traced. The section on 'Of Behaviour at School' is worth quoting as a fair enough description of what a schoolmaster thought the conduct of his pupils ought to be:

1. Behave to your teachers with humility, and to your schoolfellows with respect.
2. Do not run into the school, but advance decently and slowly to the door.

[1] Copy in the British Museum.

3. Make your bow or curtsey, when you enter, and walk straight to your seat.

4. Never talk in the school, for it interrupts yourself and others.

5. If a stranger comes in, rise and bow, or curtsey as he passes by you: but after that keep your eyes upon your book, not regarding that any is present.

6. If you have anything to say to the master, wait till he is at leisure, and then speak with modesty and plainness.

7. Observe nothing at school but your book, and never neglect that.

8. Never quarrel at school, for it shows idleness and a bad temper.

9. When the master speaks to you, rise up to hear him, and look him in the face as he speaks, with modesty and attention.

10. Begin not to answer before he has done speaking, and then bow to him respectfully, and answer with humility.

11. If you have occasion to complain of a schoolfellow, first speak to him softly, and desire him to desist.

12. If he will not, then rise up and wait an opportunity; and when the master's or usher's eye is upon you, bow and say softly, and in a few words, what your complaint is.

13. Never speak loud in school: answer a question moderately; repeat your lesson distinctly; and on no other occasion speak at all.

14. When a stranger is in school, do not stare at him.

15. If he speaks to the master or usher, governess or teacher, do not listen to it, for it is ill manners, and shews you neglect your own business to mind others.

16. If he speaks to you, rise and hear him.

17. When he has done speaking, bow and make a short and modest answer, and let your looks and gesture show respect.

18. When the school hours are over, go out, as you came in, quietly, softly, and decently.

19. Never run or crowd to get at the door, for it will be free for you in a few minutes waiting.

20. When out of the school, go home without hurry and without delay; do not run, nor do not loiter; but do this, as all things else, with discretion.

21. Do not speak at home, or elsewhere, of what has been done in school; for nothing that passes there should be told out.'

The first of the rules for behaviour at meals is worth quoting as being typical of the tone of the whole: 'Nothing shows the difference between a young gentleman and a vulgar boy so much as the behaviour in eating.'

Another Edinburgh textbook on reading is *The Town and Country Spelling Book* by Cortes Telfair (or Telfer), published in 1775.[1] It is in four parts. Part I contains single words and sentences, words with more than one syllable being divided; Part II has single words and sentences with undivided syllables; Part III contains edifying and entertaining lessons; Part IV is a comprehensive view of the pronunciation of the best speakers in London, 'designed more particularly for the use of schools at a distance from London'. Telfer had come from London, and no doubt his textbook was intended to reinforce his advertisement that 'great care will be taken that no Scotch be spoken in time of school'. An interesting innovation is a page of illustrations, black and white cuts of pictures appropriate to the various sounds. 'A' and 'a' have beside them a drawing of an apple, and 'E' and 'e' have an egg. Some of the reading lessons are simplified versions of Bible stories. The syllabic method of teaching spelling and reading produced its problems, and many textbooks, like this one, contain lengthy attacks on other authors. Telfer disapproved of the method of teaching di-syllables favoured by John Drummond and others. They attached the consonant to the second syllable, as in *ne-ver*; Telfer felt it was more natural to say *nev-er*.

William Perry was another Englishman who entered the dispute about syllabication. In his first book, published while he was still in Kelso,[2] he provides a list of rules about the syllabication of words, including the following: 'A consonant between two vowels must be joined to the former to make the first syllable; eg bal-ance, ev-i-dent, ac-cip-ient.' One of the books he published in Edinburgh was *The only Sure Guide to the English Tongue; or new pronouncing Spelling Book*, of 1776. In the preface he discusses other spelling books, in particular the popular work of Dilworth, and the errors which he says are less to be wondered at in 'North British authors like Masson, the late Mr Drummond, etc, some of whom probably never

---

[1] Copy in the British Museum.
[2] *The Man of Business and Gentleman's Assistant*, 1774.

crossed the Tweed'.[1] Perry gives examples of Masson's mistakes in pronunciation. Masson gives the following groups of words as possessing the same vowel sound: *aunt, daunt, flaunt, slaunt*: *death, deaf, bear*: *sour, tour*: *wrought, drought*: *though, through, soul*. Referring to Masson and Drummond, Perry proceeds: 'I am ready to descend to the character of an Abecedarian and prove the truth of my declaration by engaging to teach a class of youth to read and spell in one third less time than the authors themselves, or an any teacher in England or Scotland, shall do for them by their spelling books.'

As a textbook, Perry's book is interesting. He groups one-syllabled words according to rhyme, and gives lists of diphthongs. There are reading lessons for words of one syllable, as; 'When you come to school be sure to mind your book, and sit still in your place and make no noise', and; 'Let not the time you are in school be spent in play and talk, but mind what is said to you; and when you come out, do not go with boys that will curse, swear, tell lies, and do all bad things'. The same method is followed for words with more syllables, the reading exercises preserving the same high moral tone. They include a translation of a fable by Master John Marjoribanks, aged 15, done after five weeks study of French under Mr Perry.

The little volume by Mr Lawrie which was intended for the guidance of the girls in the Merchant Maiden Hospital, contains advice to the older girls on how to teach reading.[2] Pupils, it says, 'should be taught to read not in a canting, whining strain, as some ignorant people usually read the Bible and other religious books, but in a sweet and agreeable manner'.

A common method of teaching spelling, pronunciation, and meaning of words was to use specially devised dictionaries. Perry produced one for schools, *The Royal Standard English Dictionary* (1775). In it he marked what he called 'flat and slowly accented syllables' with a grave accent, and 'sharp and quickly accented syllables' with an acute one. William Scott, another Edinburgh teacher, published *A New Spelling, Pro-*

---

[1] A little hard on Arthur Masson, who was at pains for many years to advertise his visits to London and Paris, where he was acquainted with Sheridan and Diderot.
[2] *The Merchant Maiden Magazine*, printed by W Darling, Edinburgh, 1779. Copy in Edinburgh Public Library.

nouncing, and Explanatory Dictionary of the English Language probably a little later.[1] Alexander Barrie published *A Spelling and Pronouncing Dictionary* in 1794. This is clearly the work of a practical teacher. He lists words ranging from those of one letter to those of eight or nine syllables. Each list is in alphabetical order, and there is a pronunciation key. Barrie recommends—and this is some indication how such books were used— that a daily task be set for the pupils' homework, to be spelt every morning 'till they have gone over the whole'. The longest words in this dictionary, and the last are: *contraregularibility*; *honorificabilitudinity*; *anthropomorphitanianismicaliation*. Other lists of words include homonyms and synonyms, proper names, occupations, post towns of Scotland, countries and capitals, and books of the Bible. The practice of using dictionaries for the teaching of reading is characteristic of the last quarter of the eighteenth century. It owed its popularity to the well-known dictionaries of Johnson, Walker, Sheridan, and others, and no doubt by an insistence on correct pronunciation and spelling did a great deal to standardise the English language.[2]

LEARNING TO WRITE

Writing books, especially copy-books, are of all school-books the most ephemeral, and it is not surprising that few of the eighteenth century writing books published in Edinburgh have survived. There is an advertisement for a writing book in 1708,[3] but no example of it has been found. There is, however, in the British Museum, another book of the same period: *Recta Scribendi Ratio: or a Method of Writing Well; Being an Introduction to the best Forms of Letters, with Copies of the Round Hand, By Ralph Morton Writing-Master, opposite to the Tron-Church, Edinburgh, Printed and sold by the Author and at the*

---

[1] I have not seen the first edition, but there is a copy of an improved and enlarged edition, dated 1798, in Edinburgh Public Library. The first edition was advertised in *The Caledonian Mercury* in 1786.

[2] Barrie's *Dictionary* was published in 1794.

[3] *The Edinburgh Evening Courant*, 1-3 Sept 1708: *The Scots Writing Master, or a new Coppy Book, containing round hand and Italian copies . . . by the deceased Mr John Thomson that famous writing master.*

Coffee-Houses.[1] The book begins with some pages in praise of the art of writing. The advertisement at the end of this passage gives some idea of the author's purpose and audience: 'All the clerks' hands, with arithmetic, vulgar and decimal, merchants' accounts, are taught by the author; and for expedition youth may be boarded. Such as have neglected their time, may be taught privately in the author's house, or at their own habitations.' In other words, Morton was meaning to train apprentices in commerce, and his book was not intended primarily for young children. These probably learned writing from horn books, or from samples written by their masters, like the one found in Heriot's Hospital in 1952, and now preserved there.

Morton gives rules for good writing. First he stresses the importance of firmness: 'So that the hand is most firm and durable whose characters are, in their several differences, performed by the full of the pen.' Next speed is mentioned, and particularly the lifting of the pen from the page: 'The taking of the pen, and the making of any letter, or in the joining of letters, makes the hand the slower.' But most space is devoted to 'Beauty'; regularity of letters and even spacing are emphasised.

Other writing masters who advertised writing books are Samuel McArthur and Robert Godskirk (who was writing master in Heriot's Hospital and in the High School), but no specimens have been found.[2] It is a pity that no specimens of the handwriting of John McLure have been found, especially the note, mentioned by Scott, that McLure kept under his shirt at the battle of Falkirk: 'This is the body of John McLure, writing master in Edinburgh; whoever finds the same is requested to give it a Christian burial.' 'The great hand-spoiler' of Cockburn's day, William Swanson, has left no memorial.

Edmund Butterworth, who was writing master to the High School in the latter part of the eighteenth and the early part of the nineteenth century, was the author of several beautiful books on writing, including one that was published in France.

---

[1] This may be the same book as was advertised in *The Edinburgh Evening Courant*, 13-16 May 1709: *Morton's Round Hand, a Copy Book. . . . By Robert Morton a London Penman.* To be sold at the Exchange Coffee House Price 1 Shil.'

[2] McArthur's book was advertised in *The Edinburgh Evening Courant* for 7 Sept 1756, and Donaldson the bookseller advertised a Copy book in 1760.

They display the attractions of plain and ornamental writing 'for the improvement of youth or amusement of the curious'. The last phrase is perhaps significant; handwriting had become mannered and elaborate, and more and more a pre-occupation of the precious.

Teachers of writing usually also taught 'accounts', and we find examples of writing in books on book-keeping, or compendious volumes like William Perry's *Man of Business*. Some of these books, like Lawrie's little book for the Merchant Maiden Hospital, contain instructions on how to 'make a pen'. Some books generally emphasise the importance of the speedy 'round hand' in business, reflecting in this the interest in developing commerce which is characteristic of Scotland in the eighteenth century.

MATHEMATICS AND ARITHMETIC

The most popular textbook in arithmetic at the beginning of the eighteenth century was the famous *Cocker's Arithmetic*, which, published in 1678, remained a standard text for at least a century, and we find it in the lists of Edinburgh booksellers as late as the 1770s. Three Edinburgh textbooks of the late seventeenth century indicate how the subject was regarded. First is Robert Colinson's *Idea Rationaria* or *The Perfect Accomptant*, Edinburgh 1680, which is really a textbook in simple accountancy, concerned in particular with the working of the Scots staple at Campveere. James Paterson's *Scots Arithmetician*, Edinburgh 1685, on the other hand, is an arithmetic of the type of Cocker, containing many examples like the familiar one of a cistern with two cocks A and B—'set open at once, all the water will run out in 3 hours, but the cock A alone being set open it will run out in 9 hours; I demand how long it shall be a running out, the cock B alone being set open'. The third is *A Book containing Tables for finding out the Exchange of Money and Annualrents* by Alexander Heriot, Teacher of Bookkeeping, Edinburgh 1697. The contents have largely to do with book-keeping. Arithmetic, book-keeping, accountancy, and mathematics with its other practical applications were taught often by the same people, and there was no fixed dividing line between the various branches.

In 1715 Alexander Macghie published *Principles of Book-keeping explain'd to which are annexed two setts of Books of Trade*, and a second edition appeared in 1718.[1] In 1718, Robert Lundin, also an Edinburgh teacher, brought out *The reason of accompting by Debtor and Creditor, with general rules for attaining to that way of accomting*[2] for the use of his school. The opening sentence is: 'The whole art of this way of accompting consists in a perfect knowledge of a book called the leger, whose name implies its use and design, viz by it any that accompts this way, may, at any time, at a view, without trouble, be informed into any, or all the circumstances of his business.' A description follows of how to keep a Ledger, Journal, Waste-book, and so on, with examples.

1718 was also the year of publication of Alexander Malcolm's *A New Treatise of Arithmetick and Book-keeping*,[3] dedicated to the Lord Provost and Magistrates of Edinburgh. There is a great deal of detail in this book, including the following table of Long Measure:

> 3 barleycorns = 1 inch
> 12 inches = 1 foot
> 3 foot or 16 nails = 1 yard
> 45 inches = 1 ell English

This is a book for apprentices and adults. Malcolm says that he felt it was wrong that many men who 'have a great practice in numbers, should be forced to work like machines and be able to give no reason for what they do'. He had in mind not only tradesmen, but landowners, stewards, and factors. The chapter headings are sometimes curiously modern, like 'Mind the following Practical Notes'.[4] Malcolm demonstrated Long Division and Long Multiplication, and treated decimals. (As D K Wilson points out in his *History of Mathematical Teaching*

[1] Watson's list, ed G P Johnston. Edin Bibl Soc.
[2] No copy seen, but one is described in D Murray, *History of Book-keeping and Accountancy*.
[3] Copy in Aberdeen University Library.
[4] Malcolm moved to Aberdeen, where he published a *Treatise of Musick* in 1721, and *A New System of Arithmetick* in 1730.

in Scotland, the old method of Long Division, in which division was carried out by a sort of continued subtraction, was still commonly taught and practised as late as 1756.)[1]

John Wilson's *Introduction to Arithmetic*,[2] published in 1741, is a practical and interesting book, with special references to the use of arithmetic by masons and carpenters. To the student of education, the book is surprisingly modern in that it recommends what is practically the modern method of teaching subtraction by 'equal addition'. Some of the tables are even more frightening than those given by Malcolm, for in addition to English ells, there are Scotch ells, and even Flemish ells.

John Wright's *Elements of Trigonometry*, published in 1724, is a more advanced book, intended not only for those interested in the practical applications of trigonometry to navigation, but also those concerned with the theory of mathematics.[3]

Two books on book-keeping of about this period are William Hamilton's *A Compendious Method of Book-keeping*, of 1740,[4] and William Stevenson's *Book-keeping by Double Entry*, of 1764.[5]

Alexander Ewing published a number of books including *Institutes of Arithmetic* in 1756, and *A Synopsis of Practical Mathematics* in 1779.[6] In the preface to his book on arithmetic, Ewing claims that, following his methods, boys can learn arithmetic in two-thirds of the time previously devoted to the subject.

The Rector of the Canongate High School, William Panton, produced in 1771 *A Tyro's Guide to Arithmetic and Mensuration*. The title goes on to indicate that the book was intended for the use of schools and mechanics. All the usual arithmetical problems are here, from the four rules to cube root. The

[1] D K Wilson, *op cit*, Univ of London Press, 1935. (*Publications of the Scottish Council for Research in Education*, VIII.)
[2] Copy in National Library of Scotland.
[3] Copy in National Library of Scotland.
[4] Copy in National Library of Scotland. Hamilton's other claim to fame is that, according to *The Caledonian Mercury* of 23 Dec 1740, he 'invented a machine for effectually preventing the breaking of houses; which being placed behind a door or window, instantly rings a bell, fires a pistol and lights a candle, on the least attempt to force up either door or window'.
[5] Copy in National Library of Scotland. He published other books.
[6] A copy of the second is in the National Library of Scotland, with Walter Scott's signature and the date 1st Dec 1795.

mensuration side has a practical bias, and is intended to meet the needs of masons, glaziers, painters, joiners, sawyers, slaters, surveyors, and gaugers. There are problems (provided with answers) like the following: 'The Spectator's Club of fat people, though it consisted but of 15 persons, is said to weigh no less than 3 tons, how much at an equality was that per man? Answer 4 cwt.'[1]

Ewing's book on *Practical Mathematics* dealt with the practical applications of trigonometry to the problems of surveying, gauging, navigation, and gunnery, and from the time of its appearance (1779), these subjects appear to become more popular. No doubt the naval wars had to do with this. William Wilson's *Elements of Navigation* was rather earlier (1773).[2]

Melrose's *Arithmetic*, published in 1791, is a kind of arithmetic book that was familiar during the whole of the nineteenth century, and similar works may be found in use with few changes even today. The edition examined was, in fact, the 38th, of 1866.[3] There are many problems in this book, with perhaps too many long calculations, but it is a clear and practical guide.

LATIN

Robert Blau, who had been a master in the High School until he was deposed in 1685 because, according to Principal Lee, he had been a government spy, became a private teacher in Edinburgh and published a number of books on Latin. These include *Rudiments of Etymology*, 1686; *Vocabularium Duplex*, 1685; *Locutions of the Latin Tongue*, 1702; and *Etymology of the Latin Tongue in English*, 1711. Most interesting appears to be, however, *Praxis Oratoria*, 1703, which contains five orations 'by way of a comical play (both Latin and English) viz upon Diligence, Mechanicks, Arts, Learning, Latin Tongue, and Maternal Indulgence. To which are added an oration, concerning the Cocks and their Game, declaimed yearly both in Latin

---

[1] Copy in Edinburgh Public Library.
[2] *The Caledonian Mercury*, 31 Jan 1784.
[3] Copy in Edinburgh Public Library. A typical sum is 'How much whisky at 14s, 15s, 18s, and 21s per gal should be mixed that the compound may be worth 17s per gal? Answer: equal quantities of each.'

and in English by every one of the high class, the whole time of their solemn fighting.   An Inaugural Lecture of the Victor at Candlemas, holding forth to the youth the reasonableness of a limited monarchy, confirmed also by authorities out of the ancients.'[1]   Blau seems to have been an ardent Scot, for in some of the sentences given as examples of how to vary the idiom in translating, one finds the following: 'Regno Numidiae, quod vestrum est uti libet consulite', which is translated as: 'Make a kirk and a miln of your indulged children for they are your own'; and 'Livent rubigine dentes', translated as: 'Wounds have made my legs blea'.

James Kirkwood, that argumentative teacher from Linlithgow, published a revised edition of *Despauter* in 1674, and in the preface advocated the use of what are now called visual aids— pictures for helping in the teaching of history, and maps and globes for geography, and wall diagrams for Latin grammar. *Despauter* was the standard Latin grammar used in Scotland, of which there were a number of revisions.

Another attempt to sweeten *Despauter* was Thomas Watt's *Grammar made Easie*, of 1704.   Watt believed that Latin Grammar should be taught in English, but only goes part of the way in this book, leaving a good many of the rules in Latin. To the Latin, Watt at least added an English translation.   The first sentence of the book is:

> Omne marem signans nomen decet esse virile.
> Names of Gods, of Angels, of Men, of Mans Offices, hee Animals
>   are mas.

and

> Tu quae foemellam signant muliebris ponas.
> Names of Goddesses, of Women, of Womens Offices, she Animals
>   are fem.

These metrical rules are similar to those of Despauter.   Watt also published a book which throws some light on the teaching of Latin at the time: *A Vocabulary English and Latin, together with the Language of the school translated into Latin, collected*

---

[1] This is an interesting reference to the old practice of cock-fighting at Fastern's E'en.

from the Classick authors, and proposed as the best method to prevent boys speaking bad Latin, and the easiest way to teach them in a few months to converse in true Roman Latin.[1] It will be remembered that the old practice of 'disputing', which formerly took place every Saturday in the High School, was cut down to once a month by the Town Council acting on the advice of a committee of professors. It is probable that the standard of Latin used in these disputations was very low, and Watt's book was an attempt to improve it.

In 1714 appeared a Latin grammar that achieved great popularity, *Rudiments of the Latin Tongue*, by Thomas Ruddiman, Keeper of the Advocates' Library. No mere adaptation of *Despauter*, this was a new work. The book is in both English and Latin, with English on the right half and Latin on the left half of the page, for example:

De Dictionibus	*Of Words*
M. Quot sunt partes orationis?	M. How many parts of speech are there?
D. Octo: Nomen, Pronomen, Verbum, Participium, Adverbium, Praepositio, Interjectio, Conjunctio.	S. Eight: Noun, Pronoun, Verb, Participle, Adverb, Preposition, Interjection, Conjunction.

In notes at the foot of the pages are details of English grammar, conceived in terms of the grammatical conceptions of Latin. This is a neat little book, handy for scholars and teachers. It consists, as did most of its predecessors, mostly of rules; in the hands of a good teacher it was probably an admirable textbook, but it makes no concessions to the reader, and needs to be taught.[2]

James Barclay, Rector of the Grammar School of Dalkeith, who had previously been a master in the High School, published in 1758 *The Rudiments of the Latin Tongue in which the difficulties of all the parts of our Latin Grammars are made plain to the*

---

[1] *The Edinburgh Evening Courant*, 2 April 1714.
[2] Ruddiman's Grammar had its attractions for a soldier in winter quarters in the Peninsula. General Sir George Murray wrote to his brother on 16 Oct 1811, asking for it: 'The Rudiments with Penna, Amo etc' (Murray Papers in National Library of Scotland). Sir George was an old High School boy.

capacities of Children.[1] Barclay deprecated the excessive learning by heart of rules, especially in Latin, and much of his book is arranged by question and answer, eg

Of the Declension of Nouns

Q. How is a noun declined?
A. By genders, cases, and numbers.
Q. What is it you call the gender of a noun?
A. Philosophically speaking, it is the distinction of nouns according to their different sexes, male and female; but grammarians, by gender, mean nothing more than the fitness of a substantive noun to be joined to an adjective of such a termination and not to another.

As in Ruddiman's grammar, the footnotes give English grammar. One says, for example, 'There are only two genders in the English language, masculine and feminine'. There are mnemonics to help in versification:

> Would you pentameters compose
> Five feet the harmony must close

and

> Six feet Heroic verse requires
> The fifth place Dactylus admires
> The sixth Spondaeus loves; the rest
> Are the same feet where you think best.

Dr Adam's Latin Grammar[2] has already been mentioned as having been the cause of opposition to its author, and dispute between him and his staff. Based on the work of Ruddiman, and on that of Bishop Louth, it is a more attractive volume than either of these. It is a thorough book, with long vocabularies to be learned, treating matters like style and rhetoric, figures of speech, etymology, punctuation, and grammar in English as well as in Latin. It goes in fact a long way towards providing a broad general literary education. It was for many years a standard work, used all over the United Kingdom.

[1] Copy in National Library of Scotland.
[2] *Rudiments of Latin and English Grammar* by Alexander Adam. Edinburgh 1772.

MODERN LANGUAGES

French was the modern language that was popular. No reference has been traced of any textbook on German by an Edinburgh schoolmaster, and only two wrote textbooks on Italian. French was taught in the College as an additional subject, and the first French grammar to be printed in Edinburgh was primarily for the use of students in the College. It is *A short and easy French Grammar: Containing the rules of pronunciation, the Inflexion of nouns and verbs, a short syntax and prosody. . . . For the use of the Students in the University of Edinburgh*. Watson, Edinburgh 1718. The author of this grammar was William Scott, Professor of Greek in the College, and later Professor of Philosophy. As its title indicates, this is a careful grammar of the type familiar in Latin and Greek. Scott's help and advice was valuable to William (or, as he preferred to call himself later, Guillaume) Ker, who published *The Most Complete, Compendious, and Easy French Grammar for Ladies and Gentlemen* in 1729. Ker taught both privately and in the College.[1]

Ker's rival as a teacher of French in Edinburgh was James Freebairn, who published in 1734 *A New French Grammar, wherein the Defects of former Grammars are supplied, and their Errors corrected; For the Use of the Young Nobility and Gentry of Scotland*. That this contained an attack on Ker's book is obvious from the reference to 'a late one in this country which the author calls on the title page: The most Complete, Compendious, and Easy French Grammar'. Freebairn liked to stress his connections with the nobility and gentry. He taught, among others, the well-known Mrs Alison Cockburn or Rutherford.[2]

Ker published two anthologies of French prose and verse, one in 1727 and the other in 1737. The earlier volume is dedicated to 'Mademoiselle de Duglas'. The 1737 volume, entitled

---

[1] Ker's wife was French and published *A Nouvelle*, which was advertised in *The Caledonian Mercury*, 20 May 1736. No copy has been found.

[2] James Freebairn was a brother of Robert Freebairn, King's Printer. They were sons of the Rev David Freebairn who became Bishop of Edinburgh in 1722. In the 1715 Rebellion David and James came out on the Jacobite side and subsequently lived for many years on the Continent. See *Scottish Notes and Queries*, Sept 1934.

Nouveau Recueil Très Utile Pour Bien Entendre La Fable, Le Sublime, L'Histoire, et La Poésie, is dedicated to 'Madame la Comtesse D'Ancrum', and the list of subscribers contains mostly Edinburgh names, including one or two teachers, a number of students at the College, and forty-two people of the name of Ker from the Duke of Roxburghe and the Marquis of Lothian downwards. Extracts from both modern and ancient French writing are to be found in this volume.[1]

An anthology, whose editor is not known, was advertised in 1750; it included selections from 'the most celebrated wits of France', including Gil Blas, La Fontaine, Molière, Corneille, Racine, and Boileau.[2]

Arthur Masson published a number of books on French. In 1755 he proposed to publish *A System of the French Language.*[3] No trace has been found of this book, but an anthology of French by Masson appeared in 1766: this is *Recueil de Pièces Choisies . . . par Arthur Masson.*[4] The advertisement ends with 'NB. There are various pieces in this Collection which will afford agreeable entertainment to young gentlemen during the vacation.' Masson also published a work on Italian—*Rudiments of the Italian Language in Ten Lessons, with collection,* in 1771. This book, described in the *Courant* as 'The first of its kind that hath appeared in Scotland', is a workmanlike little volume.[5] Its publication at this time is interesting in view of Henry Mackenzie's statement[6] that he found it impossible when he was a young man to get tuition in Italian in Edinburgh, and indicates how much Edinburgh was developing in the last quarter of the century. Baron Charles Ricci advertised in 1766 that he was a 'former soldier in the Queen of Hungary's army', but, 'having met with several disappointments in life, he intends to teach here the Italian Language'.[7]

A French grammar intended for those whose main purpose in learning the language was commerce and trade was that

[1] Copy in the British Museum.
[2] *The Edinburgh Evening Courant,* 6 Feb 1750.
[3] *ibid,* 1 May 1755.
[4] *ibid,* 9 Aug 1766.
[5] *ibid,* 5 Jan 1771. Copy in National Library of Scotland.
[6] *Anecdotes and Egotisms.*
[7] *The Edinburgh Evening Courant,* 30 April 1766.

published by J Coomans in 1764: *French and English Grammar,
with forms of letters, inland and foreign bills of exchange.*[1]

Another writer of textbooks in French was A Scot, who published *Exercises for turning English into French, with the Grammatical rules* in 1776.[2] A similar book, published by Creech in Edinburgh (Scot's 1776 volume was published in London) was advertised in 1781.[3] Scot's next book is the only one in or on French that is definitely intended for children: *Fables Choisies a l'usage des Enfans.*[4] This is perhaps not surprising, for most of the textbooks on modern languages were meant for the young men and women and the adults who attended the classes of the numerous private teachers. Scot also published an anthology on the lines of Arthur Masson's, *Nouveau Recueil ou Mélange Littéraire, Historique, Dramatique, et Poétique*, par A Scot, AM, Membre de L'Université de Paris.[5]

One other author deserves to be mentioned, F Bottarelli, who in 1781 published *The New Italian, English, and French Dictionaries, Grammar and Exercises.*[6]

CONCLUSION

It is not pretended that these textbooks exhaust the list of those written by Edinburgh schoolmasters during the period under review, but probably enough have been described for certain general impressions to be drawn.

The first is the pervading influence of England. It is doubtful if a single one of the textbooks produced in Edinburgh was a purely Scottish product, owing nothing to English examples. The spelling books on the 'syllabication' method followed English models, and the arithmetic texts were in a true sense 'according to Cocker'. Possibly the grammars of Ruddiman and Adam were the most original of all the textbooks, but even they, like most Latin grammars, were inevitably derivative. The 'round hand' introduced at the beginning of the century for

[1] *The Edinburgh Evening Courant*, 17 Nov 1764.
[2] *The Caledonian Mercury*, 24 Feb 1776.
[3] *The Edinburgh Evening Courant* 25 Aug 1781. *Rudiments and Practical Exercises for Learning the French Language* by A Scot, AM.
[4] *ibid*, 11 Jan 1783.
[5] *The Caledonian Mercury*, 20 Oct 1784.
[6] *The Edinburgh Evening Courant*, 24 Feb 1781.

speedy writing in commerce, came to Scotland from England. Edinburgh was the centre in Scotland from which new ideas from England were spread over Scotland. The Edinburgh textbooks may not always have been the best in Scotland, but because of the concentration of the printing trade in Edinburgh, the city produced many more books than the other towns. Edinburgh booksellers, too, had arrangements with London booksellers, and acted as their agents. James Watson includes in his advertisements in the Edinburgh papers in the first twenty years of the century a considerable number of English school textbooks.

The taste in schoolbooks changed remarkably in the course of the century. Spelling books in the early days were mere lists of letters and words to be memorised; at the end of the century they were illustrated and contained stories. Latin grammars were no longer entirely in Latin, being more palatable at least to the extent that they were partly in English. Textbooks appeared—none of them written by Edinburgh teachers—in history and geography. Various reasons have been put forward for the change of tone in schoolbooks in the course of the eighteenth century—the influence of John Newbery's charming little books,[1] the increase in the number of children who were taught to read, the effects of the evangelical movement.

Outside influences weighed in the development of certain subjects. At the end of the seventeenth and beginning of the eighteenth century, the time of Darien and the Treaty of Union, there are many references to the importance of book-keeping, accounts, and fluent writing. Shorthand is seldom mentioned: in one of the early references, in 1740, its virtues are described not as commercial but as connected with the taking down of sermons and speeches.[2] Later in the century, after 1760 or so,

---

[1] One of them contains a definite reference to Edinburgh. The *Lilliputian Magazine*, published by Newbery in 1752, contains among other items alleged to be contributions from different parts of the country 'The Student. A New Country Dance, composed by Master Willie Duff of Edinburgh'. (Copy in British Museum.)

[2] *The Caledonian Mercury*, 15 July 1740. 'Thomas Cumming from London . . . teaches the excellent and useful art of stenography . . . by which any who can but tolerably write long hand, may be taught to take down from the speaker's mouth, any sermon, speech, lecture, trial, etc.'

a considerable number of books are written on the practical applications of mathematics to navigation, fortification, gunnery; useful in a time of expanding maritime trade, and colonial wars. Land-surveying, important to the 'improving lairds', also had a mathematical basis. After the publication of Johnson's Dictionary, a number of dictionaries were published for use in schools as part of the teaching of reading.

Finally, it is interesting to note that textbooks were written by private teachers as well as by masters in the well-established schools. Masson's books must have had large circulations throughout Scotland, and William Perry, in spite of financial trouble, claimed to make a reasonable living from his schoolbooks. The works of Adam and Ruddiman were known all over the United Kingdom. It seems a fair deduction that the teachers of Edinburgh, public and private, reached a high professional standard in their day.

Chapter VII

RETROSPECT

THE schools in Edinburgh at the beginning of the period under review were few and limited compared with those at the end. When, in 1706, the Presbytery of Edinburgh conducted a visitation of the city, the Lord Provost and Magistrates were asked the customary question about the provision of schools, the reply was as follows:

'. . . there is a high school in this city, whereof Mr William Skeen is principal master, and that he has four Doctors or under teachers and that Mr Skeen has been in that station since some time before the late Revolution, but they do not know whether he has subscribed the Confession of faith or not. But all the Doctors that has been admitted since that time have done it, and both Master and under teachers are provided with suitable maintenance, and it is hoped they are qualified for their stations and are diligent and faithful therein. . . .

'. . . That these of this place had reason to bless God who had put it in the hearts of many charitable persons to provide so liberally for the help of the poor, there being several hospitals erected for that end in this place, particularly a famous hospital erected by George Heriot many years ago, which maintains and educates a great number of boys . . . a new hospital lately founded by the Company of Merchants and another by the several Incorporations of Trades in this place, both of them for young girls, to which several charitable persons have contributed considerably.

'. . . and there was lately a free school erected by the Town Council for teaching the poor to read, to which a great many do resort.

'. . . and that there are French papists who keep schools in this city.'

A report of one of the Presbytery's committees in the following year adds the information that there were also

'diverse private schools'.[1] Other visitations of the time refer
to the Canongate High School and the Grammar School of
South Leith.

It was a different picture that Thomas Brown painted in 1791.[2]
The High School of Edinburgh was then a flourishing school of
between 400 and 500 pupils, with a considerable reputation.
Heriot's Hospital housed more than 100 boys, and Watson's
Hospital 60 boys. Of the two long-established girls' hospitals,
the Merchant Maiden Hospital accommodated 70 girls and the
Trades Maiden Hospital 50 girls. There were also schools in
the Charity Workhouses and in the Orphan Hospital. The
town's four English schools were popular and successful. There
were certainly two, probably more, Charity schools, and a
considerable number of private schools of all kinds. Brown
says: 'There are likewise many other private schools in Edinburgh
for all languages; and in general every kind of education is to
be had here in great perfection, and at a very cheap rate.'[3]

That there should be more schools at the end of the century
than at the beginning is scarcely surprising, for the population
of the city had grown from 50,000 to 100,000. The founding
of schools, however, did not proceed steadily with the growth of
population. Quite suddenly, in or about the year 1760, there is
an increase in the number of schools and of teachers. The
town's English schools were founded in 1759, and the short-
lived Charity Working schools. At this time occurs also an
increase in the numbers of private teachers, notably of teachers
of English. From the same period date many of the fashionable
boarding schools for girls.

To the reader of the records of the period, whether in the
minutes of public bodies or in the newspapers of the day, the
great variety of subjects that became available in Edinburgh in
the last forty years of the century is most impressive. In 1718,
French was taught in the College but seldom outside it: by 1770,
French was professed by many private teachers, it was an
accepted accomplishment in girls' boarding schools, and High
School boys like Walter Scott were taught French privately

[1] Edinburgh Presbytery Minutes, 15 Oct 1707.
[2] Brown, *op cit*, pp 42-8.
[3] Brown, *op cit*, p 43.

by their tutors. There were private teachers of other modern languages as well as of the classical tongues. There was a similar variety in the mathematical subjects. In the early years of the century, arithmetic was taught in English schools and by private teachers usually in the form of 'Accompts': as the century progressed there were taught not only branches like geometry, algebra, trigonometry, but also many forms of applied mathematics, like navigation, fortification, gunnery, and gauging. An interest in book-keeping developed steadily, particularly with the opening of private schools with the name of Mercantile Academies.

The treatment of the basic subjects in English schools and High Schools became enriched in the course of the eighteenth century. In English schools in the early days, the reading matter was limited to the Bible, the Shorter Catechism, and brief moral tales, but the popularity of 'Collections' like Arthur Masson's well-known work meant that selections from history, poetry, and belles lettres were read in many schools. In the High School of Edinburgh a teacher like Dr Adam added to the rather narrow Latin course subjects like English grammar, philology, ancient and modern history and geography, and some knowledge of Greek. This enriching of the course of education was part of a general humanising of education, which becomes apparent also in other parts of the United Kingdom in the later years of the eighteenth century. The textbooks of the time reflect this trend; they are more interesting and attempt to understand more of the child's point of view than the dry, uncompromising volumes of the early part of the century. But it would create a false impression to stress this change too much, as evidence in plenty exists of harsh punishment and unenlightened teaching methods.

While it is true that the High Schools did not profess to be anything other than Latin schools, and that it was only in the hands of cultured and able teachers that their instruction was widened to include history, geography, philology, and so on, it is also true that opportunities for instruction in the other subjects of a general education were amply available to High School boys elsewhere in Edinburgh. They might learn writing and 'Accompts' from the writing master attached to the High

School of Edinburgh, but many, including Scott and Cockburn, learned these subjects in private schools. Boys whose parents wished them to learn particular subjects, were sent to private teachers. In a sense, though the normal traditional course provided in the three High Schools of Edinburgh, Canongate, and South Leith was narrow, the education that could be provided for a High School boy in the city was extremely wide. It is necessary to stress this point to illustrate the important place that private teachers held.

Though it is true that in English schools and Charity schools the subjects and methods at the end of the century were rather more suited to the needs of children than at the beginning, one must be careful not to give the impression that the improvement was either noticeable or widespread. In these schools the object was to teach reading, writing, a little arithmetic, some knowledge of the principles of religion, the tunes commonly used in church, and very little more. A stay of three or four years was the longest schooling even for those who intended to proceed to the High Schools. As late as 1781 the ministers reporting on Wightman's Charity School noted that 'after all that has been done, the education of a great number of poor children is totally neglected'. Every now and then, even late in the century, there are echoes in school reports of the phrase used in 1739 in connection with the Orphan Hospital, 'to sow the seeds of industry in their very infant years', which was an attitude likely to commend itself to both the commercial and the philanthropic ideas of subscribers.

The place of Edinburgh in any description of Scottish education in the eighteenth century is exceptional. Its English schools developed early, and there were many more private schools and teachers than in the other burghs. Boys belonging to families of distinction from different parts of the country came to Edinburgh to attend the private schools and the High School. Their sisters came to Edinburgh boarding schools to learn the domestic arts, a little French, music, and dancing, and something of city life. The city came to be regarded as a centre of education, and because of that it attracted even more teachers and pupils. Private teachers covered such a wide range of subjects in the later years of the eighteenth century that they provided for the intelligent young men all the variety of a polytechnic, and supplemented in this way the humanities and sciences of the rapidly growing College.

Though Edinburgh was different from the other Scottish burghs because of its hospital schools and private schools, yet the general organisation of English school and High School was typically Scottish. This arrangement was the counterpart in the towns of the parish school system, a fact which has not been sufficiently stressed in histories of Scottish education. It has been assumed in these histories that the parish schools represent alone the tradition of Scottish education. No doubt the parish schools, in which children of all classes were taught from the rudiments of reading and writing to Latin and even Greek of University level, stood for democratic ideas which appeal to many. But they were not the only schools in eighteenth century Scotland, nor at that time perhaps the most influential schools, and it is hoped that the details provided in the present study have shown how there grew up in Edinburgh the system of English school and High School which, in the course of the following century, gradually developed into the arrangement in force today of primary and secondary schools.

It was a system that provided schooling, either free or at modest rates, for all. In eighteenth-century Edinburgh social class was important. There were degrees of distinction in the private schools. (A school like Mr Mundell's was very exclusive). Among the High Schools, the High School of Edinburgh was socially the most desirable. Besides the sons of burgesses, the High School attracted the sons of the landed gentry and even of the nobility. For example, the annual subscription of 1s as a minimum for the High School library was collected in March 'before the Gentlemen's children from the Country leave the Town',[1] and the library lists contain the names of many sons of noble families. But there was always an overwhelming majority of boys from the families of professional men, merchants, and tradesmen, whose presence, along with that of boys from Heriot's Hospital, ensured a certain democratic quality. The High Schools of Canongate and South Leith served in the main the great mass of middle- and working-class families in their neigh-

[1] Minutes of the Town Council of Edinburgh, 23 May 1770.

bourhoods. At the elementary level, ordinary people sent their children to the English schools and the less expensive private schools. With establishments like these, private schools in considerable variety, Hospital schools for the children of burgesses in distressed circumstances, and Charity schools for the poor, Edinburgh may be said to have been generously provided with schools in the eighteenth century.

Appendix I

THE TEACHING OF SCOTS

THE earliest reference to the use of the Scots tongue in schools appears to be in the list of school texts of which William Nudrye was given a monopoly in 1559. This list, in *Registrum Secreti Sigilli* XXX fol 5a, includes: *Ane Schort Introductioun: Elementary digestit into sevin breve tables for the commodius expeditioun of thame that are desirous to read and write the Scottis toung*, and *Ane instructioun for bairnis to be lernit in Scottis and Latin*. The Statutes drawn up in 1627 for Heriot's Hospital say that the Schoolmaster shall 'teach the Scholeris to read and wreat Scottis'.

In the Town Council minutes (12 Feb 1658), James Chalmers was given a licence to keep a vulgar school, 'for teaching of scholars to read and write Scots and only to read Latin before they go to the Grammar School'. In 1660 (7 Nov 1660) Patrick Kellie was allowed to keep a vulgar school, the subjects of instruction being arithmetic, 'reading Scots', writing, and reading of writing, drawing up accounts, and playing the cithern.

Grant's *Burgh Schools* contains mention of the teaching of Scots in Peebles (1655), Glasgow (1663), Dumfries (1663), Leith (1681), and Stranraer (1686).

Appendix II

THE ESTABLISHMENT OF THE FIRST CHARITY SCHOOL IN EDINBURGH

THE minute of the Town Council for 24 Feb 1699 reads as follows: 'Bailie Cunningham and Bailie Warrender reported that whereas there are now many children in Edinburgh whose parents and relations are not able in those hard times to pay quarter payments to school-masters for their children's education at schools, for remedy whereof it is proposed that there be a free school forthwith set up in Edinburgh to teach such children. And that the same school be immediately effectual it was their opinion that George Clark precentor to the Tolbooth Kirk be employed according to the under-written articles. First that the said George Clark take in as many of the said children of both sex as possible one man can teach. Secondly, that the said George Clark faithfully teach these children to read English, writing, common tunes of music, some arithmetic, and his wife to teach the girls to work stockings. Thirdly that the said George Clark teach every week-day from nine in the forenoon to twelve and from two in the afternoon to five except Saturday afternoon. That the said George Clark shall teach the said children gratis without any payment of money or other reward whatsoever from the children or their parents or relations. Fifthly that the said George in the meantime accommodate forty children in his own house and that the Town furnish him firing until a better conveniency be provided. Sixthly that the said George Clark shall have Ten Pounds Sterling for his salary.' This was approved and the direction of the school was given to the Town Council's Committee of the Poor, 'who are hereby appointed to set and give such rules and orders anent the management thereof as they shall find just, with preference always to all the Good Town's pensioners' children and foundlings'.

Appendix III

THE FOUNDATION OF THE TOWN'S ENGLISH SCHOOLS AND CHARITY WORKING SCHOOLS

THE Town Council minutes for 29 Dec 1758 give the following account of a report by the Lord Provost, George Drummond:

'They having met the said committee (of the Presbytery) and considered the present state of the English schools within this city, they found that the number taught by men amounted to twenty-four whereof two are Charity schools, and of the remaining twenty two there are four or five at least in which each scholar must pay at the rate of half a guinea per quarter, which with coal money and other perquisites included raises the expense of their education at these schools at a medium to £2 10s or £2 15s per annum. There is one school whereof the master exacts no more than three shillings per quarter, four schoolmasters who demand four shillings per quarter exclusive of perquisites, and all the rest five shillings per quarter besides perquisites. Exclusive of the two Charity schools, there are only nine of these masters who are of the communion of the established Church—all the rest are either nonjurors, seceders, Cameronians, etc. The number of scholars at each of these schools taken at a medium does not exceed thirty. Besides these twenty four schools there are five or six more taught by women at different prices. The number of scholars at each of these does not exceed fifteen. Hence it appears that the number of scholars taught annually at all the schools of this city of every denomination taken at a medium amounts to about eight hundred—and though it is not easy to ascertain the number of children in this city fit to go to school, yet on the lowest calculation they cannot be fewer than three thousand—consequently there are two thousand children who are not sent to any school, and of whose education it is impossible to give any account. It is further to be observed that of the above-

mentioned nine schoolmasters who are of the communion of
the established Church, there are some of them especially of
those who take the highest prices, who do not teach any
Catechism, and who have excluded from their schools the
laudable practice of causing the scholars read the Holy Scriptures, and almost every other means of religious instruction.
And with respect to the other schools taught by nonjurors,
seceders, etc, whatever instructions their scholars may receive
concerning the principles of religion in general, yet it may be
most reasonably supposed they are bound up with prejudices
and aversion either against the established Government or
established Church. So that of the above eight hundred scholars
how many are there of them who have not the benefit of being
properly instructed in religious matters. From the above
facts it is too evident that the education of the young children of
this city is at present on a bad footing, great numbers of them
are altogether neglected, and of those who are sent to school to
learn to read, there are many who are not taught the principles of
religion at all, or at least as they ought to be. This is an evil
of such shameful and pernicious consequences as loudly calls on
all ranks and conditions of men in this city to assist in applying
a proper remedy to it, and accordingly it is humbly proposed,
that besides the two Charity schools above-mentioned, three
more schools should be erected in this city, at the expense and
under the direction of the Society for Propagating Christian
Knowledge, and besides these, that there should be four more
schools erected by the Honourable Magistrates and Council of
this city.'

P

Appendix IV

SPINNING SCHOOLS IN EDINBURGH

In 1727, a spinning school was set up in Edinburgh, as the result of an agreement between the Town Council and Mrs Christian Miller, formerly Christian Shaw of Bargarran and widow of the minister of Kilmaurs. In her younger days, Christian Shaw was accused of witchcraft: William Roughead gives an account of her early experiences in *The Riddle of the Ruthvens*.

The school was for thirty girls, ten of whom could be nominated by the Town Council from the Merchant Maiden and Trades Maiden Hospitals. Mrs Miller was to teach them 'to spin flax into fine yarn fitt for making thred or camrick' and also 'the twisting of threed bleching, milning Hanking or Reeling Back rowing and upmaking of the same'. A considerable part of the profits of the undertaking went to Mrs Miller, who had to maintain a trained staff, but a share went to the Hospitals and some part to the girls. Mrs Miller was to receive £50 a year from the ale duty money. The Town Council supplied spinning wheels.

Mrs Miller also agreed to teach 'six poor apprentices to be presented out of the Boys in Heriots Hospitall and in default thereof any other poor boys in the weaving of Tape or knittings for a term of four years'.

The original contract was for nine years, and it was renewed in 1736. Full details are in the City Archives, Moses Bundle, 157, No. 6023, and Moses Bundle 160, No. 6135. See also Irene F M Dean, *Scottish Spinning Schools* (*Publications of the Scottish Council for Research in Education*, I), and Chambers's *Domestic Annals of Scotland*, where Mrs Miller is recognised as the first person to introduce the spinning of fine linen thread into Scotland.

Appendix V

ACADEMIES

HISTORIANS of Scottish education from Grant onwards have failed to note or to emphasise how definitely Perth Academy was founded on the model of the dissenting academies of England. Edward Smart, in *The History of Perth Academy* (Perth 1932) makes this quite clear by quoting in full the report made by the Rev James Bonnar, who had been asked to advise the Perth Town Council. The relevant passages are as follows:

'Thus in times long past, all learning was made to consist in the grammatical knowledge of dead languages, and skill in metaphysical subtleties, while what had an immediate reference to life and practice was despised. But Providence has cast our lot in happier times, when things begin to be valued according to their use, and men of the greatest abilities have employed their skill in making the sciences contribute not only to the improvement of the physician, lawyer, and divine, but to the improvement of the merchant, mechanic, and farmer, in their respective arts. . . . Although our different universities are at this time filled with men of distinguished abilities, yet both the time necessary for completing a course of education there, and the vast expense of such attendance, must prove an insurmountable bar in the way of the greater part who have inclination and capacity for these studies. The people of England have been so fully convinced of this, that we find private academies established in almost every great town, where not only the languages but those sciences which are of the greatest use in life, are taught in a compendious and practical manner. The example, however, has not been sufficiently attended to in Scotland, where scarce any institution of that kind is to be found.'

The above passage is quoted from the Perth Town Council minutes of 27 Oct 1760. Details of the dissenting academies in England and Wales, and interesting notes on their links with the Scottish Universities are to be found in J W Ashley Smith, *The Birth of Modern Education, the contribution of the Dissenting Academies* 1660-1800, London 1954.

Appendix VI

THE CONSTITUTION OF THE
EDINBURGH SCHOOL OF ST LUKE

THE following is taken from the *Edinburgh Annual Register*, Edinburgh, 1816, ccclxxii:
'At Edinburgh the eighteenth day of October A.Dom. MDCCXXIX.

We Subscribers Painters and Lovers of Painting, Fellows of the Edinburgh School of St Luke for the encouragement of these excelent Arts of Painting, Sculpture, Architecture etc and Improvement of the Students: Have agreed to erect a publict Academy, whereinto every One that inclines on aplication to our Director and Council, shal be admited on paying a smal sum for defraying Charges of Figure and Lights etc. For further encouragement Some of our Members who have a fine colection of Models in Plaister from the best Antique Statues are to lend the use of them to the Academy.

To prevent all disorder the present Members have Unanimously agreed on the observation of the Folowing Rules.

I.   To meet anualy on the eighteenth day of October, being the Feast of St Luke our Patron, to chuse a Director, Treasurer, and Secretary, and four Common Councellours for the ensuing Year, of which Council of Seven there Shal ever be four Mr Painters.   This sd. Council to be chosen yearly, and may or not be rechosen, but upon no account to continue above two Years at a Time.

II.   That the Sederunts of the Society be Registrated in a Book to be kept by the Secretary for the time being.

III.   The Academy to meet on the first of November Jajvii and twenty nine years, and to continou till the last of February, four times a week, viz. on Mundays, Tusdays, Thursdays, and Fridays, at five o'clock at night, and to draw the space of two hours. To meet again on the first of June, and continue till the last of July on the for said days of the week; but the two Drawing hours to be in the morning from six to eight. The Summer Season being chiefly design'd for Drawing from Antique Models and Drawghts of the best Masters of Foraigne Schools by a Sky Light; for which Purpose, a large Portfolio to be kept in the Academy for preserving all curious Drawings allready given, or that may be given for that end.

IV. On Placing of every new Figure, those present to draw Lots for the choise of their Seats.

V. That every Member acording to his Seniority shd be allowed in his turn to place or put the Figure in whatever Posture he pleases, or have it in his power to depute annother to do it for him, and to have the first choise of his Seat.

VI. All Noblemen, Gentlemen, Patrons, Painters, and lovers of Painting who shal Contribute to the Carrying on the Designe (if they do not incline to draw Themselves) Shal have the Privilege by a written Order to our Director, to assign the Right to any Young Artist whom he is pleased to Patronize.

Linton Garlies	William Robertson	Geo. Marshall, Preses
William Adam	Hugh Clerk, jun.	Richd. Cooper, Treasurer
Gilb. Elliot		Roderick Chalmers, Secretary
Andrew Hay		John Alexander
Ja. McEuen		And. McIlvraith
Ja. Balfour		Ja. Norie
Mark Sandilands		Alexr. Guthrie
Allan Ramsay		Th. Trotter
		John Patoun
		Jas. Norie, junior
		Allan Ramsay, junior
		Dav. Eizat
		James Clerk
		Alexr. Clerk
		Wm. Denune
		W. Trotter
		David Cleland
		Robert Yelton'

SELECTED BIBLIOGRAPHY

I MANUSCRIPT SOURCES

Minutes of the Town Council of Edinburgh   (City Chambers)
Minutes of the Presbytery of Edinburgh.   Library of the Church of
Scotland (now in HM Record Office)
Minutes of the Society in Scotland for Propagating Christian Know-
ledge (HM Record Office)

II PERIODICALS

The Caledonian Mercury
The Edinburgh Evening Courant

III OFFICIAL REPORTS

Acts of the Parliament of Scotland
Registrum Secreti Sigilli
Municipal Corporations Report, 1835

IV BOOKS

*Account of the Rise of the Society in Scotland, for propagating Christian
Knowledge*, 2nd edition, Edinburgh: printed for Wm Brown & Co,
1720
ARNOT, H   *The History of Edinburgh from the earliest ages to the year
1780*, Edinburgh: Wm Creech, 1779
Book of the Old Edinburgh Club, Edinburgh: T & A Constable
BROWN, T   *History of the Shires of Scotland*, Glasgow: 1791
CHALMERS, G   *Life of Thomas Ruddiman*, London: John Stockdale,
Edinburgh: Wm Laing, 1794
CHAMBERS, R   *Domestic Annals of Scotland*, Edinburgh: W & R
Chambers, 1858 and 1861
COCKBURN, H   *Memorials of his Time*, Edinburgh: Robert Grant, 1946
Colston, J   *The Incorporated Trades of Edinburgh*, Edinburgh:
Colston & Co, 1891
DEAN, I F M   *Scottish Spinning Schools*, Research Council Publication
No I, London: University of London Press Ltd, 1930
DIBDIN, J C   *Annals of the Edinburgh Stage*, Edinburgh: Richard
Cameron, 1888
Edinburgh, 1329-1929, Edinburgh: Oliver & Boyd, 1929

ERSKINE, J (Lord Grange) *Diary of a Senator of the College of Justice*, ed Maidment

FERGUSON, T *Dawn of Scottish Welfare*, Edinburgh: T Nelson & Sons Ltd, 1948

GOUDIE, G *David Laing, A Memoir*, Edinburgh: T & A Constable, privately printed, 1913

GRANT, J *History of the Burgh Schools of Scotland*, Glasgow: Wm Collins, Sons & Co, 1876

GRANT, Sir Alexander *The Story of the University of Edinburgh*, London: Longmans, Green & Co, 1884

HENDERSON, A *An Account of the Life and Character of Alexander Adam LLD, Rector of the High School of Edinburgh*, Edinburgh: Printed by D Schaw & Son, 1810

HERON, A *The Rise and Progress of the Company of Merchants of the City of Edinburgh 1681-1902*, Edinburgh: T & T Clark, 1903

JONES, M G *The Charity School Movement in the XVIII Century*, Cambridge: The University Press, 1938

JOYCE, M *Edinburgh: The Golden Age*, London: Longmans, Green, 1951

MACKAY, A *A Sketch of the History of Leith Academy*, Leith: Printed by Wm F Duff & Co, 1934

MACKENZIE, H *Anecdotes and Egotisms, 1745-1831*, Ed, by H W Thompson, Oxford: The University Press, 1927

MASON, John *History of Trinity House of Leith*, Glasgow: 1957

MATHIESON, W L *Scotland and the Union*, Glasgow: James Maclehose & Sons, 1905

MATHIESON, W L *The Awakening of Scotland*, Glasgow: James Maclehose & Sons, 1910

MORGAN A and HANNAY, R K *University of Edinburgh, Charters, Statutes and Acts of the Town Council and the Senatus, 1583-1858*, Edinburgh: Oliver & Boyd, 1937

MORGAN A *Rise and Progress of Scottish Education*, Edinburgh: Oliver & Boyd, 1927

Municipal Corporations Report, 1835

MURRAY, D *Chapters in the history of book-keeping, accountancy, and commercial arithmetic*, Glasgow: Jackson, Wylie, 1930

PATRICK, M *Four Centuries of Scottish Psalmody*, Oxford: the University Press, 1949

PLANT, M *The Domestic Life of Scotland in the 18th Century*, Edinburgh: Edinburgh University Publications, 1952
1934

ROSS, W C A *The Royal High School*, Edinburgh: Oliver & Boyd, 1934.

ROUGHEAD, W *Glengarry's Way*, Edinburgh: W Greene & Son Ltd, 1922

ROUGHEAD, W *The Riddle of the Ruthvens*, Edinburgh: Grant & Murray Ltd, 1936

Rules for the Government and Order of the Merchant Maiden Hospital, Edinburgh: 1776

SCOTT, H   *Fasti Ecclesiae Scoticanae*, Edinburgh: Oliver & Boyd, 1915

South Leith Records, Second Series, Leith: Mackenzie & Storrie, 1925

Statutes and Rules of George Watson's Hospital, Edinburgh: 1755 Printed by Hamilton, Balfour and Neill

STEVEN, W   *History of George Heriot's Hospital*, Edinburgh: Bell and Bradfute, 1859

STEVEN, W   *The High School of Edinburgh*, Edinburgh: Maclachlan and Stewart, 1849

The Edinburgh Directory, 1793-1800, Edinburgh: Peter Williamson

The Rules and Constitutions of the Trades Maiden Hospital, Edinburgh: 1734

TOPHAM, E   *Letters from Edinburgh 1774-75*, London: Printed for J Dodsley, Pall Mall, 1776

Williamson's Directory, 1773-1792, Edinburgh: Peter Williamson

WILSON, D K   *The History of Mathematical Teaching in Scotland*, Research Council Publication No VIII, London: University of London Press Ltd, 1935

WOOD, M   *The Lord Provosts of Edinburgh*, Edinburgh : Printed for Lord Provost Sir Thomas B Whitson, by T & A Constable, 1932

INDEX OF NAMES

233

INDEX OF TOPICS

237